Ethnic Conflict and Religion

Théo Tschuy

CHALLENGE
TO THE CHURCHES

WCC Publications, Geneva

Cover design: Stephen Raw

ISBN 2-8254-1190-6

© 1997 WCC Publications, World Council of Churches,
150 route de Ferney, 1211 Geneva 2, Switzerland

Printed in Switzerland

Table of Contents

To my children and grandchildren
whose only space is this earth
and whose only time is the present

I am grateful to the following persons for the time, thematic suggestions and critical comments generously offered: Paul Abrecht, S. Wesley Ariarajah, Branco Bosknjakovic, Dwain Epps, Tarek Mitri, Teny Pirri-Simonian, Julio de Santa Ana, Baldwin Sjollema and Lukas Vischer. Each has contributed generously out of his or her vast store of knowledge and personal experience. A special word of thanks goes to Pierre Beffa (Ecumenical Centre Library) and Professor Curt Gasteyger (Institut Universitaire de Hautes Etudes Internationales, University of Geneva), who kindly supplied me with indispensable background materials. For any errors of judgment or factual mistakes, however, I alone am responsible.

Introduction

A staggering death toll

According to statistics compiled by US political scientist R.J. Rummel, no fewer than 170 million human beings were murdered by their own governments between 1900 and 1987.[1] These figures shed new light on the overriding significance of internal conflicts in the 20th century, because their victims have far outnumbered those of the wars between states. By comparison, an estimated 15 million and 50 million persons perished in war action during the first and second world wars respectively. Ethnic conflicts must be seen within this larger context, even though it is impossible to determine precisely who among these victims died because of their "ethnic" identity.

Rummel's statistics need some explanation. First, these figures refer to victims who lost their lives not on "official" front-line duty or during bombing raids carried out by foreign air forces, but *within* a territory for which a given government bore juridical and administrative responsibility. Second, these killings were deliberate or implicit actions for which the government in charge bore full responsibility, because they took place within its own national frontiers or within occupied territories for whose administration it had assumed full legal responsibility (for instance, the areas occupied by Germany and Japan during the second world war or colonies belonging to Great Britain up to decolonization). In the case of civil wars these deaths took place in territories over which one of the contesting parties had taken effective control. It is understandable that such situations make the authorities nervous; it is far less understandable that this should lead them to mistreat the population and deliberately commit mass executions. The notable population losses in China, for instance, were largely due to the coincidence of its long and bloody civil war with the Japanese invasion. Such multiple upheavals produce behind-the-front executions, forced marches and famines in most social revolutions, but this was especially severe in the case of China. Russia and later the Soviet Union suffered heavy losses for similar reasons. The first world war helped to unleash the revolution of 1917. This was followed by reprisals during and after the ensuing civil war, the extermination of certain social classes like the Ukrainian *kulaks* (landowners) and moves against ethnic minorities considered ideologically "unreliable", such as the Tatars, the Caucasian peoples and the Jews. Although the Soviet Union persecuted all religions on ideological grounds, considering believers and religious bodies backwards and politically untrustworthy, ethnic or national groups marked by certain religious faiths whose religion tended to strengthen their spirit of resistance — such as Jews, Roman Catholics and adherents of Eastern Catholic or Uniate churches — came under special pressure.

Then there was the blood spilled during the colonial era. Down to the last decades of the colonial system, nations which saw themselves as "civilized" and "Christian" caused enormous human losses. Whether one looks at Spain, Portugal, France, Germany or Britain, the military campaigns for conquest or subduing rebels were always carried out in a spirit of racial and cultural superiority. Furthermore, since the colonial system could function only because the foreign occupiers were past masters of playing off one ethnic or religious group against another, countless conflicts of this type continue into the present.

One of the aspects of colonialism whose repercussions continue to be felt today was the settlement of large numbers of Europeans on other continents. In the Americas, South Africa, Australia and New Zealand they have taken over vast areas outright, conquering, marginalizing and eliminating the local populations. New European civilizations have arisen, and the descendants of the settlers are generally ignorant of and indifferent to the horrors of conquest. The resurgence of black and American Indian consciousness and white reaction to it can become another cause for racial or ethnic conflict. A source of further potential problems is the massive migrations from the poorer regions of Eastern Europe, the Mediterranean and sub-Saharan Africa to Western Europe, and from Latin America to the United States and Canada. This creates new racial or ethnic minorities which are often resented by local populations. Its grave political consequences can be seen in the rise of overt racism in France. Similar migrations take place from the rural areas in Latin America to the cities and from the poorer regions of Asia to the Middle East or to the more prosperous "New Tiger" economies.

The "murder by government" we have described sharpens our focus on the new ethnic conflicts that have broken out since 1989. A new stage in history seems to have been reached. The more than fifty ethnic conflicts going on in the world today have a multiplicity of causes, and it is difficult to classify them into a coherent pattern. While we cannot yet understand all of the reasons for outbreaks such as those in the former Yugoslavia and Rwanda, we may establish a few working hypotheses about the contributing factors which operate at different levels and often in contradictory ways. These include:

1. The *break-up of multinational states* (such as the Soviet Union and Yugoslavia after 1989).

2. Dissatisfaction with *the failure of decolonization* to bring the expected economic prosperity.

3. *Population pressures*, leading to increased competition over land and diminishing resources, many of which are already appropriated by the more powerful economies.

4. *Weakening of the nation-state* due to a globalized economy, instant worldwide communication, transnational migration and intermingling of populations, the growth of international and regional organizations and self-assertion within national borders.

5. *Weakening influence of traditional religion and ideology*, coupled with a growth of new religions and of fundamentalism.

6. *New approaches and methods of history*, such as oral history, studies of neglected social groups, including women, better awareness among the poor of the mechanisms of oppression and "poverty creation", local actions for self-help.

7. *New forms of networking* made possible by modern forms of communication and travel.

8. *Improved legal standards for the protection of minorities and ethnic groups*, both at international and national levels, providing legitimacy for the aspirations of the disfavoured.

Defining terms

Already in this brief overview we have used several terms which will recur frequently throughout this book. It will be helpful at the outset to define some of these, even though (as we shall see) this is by no means a simple and straightforward exercise.

To begin with, it is not clear that the terms *race* and *ethnicity* can be effectively distinguished. The English word "race" is derived from the Latin *ratio* (reason or understanding), which became part of European scientific language during the 16th century, when it was first used to classify plant and animal species. During the 19th century the term was absorbed into European colonialist ideology and became subverted, with the help of social Darwinism, to justify the power and domination of white Europeans over non-white colonized peoples. This "classification" was not used to establish scientific anthropological categories but simply to "prove" white superiority; and such pseudo-scientific abuse became known as "racism".

Within Europe, however, "race" took on a secondary, though no less destructive connotation. It came to be applied to a supposed distinction between "superior" and "inferior" European populations, an ideology that reached its culmination in Hitler's National Socialism, which classified Germanic northern "races" as superior to Jews, Slavs, Gypsies and blacks. This racist ideology was used not only to dominate inferior "races", but to destroy them outright. The Nazis, though defeated in war, have been succeeded by imitators such as neo-Nazis in Europe and a great variety of white supremacist groups in North America.

The term "ethnicity" comes from the Greek *ethnos* (people or nation). It is used today to designate a group of persons of similar language, culture and often (but not always) religion. Ethnicities are often, but not necessarily, identical with the population inhabiting a specific nation-state. The fact that certain ethnic groups feel superior to others and engage in warfare to subdue or even to exterminate them places ethnocentrism in the same category as racism, even though the term sounds less aggressive. A consultant at a 1994 World Council of Churches meeting on racism, ethnicity and indigenous peoples offered a shorthand definition: racism is based on power and privilege, while ethnicity derives from blood and belonging. Obviously the two terms overlap, and they are not used here as hard and fast socio-political categories.

The root of the term "nation" is the Latin *natio* (those *born* from a common ancestry). Originally equivalent to the Greek *ethnos*, people, it took on different connotations during the course of history. At the time of the French Revolution, *la nation*, *the* people, stood in opposition to the declining monarchy and the nobility. Soon the expression began to be used for all the inhabitants of a country who lived within given frontiers, which were controlled by their (presumably democratic) government. From there it was a short step to insisting on one common language, uniform administrative structures, fixed boundaries, armies and if possible an identical ideology for all.

During the 19th and early 20th centuries "nation-states" began to replace multi-national empires and ultimately became the political model after 1918. Inheriting the mystique that had formerly surrounded the monarch, the nation-state developed national "theologies", public ceremonies, national hymns, particular views of history, notions of the sacredness of frontiers and the need for laying down one's life for the nation. The model, invented in Europe, was exported overseas, where post-colonial states adopted it whether it was suitable for them or not.

While the nation-state ideology is declining in Europe it remains unbroken in the United States. Most nation-state ideologies are formulated by the dominant power sectors in a given state, who are often able to impose their beliefs on the rest of the population, if necessary by force of arms. During the cold war the great powers pushed unstable governments throughout the world to transform their countries into national security states. These became major violators of human rights and initiators of social and ethnic conflicts.

The term *ideology* refers to a set of ideas about politics, social organization and philosophy which are put together on the basis of a presumably logical guiding principle. Such currents of thought do not of course necessarily remain confined to national territory; liberal or Marxist ideologies are obvious examples of trans-national ideologies. However, when applied to a single state or to a group of states, ideology can be used with deadly efficiency by a ruling group against its own people or against other states.

These definitions, brief as they are, point to some of the negative factors leading to the type of conflict with which this book is concerned. Over against these destructive elements, it is important to emphasize the constructive role to which religion is called, its potential for peace in opposition to such deadly forces. Universal religions commonly demand unconditional obedience to a supreme deity that is not limited to any single territory or ethnic group. As creator of the universe and of the earth, this deity is the father and the mother of *all* human beings, implying that all human beings are fellow creatures called to treat each other with respect and love. Organizing life together imposes certain conditions, among them justice, respect for human rights, ecological sustainability and life in community. Religions also have conceptions of the origins and fulfilment of the earth and humanity which provide meaning for life and death above and beyond the confines of time and space.

Such convictions, which stand in stark opposition to narrow ethnicity, nation-alism and ideology, can serve as guidelines to help religious institutions and local religious communities deal with their conflicting loyalties and capacities for peace-making in the context of ethnic conflicts. Without examining these matters of principle, they run the risk of being taken in by the forces of this world.

In this book, the expressions "religion", "Christianity" and "church" or "churches" are often used without any clear distinction between them. This is due to the fact that several of the major religions fall under the purview of this study, but its conclusions are basically addressed to Christians. It is nevertheless assumed that ethnic conflicts cannot be effectively confronted and resolved without the unhesitating cooperation of all religions.

An ecumenical issue

The central concern in this book with how ethnic conflicts and religion are related is not a new issue on the agenda of the World Council of Churches. The WCC has since its founding in 1948 (and through its predecessor organizations since the early 1920s) consistently called on its member churches to be involved in the struggle against human rights abuses, racism and genocide — as part of the search for Christian unity and the unity of humankind. Major examples of such involvement include the substantial study of colonial racism by the International Missionary Council, submitted by ecumenical pioneer J.H. Oldham to the world missionary conference in Jerusalem in 1928; the strong stand by the Life and Work world conference in Oxford in 1937 against National Socialist racism and the "divinization" of the totalitarian state; the rescue of persecuted Jews during the second world war by what was then the WCC "in process of formation", in conjunction with the World Jewish Congress; cooperation of the WCC Department on Church and Society with the churches in newly independent countries of Asia and Africa on nation-building; the creation in 1969 of the Programme to Combat Racism (PCR); and multi-faceted support for human rights activities over the years in many parts of the globe.

Under the impact of the ethnic crises in Bosnia and Rwanda, the WCC joined with the Lutheran World Federation and the World Alliance of Reformed Churches to organize in November 1994 a consultation in Colombo, Sri Lanka, on "Ethnicity and Nationalism: A Challenge to the Churches". Judging the role of the Christian community in these conflicts to be "difficult and often ambiguous", the participants suggested that the theological concept of the kingdom of God in the different church traditions should be explored afresh, because it might provide a key to help churches rethink their relations to nationalism and ethnicity. The consultation, after reviewing several contemporary ethnic conflicts, called on the churches to reassess their history critically and to evaluate their own involvement and their inadvertent support for nationalist and ethnocentric ambitions. They were asked to explore their relations with people of other faiths and to become servants of the "reconciliation of God at the local level". The text of the report from this consultation is published as an appendix to this book (pp.150-56). [2]

Following this lead, there was further reflection on ethnicity during a meeting of the WCC Working Group on Racism, Indigenous Peoples and Ethnicity (Unit III) in Berlin in January 1996. Those taking part did not hesitate to analyze the often questionable contribution of some churches to the historical formation of distinct ethnicities. While recognizing that churches have sometimes provided identity and security to threatened communities, the report of this meeting notes that churches have also given support and legitimation to ethnic and national values and elites which threaten other ethnic groups. "In some countries the church presents itself as being the backbone of the nation and of nation-state building. This is the case, among others, of the Orthodox churches in Eastern Europe, a process which is still going on." This involvement has led to fragmentation, competition, rivalry and violence, especially where "official churches" have been connected with the majority population and with governments. Territories come to be considered as ethnic property:

> Churches provide legitimacy for the re-emergence of ethnic nationalism. In some countries, ethnic nationalism serves as alternate legitimation of elites, previously legitimated by communist ideology... Inter-ethnic wars cover religious, confessional disputes and conflicts. Some churches, while professing conciliatory intervention, are often feeding the very conflicts (frequently violent) which they are supposed to conciliate. [3]

Several months later, in September 1996, the moderator of the WCC central committee, Catholicos Aram I of the Armenian Apostolic Church (Cilicia), outlined in an address to the meeting of that committee in Geneva some positive patterns for an ecumenical policy regarding ethnic conflicts. He urged WCC member churches

> to manifest themselves as a conciliar fellowship of mutual commitment which goes beyond ethnic, national, geographic and cultural identities and confines. They must see the prevention of ethnic conflicts as a long-term task and as a process, a process which is intended to re-affirm our long-standing commitment to a just society, participatory democracy, a community of diversities and ethically sustainable humanity. [4]

This book looks at nine ethnic conflicts in which religion plays a significant role. Both the conflicts and the way religion functions in them vary from situation to situation. While the first two — Armenia 1915 and the Jewish holocaust — belong to the past and can therefore be looked at more "objectively", the others continue into the present, and any account of them must remain open-ended and somewhat vague. They unfolded almost from day to day while this study was being written and have developed further since then.

Following these case studies, some of the insights emerging will be further explored through four foci, especially the question of how ethnic conflicts and religion interact and what guidelines might be further developed for a more dynamic ecumenical approach to them. These findings do not of course exhaust the possibilities for prevention of such conflicts, but are meant to induce readers to further reflection and action of their own. It should be added that although this study has been requested by the WCC, it does not purport to represent the official views of that organization nor does it attempt to describe all of its extensive activities in the field of racial and ethnic conflicts.

The chapters that follow make sobering reading. They tell of human entanglements and betrayals, of depravity and sin, of religious bigotry and disobedience to divine commandments. But they also tell of the incredible courage and indomitable will to survive and to begin life afresh among individuals and entire communities who in the midst of adversity are "touched by the grace of God".

It seems to me that Christians and adherents of other faiths who are concerned about future outbreaks of ethnic and racial violence must raise one question insistently: How can an *early warning system* be set up in order to prevent such murderous crises? Churches and other religious structures and their leaders are close enough to their peoples to know what is going on. They cannot escape their responsibility. What effective methods can they develop to calm dangerous situations, to convey a message of peace and reconciliation when they see threatening situations, to act as mediators, to communicate effectively and courageously with their governments and to the international community? There must be no limit to such imaginative action, always in the knowledge that "disunity costs lives", aware that also indifference can have deadly consequences. For once a conflict has broken out, no statement by religious leaders, no matter how well meant, will make the evildoers sheathe their drawn swords.

NOTES

[1] R.J. Rummel, *Death by Government: Genocide and Mass Murder Since 1900*, New Brunswick NJ (USA), Transaction Publishers, 1994. According to Rummel's figures, three countries account for the largest number of losses, which he classifies as *deka-murders* (tens of millions): the Soviet Union (61.9 million from 1917 to 1987), China (10.1 million by the Kuomintang, 1928-1949, and 35.2 million under communist rule) and Germany (20.9 million from 1933 to 1945). To the next largest category, classified as *mega-murders* (between one and ten million), belong Japan (6 million from 1931 to 1945), China (3.5 million from 1923 to 1928), Cambodia (2 million from 1975 to 1979), Turkey (1.9 million from 1909 to 1918), Vietnam (1.7 million from 1945 to 1987), Poland (1.6 million from 1945 to 1948), Pakistan (1.5 million from 1958 to 1987), Yugoslavia (1 million under Tito, 1944-1987), North Korea (1.7 million from 1948 to 1987), Mexico (1.4 million from 1900 to 1920) and Russia (1 million from 1900 to 1917).

[2] Several papers from the consultation were published in *The Ecumenical Review*, Vol. 47, no. 2, Apr. 1995, pp.225ff.

[3] Cf. Minutes of the WCC Working Group on Racism, Berlin, 11-18 January 1996, Geneva, WCC Programme Unit III, 1996, p.19.

[4] *The Ecumenical Review*, Vol. 49, no. 1, Jan. 1997, p.101.

1
Armenia 1915

In a 1984 WCC report on Armenia, Ninan Koshy wrote:

The Armenian churches have a special claim on the World Council of Churches. As the Armenian churches uniquely represent the Armenian people, their membership in the WCC provides them with one major international forum for the Armenian people. Their concerns therefore need to be especially recognized by the ecumenical movement, and all efforts should be made to mobilize international support for their legitimate concerns. Even though the Armenian churches have played a significant role in the ecumenical movement, their history and their special plight are not widely known among the churches. Their witness as churches is all the more significant when one considers what suffering the Armenian people have gone through. [1]

Unfortunately, few significant efforts have been undertaken by WCC member churches to mobilize support for this nation, which was the first in the 20th century to suffer mass genocide; and with the passing of time even the memory of the tragedy is falling into oblivion. For the sake of its own integrity the ecumenical movement should re-examine its obligations in the light of the above statement.

A long Christian history

Since time immemorial, the Armenians, a people of skilled artisans and enterprising merchants, have inhabited the vast mountain region between the Taurus mountains on the northeastern coast of the Mediterranean across Anatolia to the Black and Caspian Seas. The present-day independent state of (formerly Russian Czarist and Soviet) Armenia covers a mere one-tenth of a once considerable territory. The early Armenians raised cattle and established intensive forms of agriculture with elaborate irrigation systems. Armenia lies on the crossroads between Asia and Europe and between the Fertile Crescent and Russia; and some great rivers, including the Tigris and the Euphrates have their source in Armenia. Trading and early forms of banking followed naturally.

Unfortunately, these very advantages have made Armenia a strategic region, which the great powers of different eras have invaded again and again. Thus Ararat, Armenia's sacred mountain, mentioned in Genesis as the place where Noah's ark landed after the great flood, rises today on Turkish soil.

The Armenians were already known to the ancient Babylonians, and their kingdom, centred on Lake Van, fought off the invading Assyrians. In the 6th century B.C., Medes and Persians reduced Armenia to a vassal state. After the defeat of the Persian empire by Alexander the Great in 331 B.C., Armenia became a satrapy of the Seleucid kingdom, only to be caught up in a centuries-long seesaw struggle between the Romans and — once again — the Persians.

Christian faith probably entered Armenia at an early stage. The Armenian heartlands were near to Galatia, to whose Christian communities Paul sent one of his letters; and there were almost certainly Armenians in the Christian congregations in Syria. The apostles Thaddaeus and Bartholomew brought the gospel to Armenia directly and were martyred there. The existence of many Christians during the persecution under Decius (c. A.D. 250) is reported, and early sources mention a Christian called Merusanes as bishop over the Armenians in 254. In 301, King Tiridates III, his family and many others were baptized by Gregory the Illuminator. Tiridates outlawed pagan religions and ordered his subjects to accept the Christian faith, making Armenia the first Christian nation in history. Pagan priests and their families converted en masse and transmitted the new faith to the people. The king named Gregory to be head (catholicos) of the Armenian church.

The church adopted an Orthodox structure, with a rich liturgical and monastic life, but for political reasons remained outside the canonical sphere of the patriarchate of Constantinople. Theologically, it is monophysite (understanding Christ as having *one* divine-human nature), and is thus part of what is called the Oriental Orthodox family. At Etchmiadzine in eastern Armenia, Gregory established the church's ecclesiastical and monastic centre. The Bible was translated into Armenian in 410, shortly after the alphabet had been fixed. The writings of the church fathers were also translated; and out of this a rich general literature developed alongside the arts and trades.

In the wake of the Crusades the Dominican order penetrated Armenia and set up one of the first Uniate churches. The Armenian Orthodox liturgy was maintained though pruned to Roman standards. Priests were allowed to marry as heretofore, but the bishop of Rome and not the catholicos was recognized as head of the church. During the late 19th century Protestant missions began to make inroads into Armenia, so that today several Armenian Evangelical churches also exist.

The continuous dual pressure of the Byzantine empire and Persia began to weaken Armenia. Under Arab domination (640-1064) the country broke up into several smaller rival kingdoms. Even so, monastic life and literature continued to develop. The magnificent Surp Chatch (Sacred Cross) centre was built on Achtamar Island in Lake Van in 915 and served as the seat of the catholicos from 939 to 959.

A thousand years of persecution
The real tragedy of Armenia began in 1064 when Turkish Seljuks from central Asia conquered the city of Ani in eastern Armenia. Many Armenians fled to Cilicia near the Mediterranean coast, where an Armenian kingdom survived for another 300 years before falling to the Egyptian Mameluks in 1375. One result of this was the setting up of a second catholicosate in Cilicia, whose existence became a source of uneasy tension within the church. As of 1220 eastern and northern Armenia became subject to destructive Mongol attacks under Gengis Khan. The Mongols were followed in 1387 by the Tatars under Tamerlane. Although his empire, extending from China to Moscow, was short-lived, his

twenty-year rule is recalled as one of the most severe in Armenia's tortured history.

However the worst catastrophe that befell the Armenian people was the domination by the Ottoman Turks from 1375 until 1918, culminating in the genocide of 1915. Under Sultan Osman the Turks adopted Islam in 1299. On 29 May 1453, Constantinople, weakened by the invading Crusaders from Western Europe, fell to Sultan Muhammed II, who rode into the Hagia Sophia, Christianity's most beautiful cathedral, on horseback. The crescent replaced the cross. In due time all of southeastern Europe up to Vienna fell under Ottoman domination. Except for Russia, this included virtually all of the nations that adhered to the Orthodox faith. Likewise most Arab countries from Iraq to Morocco came under Turkish suzerainty.

Long warfare had substantially reduced the Armenian population. In 1514 the Ottomans conquered much of the eastern part of the country, which had been subjected to the Persian empire. Sultan Selim I ordered the Sunnite Muslim Kurds to occupy the area, in order to defend it against the Shi'ite Muslim Persians and to keep an eye on the Christian Armenians. The Kurds exploited the already impoverished Armenians, imposing taxes at will and abducting their wives and daughters.

The Ottoman empire also imposed on the Armenians and its other Christian subjects a head tax (*karadj*), which gave the taxpayer the right to "carry his head on his shoulders" from one year to the next, a military tax on each male above the age of three months up to old age (although Christians were excluded from serving in the armed forces) and special taxes to cover the costs of its almost continuous wars. Christians were also obliged to accommodate Muslim guests for three days at no charge and each year to deliver to the sultan a number of boys between the ages of four and eight, called the *Devishirmé*. [2] These boys were taken from their families, circumcised and reared in the Islamic faith and Turkish culture. After a rugged military training they were incorporated in the janissary corps, which was used with deadly efficiency, usually against Christian enemies. Under the rule of Suleiman the Magnificent (1520-1566) no fewer than 40,000 such boys were taken away from their families. The story of the janissaries is one of the most brutal violations of human rights in history.

Under such circumstances, the Armenian Orthodox Church represented the last remaining visible form of identity and cohesion for the entire people. The catholicos, once the right hand of the king, now became the supreme representative of the tortured nation in the Ottoman *millet* system under which each non-Muslim religious community was recognized as an entity with its own internal traditions and laws. Often addressed as *Wehapar* (Majesty), the catholicos also had the duty to pass on and explain the sultan's decrees, and if any problem arose within the Armenian community, the catholicos was held responsible, often at the price of his head. [3]

A time of betrayal

In the late 18th century the Armenians began to awaken from their long mental stupor. Literature and cultural life came alive, and travellers brought news of political developments in Western Europe and North America. Orthodox Russia was becoming a great power and occupied the northern shore of the Black Sea and Transcaucasia. Other Christian nations under the Ottoman yoke, beginning with the Greeks and Serbians, began to rebel. In 1828 the Russians under Alexander II entered eastern Armenia, which had been controlled by the Persians. But the Russians, Orthodox as they might be in their faith, signalled no intention of moving into western Armenia. On the contrary, they began immediately with a massive Russification programme of church, school and society — precisely in the areas the Armenians had kept free from the Turks.

After this disappointing encounter with another Christian nation, the Armenians set their hopes on the Western European powers which had helped the Greeks to regain their independence. Encouraging signs came from France, which had halted the massacre of the Maronites in Lebanon in 1860, placing that country under its virtual protectorate, and had intervened again on behalf of the Armenian community in Zeitun in 1867. In fact, the European powers had no intention of dismantling or weakening the Ottoman empire, fearing that Russia might then seek control over the strategic Dardanelles and come uncomfortably close to the Suez Canal. Treating Turkey with kid gloves has remained a constant political pattern by the Western powers to this day. Moreover, Armenia was militarily far less accessible to the West than Greece and dangerously close to Czarist Russia. To intervene there would be risky.

Aware of its almost invulnerable strategic position, the Ottoman empire under Sultan Abdul Hamid (1876-1915) showed no restraint in making the Armenians suffer for daring to expect their liberation. In the treaty of San Stefano (1878), which ended the Russo-Turkish war, Romania, Serbia and Montenegro obtained their independence, Bulgaria became an autonomous principality, Bosnia-Herzegovina was occupied by Austria-Hungary and Cyprus was "leased" to the British. The Armenians were merely granted internal autonomy, to be guaranteed by the powers of the day: Russia, Great Britain, Austria-Hungary, France, Germany and Italy. On paper at least they obtained full equal rights.

Although the Russians and the British considered themselves the special protectors of the Armenians and of the other Christians, their rivalry cancelled the effectiveness of this "guarantee", and the cunning and ruthless Abdul Hamid knew how to play the powers against each other. He soon realized that they would never compel him to honour the terms of the San Stefano treaty regarding the Armenians, whom he considered the most disruptive and obnoxious elements of all his subject peoples and for whom he had developed a profound hatred. On them he could take revenge for his humiliation. San Stefano thus contained the seeds for the massacre of 1915.

Even so Armenian reformist and revolutionary circles began in 1885 to clamour for the implementation of the Armenian clauses of San Stefano. They did not realize that Russia, frustrated that San Stefano had prevented it from controlling the Dardanelles, had lost interest in the Armenians and was expanding into Central Asia. The British, worried as ever about the Suez Canal, had occupied Egypt in 1881, and were also turning their eyes away from Armenia. It was a clear betrayal for *raisons d'état*.

Yet not all hope was lost. The Turkish people themselves were beginning to clamour for a revolutionary transformation of their corrupt state. The newly established party of the "Young Turks" was demanding that every inhabitant of Turkey be granted the same civic rights as had been established in Western European countries, without regard to race or religion. In fact, however, it would be from Turkish nationalism that the Armenians would meet their greatest danger.

The crisis of the Ottoman empire

Angered by Armenian restlessness, Abdul Hamid disregarded the stipulations of the San Stefano treaty and allowed Kurdish nomads to organize paramilitary regiments, who were permitted to engage in theft, rape, burning and general destruction. In 1894, when exasperated Armenians in the Sassun region attacked gendarmes who had tried to confiscate from them what little they had left, they were declared to be in a state of rebellion against the sultan. Abdul Hamid sent in his regular troops, who indiscriminately murdered 600 men, women and children and destroyed 27 villages. [4]

The European powers protested and extracted from Abdul Hamid another pledge to stop the repression and to implement the reforms promised at San Stefano. Britain and France forced the Turkish government to accept a political restructuring of its eastern provinces. But rather than keeping his promise, the sultan became increasingly convinced that only the complete extinction of the Armenians would make foreign powers end their "interference" in Turkey's internal affairs.

Counting on the empire's weakness and on foreign help, Armenian nationalists felt the moment had come to exert further pressure. On 30 September 1895 two thousand Armenians marched through the streets of Constantinople to present their grievances to the grand vizir. The authorities provoked a counter-demonstration, and in the ensuing street fighting gendarmes killed several hundred Armenian demonstrators.

Immediately Abdul Hamid issued a proclamation that the Armenians had intended to murder the grand vizir. The response was predictable: mobs immediately initiated massacres in Constantinople and in ten provinces. By the end of the year over 88,000 Armenians had been massacred, 2500 villages and towns looted and burned, 568 churches and 77 monasteries destroyed and 328 churches converted into mosques. Over half a million Armenians lost all their possessions. In Urfa the massacres were especially brutal, though many Muslim Turks defended the Armenians with their own lives. On 28-29 December about 3000 men, women and children who had taken refuge in the great Armenian cathedral were burned alive. Altogether 8000 persons were murdered in Urfa. Their bodies lay about unburied for days until the authorities forced the Jews to carry them to mass graves alongside the city walls, a task that took an entire week. [5]

These massacres were not wild mob actions but were carried out according to careful plans. Usually, a bugle signalled the beginning of the killings on Fridays right after noonday prayers at the mosque. Armed bands, accompanied by Turkish military units, would attack the unsuspecting Armenians in the streets, in their shops or in their homes, which were looted. Men and boys were killed; women and girls led away. The local authorities in Arabkir issued the following order:

> All of Muhammed's sons are called to fulfill their duty, which is to kill all Armenians, to loot and burn their houses. Not one single Armenian must be spared. This is the Sultan's command. Whoever does not obey this command shall be considered to be an Armenian and will be killed as such. Therefore each Muslim must show obedience to the government and kill first those Christians who up to now have lived in friendship with him. [6]

Asked by Western governments to explain the massacres, the Turkish authorities said that they had been forced put down a vast uprising. The "Christian powers" were satisfied with this "explanation".

The Young Turk revolution

The Armenians and other nationalities welcomed the 1908 revolution of the Young Turks, who stripped Abdul Hamid of his powers while leaving him formally in office. Originally a group of progressive young civilians and army officers who reacted against Abdul Hamid's obscurantist policies, the Young Turks became anxious over rumours that the European powers planned to carve up the remnants of the Ottoman empire. For a time it seemed that they intended to create a modern state along Western European lines, in which all ethnic, racial and religious differences were to be eliminated. But their appeal to the spirit of nationalism in order to carry out their reforms in turn awakened separatist and nationalist spirits among all the hitherto oppressed peoples. Revolts broke out everywhere. These in turn led to Turkish counter-nationalism, ably agitated by Abdul Hamid and the reactionary Muslim clergy and growing as bad news continued to come: the annexation of Bosnia-Herzegovina by Austria-Hungary in 1908, the liberation of Crete in 1909, the disastrous Italian and Balkan wars of 1911-14 and the outbreak of the first world war, which Turkey fought on the side of the losers. When Abdul Hamid briefly regained his throne with the help of reactionary clergy, he organized a militarily executed massacre of between 20,000 and 25,000 Armenians in the regions of Adana and Aleppo.

In 1915 the Young Turks replaced Abdul Hamid by his brother, Muhammed V. To retain the favour of the military and the mob, they shifted their policy and adopted an ultra-nationalist Turkish position, though without Islamic religiosity. Ominously, when they regained power, they neither apologized to the Armenians for the massacres at Adana and Aleppo, nor court-martialled the responsible officers and soldiers. In time the Young Turk clique turned into a populist-nationalist dictatorship which began to propagate the pan-Turkish movement, promoting the superiority of Turks over all other peoples and the notion that all nationalities must be absorbed into one single Turkish race.

Aiming to renew the declining empire, the Young Turks ended up appealing to the most chauvinist and racist instincts of the Ottomans. As the empire lost its remaining North African and European possessions, refugees from the lost provinces were settled in Armenia, resulting in new looting and violence as Armenians were pushed from their ancestral homes.

The genocide of 1915

The outbreak of the first world war decided Armenia's ultimate fate. On 12 November 1914 Turkey, as Germany's ally, declared war on Russia and the Western Allies, even though it was obvious that, surrounded by powerful enemies on all sides, it could not possibly win. There were a few initial successes, including a superhuman defence of the strategic Dardanelles narrows against allied attack, inspired by Mustafa Kemal Pasha, one of the Young Turk leaders; but after this victory the Turkish armies retreated on all fronts. Insecure and obsessed by treason, the government decided to make the final move against the Armenians and exterminate them once and for all. It did not matter that Armenian soldiers were fighting for Turkey and that their church and community leaders had repeatedly assured the government of their loyalty.

The massacres began on 24 April 1915, when all the leading Armenians of Constantinople were arrested, led away and murdered. According to a well-established plan the genocide proceeded in four phases:

1. Armenian military units within the Turkish armed forces were disarmed and their members killed. This made the people virtually defenceless.
2. Local notables and spiritual leaders were arrested, deported and murdered. The Armenians were thereby deprived of their leadership.
3. The demoralized Armenian civilian population was thus easily disarmed. Simultaneously, the government formed special killer units of Kurds, Cherkessians and ordinary criminal bands, aided by army and police units, with some logistical help from German military staff officers.
4. The large mass of Armenians was deported to camps or to desert regions, where they were tortured or starved to death. Women and young girls were usually raped, and many were sold into slavery in distant parts of the Arabian peninsula and Transcaucasia. For months afterwards the sides of the roads along which the emaciated columns had marched remained littered with desiccated bodies and skeletons. The Armenians of Trebizond were loaded onto ships and thrown into the Black Sea.

When the US government learned of the beginning of the genocide, it offered to send as many ships as were necessary to take away the threatened Armenians, but the Turkish government refused.

Such a vast extermination programme could not have been carried out without the active participation of the local population, which on the instructions of the minister of the interior Talaat Bey had been stirred up by the mullahs during the previous weeks. Yet despite this pressure, many courageous Turks and Arabs refused to join the violence, and some went to great personal risk to hide Armenian families and help them to flee to safety.[7] But this was not enough to stop the horror. Men and boys continued to be led outside the population centres and gunned down. Men, women and children, including the elderly and the sick, were compelled to march to a destination which Talaat Bey himself said was "nowhere". Whenever the columns passed a town, the most beautiful girls and women and the young boys were exhibited and sold into slavery; and thousands of women and children ended up in Turkish harems or Bedouin tents, where they served as sex objects and cheap labour. Of the 18,000 Armenians deported from

Kharput and Sivas only 350 reached Aleppo; of 1900 from Erzerum a mere eleven survived. Between twenty and twenty-five thousand women and children were brutally murdered by the cavalry brigade that had deported them from Erzingian and by Kurdish bands they met along the way. Their bodies were thrown into the Euphrates. The largest life-giving river of the Fertile Crescent became a river of death. For months bodies could be seen floating as far down as Baghdad. [8]

According to statistics published by the Armenian Patriarchate in Constantinople, there were 1,845,450 Armenians in the Ottoman empire, including 76,500 Uniate Catholics and 40,950 Protestants. Of these, 1,396,350 were deported or murdered outright, 204,700 managed to stay alive and 244,400 fled abroad. The rest who survived were forced to convert. Those churches which were not destroyed were transformed into mosques or Turkish schools. The losses would have been worse if the Turkish government had not been impeded by German protests against the deportation of the 20,000 Armenians remaining in Constantinople after the community leadership had been deported and murdered. [9]

One bright exception to the story of death and destruction was the heroic defence of the Armenian villagers on Musa Dagh ("Moses Mountain"), near Aleppo. With few weapons and barely any food, they fought off the Turks for nearly seven weeks, until they were discovered by French warships, which saved 4058 survivors. *The Forty Days of Musa Dagh* by the German Jewish writer Franz Werfel is a literary monument to their courage. On a visit to Damascus in 1929 Werfel had seen undernourished and maimed Armenian refugee children working in a carpet factory. He wrote the novel during the winter of 1932-33 — the same winter that Adolf Hitler took power in Germany. [10]

Among the Turks who opposed the measures of their fanaticized government were some highly placed officials, including Halil Bey, the president of parliament, Ahmed Riza, a former president of parliament, various senators, Grand Vizir Said Halim Pasha, and the Sheikh-ul-Islam, Turkey's highest spiritual leader. Some local district governors who refused to carry out the order for the Armenian genocide had to pay for it with their lives. Certain mullahs considered the murder of Armenians a shame for the country and a sin against God; and Muslim families who refused to participate in mob action protected so many Armenians that the government issued a second warning that all those who hid Armenians would be deported or killed as if they were themselves Armenians.

Moreover, despite the assistance provided by German staff officers in the preparation for the mass murder, other German officers voiced their protest, and the German management of the Berlin-Baghdad railway refused to hand over its Armenian employees, saying that they were its most capable workers. A Kurdish tribe, the Dersim, not only did not take part in the genocide but also opened up its territory to Armenian refugees and protected them. [11]

A new betrayal

In 1919 the victorious Western nations (by that time the Russians were caught up in their revolution) decided to detach both the Arab provinces and Armenia from Turkey. The refugees abroad were encouraged to return, and both the United States and France planned to occupy Armenia for its military protection. According to the peace treaty of Sèvres in 1920 an Armenian territory — though without Cilicia and other areas in southeastern Anatolia — was set aside for the establishment of an independent republic. [12] But the Western powers became so involved in their own internal disputes that they never managed to send in troops in order to ensure Armenia's territorial integrity. US President Woodrow Wilson, who had backed the Armenians' cause, was overruled by the senate and by cynical European politicians. General James G. Harbord, the deputy chief of staff of the US army, who was involved in the negotiations with the Allies, called this "the most colossal crime in history".

Mustafa Kemal Pasha, later to become president of the republic and take the name Atatürk (father of the Turks), decided to take advantage of this virtual abandonment of the Armenians. He refused to recognize the treaty of Sèvres, and established the Turkish Republic. After expelling more than a million Greeks from their ancient homelands in Asia Minor, he joined with the Red Army coming from the east and ended the precarious independence of Armenia. Where the two armies met the new frontier was drawn between the Turkish Republic and the Soviet Union. The eastern remnant became the Socialist Republic of Armenia. The much larger western part was incorporated into the Turkish Republic and ceased to exist as a political entity. Thousands more Armenians were murdered and the rest went into exile.

In 1923 representatives of the Western powers and Turkey met in Lausanne to ratify the new power constellation. For the West an old strategic policy was reconfirmed, namely to have a strong Turkey as a barrier keeping a revolutionary Soviet Union away from the oil fields of Iraq and from the Suez Canal, Britain's lifeline to India. The Turkish pledges to preserve Armenian culture, schools and religion were worthless. The ageing officers of the Young Turk movement were carrying out identical policies as their arch-enemy, Abdul Hamid.

Having lost interest in Armenia, the West has continued to rationalize preservation of a "strong Turkey" within its present borders. Meanwhile, the occasional media references to the terrifying Armenian genocide generally use qualifiers such "alleged" or "asserted", though the archives are full of documentation regarding the annihilation of this people.

Turkey itself utterly denies the fact of the Armenian genocide. Neither the Turkish state nor Turkish officials have ever admitted the facts, much less any sense of guilt or remorse. One Turkish publication entitled *Setting the Record Straight on Armenian Propaganda against Turkey* even claims that "recent scholarly research" has shown that the accounts of massacres were invented by Armenian nationalists in Paris and London and disseminated worldwide by British intelligence. [13]

Such a "revision" of history is hardly made more credible by the behaviour of subsequent Turkish governments: the detention and torture of political opponents, the occupation of northern Cyprus, the pitiless warfare against the Kurds in southeastern Asia Minor, even sending airplanes and troops into Iraq (usually with NATO and American approval). In many ways this recalls elements of the Armenian genocide of 1915. Ironically, it was the forebears of the same Kurds from among whom the Turkish government had recruited some of its worst killers of Armenians. To these obvious misdeeds, the great powers of today keep their eyes closed, for not only does Turkey remain a "key ally", but it is now also seen as a great potential market.

The future of the Armenian people

But the Armenian people refuses to die. The former Soviet republic, now independent, has waged war against Azerbaijan to recuperate Nagorno-Karabagh, which Stalin had detached against Armenia's will. Attacks against Turkish diplomatic missions and installations indicate that a new generation is overcoming the stupor caused by the genocide. While most Armenians reject terrorism, many note that the Jewish people were not squeamish about the methods they used to regain their ancient homeland. There are apparent contacts with the Kurdish leadership to reconsider a common political future.

From its side, Turkey, despite an outward show of military strength, has a weak economy and an unstable political system (which have frustrated its aspirations to membership of the European Union). Thus it would seem to have every interest in reaching a permanent settlement of its combined Armenian-Kurdish problem. But the current rise of Islamic fundamentalism, which feeds on poverty and spiritual disorientation, is likely to be a growing impediment to coming to grips with its past and creating a better future.

Outside the independent former Soviet republic, the Armenian diaspora disposes of considerable human and economic resources which could be invested in an area that has experienced nothing but economic decline ever since 1915. Large communities of this two-million-member diaspora are found in North America (600,000), Lebanon and Syria (450,000), Iran and France (300,000 each), Latin America (150,000), Turkey (50,000, mainly in Istanbul) and Australia (50,000). [14]

The two catholicosates of the Armenian Apostolic Church have been active members of the WCC since 1962; the smaller Protestant Armenian churches since 1948. As the oldest national church in history, the Armenian Apostolic Church has a distinctive character and rich religious expression marked by its long and untold suffering. The church leadership is trying to hold this worldwide community together against tendencies to pull it apart, including the fact that Armenian is no longer the spoken language of the new generation, which has become integrated into different national cultures. Moreover, as a result of the recent upheavals in Lebanon and other countries of the Middle East, a growing number of Armenians are continuing to leave the region.

Ninan Koshy suggests some possibilities of action:

Whatever the claims of Armenians and whatever the denials of Turkey, the solution, any solution can only be found through dialogue. It is here that the ecumenical community may make its most profound contribution. Dialogue is not an "easy way out". It is full of risks and requires great courage. Dialogue must be initiated by the strong. Armenians may be strong in courage, but they are weak in political influence. It is here that churches could pool their persuasive powers to bring the Armenian cause on the world agenda once again. And the Turkish government should be encouraged by its friends to take the necessary first steps towards dialogue. [15]

Pursuing this line of thought raises two immediate questions. The first concerns the need for a fresh reading of history which is acceptable to the descendants of both sides, a rereading based not on questionable compromise but on a critical examination of documents and historical facts. From there to forgiveness and reconciliation is still a great distance. Well-meant admonitions of the Turkish authorities have probably not even been heard, and the present rise of Islamic fundamentalism no doubt makes it more unlikely that they will be. Yet the fact that in 1915 there were Turks and Kurds, including mullahs, who protested against the mass murder of Armenians could be a sign that not all doors are closed. Can the spiritual heirs of these people be found? Could a dialogue be established at least with them?

Moreover, Turkey should have a political interest in lifting the moral cloud that has hung over it since 1915. Without a readiness by Turkey to acknowledge this moral problem, the international community can hardly be expected to welcome the Turkish state as a full partner. Strategic or market considerations are no longer enough at a time when geopolitics are changing. However, the initiative for such a dialogue should not come from the Armenians, who are the ones who have suffered from the genocide. The first move for recalling history must come from the international community; and the ecumenical movement, which has already expressed concern, could take a leading role in this. Once a dialogue has started and shown signs of promise, the Armenians will of course come in and pursue the effort.

The second question relates to another possibility that lies dormant in the ecumenical fellowship. It has been rightly said that the Armenian genocide has largely dropped out of the mind of the churches except for the Armenian churches. This is in sharp contrast to the Jewish holocaust, which is still very much alive in the consciousness of the churches. Christians in Western countries, especially France, Germany, Britain and the United States, and in Russia have never faced up to their historical debt towards the Armenian people due to the inexcusable silence of their forebears when their governments delivered Armenia to its enemies. This is in no way to detract from the magnificent relief work which Western churches provided after the massacres of 1885 and especially during the decades after the first world war. But charitable work does not replace political action. This involves more than establishing a joint committee of church historians — although this in itself would be of great value — but a belated acknowledgment to Armenian Christians that betrayal *did* take place, which led to both genocide and loss of country. It is a search for an historical conscience, which is the first step towards a revitalization of the Armenian concern within the ecumenical fellowship.

The silence of the churches in 1915 had deeper consequences. By allowing their governments not to face up to the Armenian massacres, the churches of the countries most concerned indirectly opened the way for the German National Socialists to prepare the Jewish holocaust less than a generation later. To this we turn in the next chapter.

NOTES

1 *Armenia: The Continuing Tragedy*, Geneva, WCC Commission of the Churches on International Affairs Background Paper no. 1, 1984, p.5.

2 Cf. Karl Meyer, *Armenien und die Schweiz*, Bern, Blaukreuz Verlag, 1974, p.30.

3 *Ibid.*, p.31.

4 *Ibid.*, p.36.

5 *Ibid.*, pp.37f.

6 Cited by Meyer, *ibid.*, p.38. Among other Christians to suffer massacres at the hands of the Ottomans during the 19th century were 50,000 Greeks on the island of Chios in 1822, 12,000 Maronites and Syrian Orthodox in Lebanon in 1860, 25,000 Greek Orthodox in Bulgaria in 1876 and 55,000 Greeks in Crete, Macedonia, Epirus and Thessaly from 1896 to 1898 (*ibid.*, p.257).

7 *Armenia: The Continuing Tragedy*, p.13.

8 Meyer, *op. cit.*, pp.93f., 97.

9 *Ibid.*, pp.104f.

10 Introductory note to Franz Werfel, *The Forty Days of Musa Dagh*, New York, Viking, 1934.

11 Meyer, *op. cit.*, pp.105f.

12 For the relevant paragraphs of the Treaty of Sèvres, see *Armenia: The Continuing Tragedy*, pp.36-41.

13 *Ibid.*, p.14.

14 *Ibid.*, p.19.

15 *Ibid.*, pp.32f.

2
The Jewish Holocaust

When Adolf Hitler (1889-1945) took the final decision to eliminate Europe's Jews in 1941, one of his advisors is said to have expressed the fear that the world would violently protest. Hitler answered no, the world had not reacted when the Armenians were murdered, and it would not do so now. Six million Jews were wiped out, gassed and burned in industrial furnaces despite two thousand years of Christian worship, preaching and education in Europe. Or perhaps — more disturbing — *because* of it.

Born and reared a Roman Catholic, Hitler knew that antisemitism was too deeply ingrained in the life and thought of the churches to make Christians rise as a body and shield their Jewish fellow human beings — even though the Hebrew Bible is also part of Christian holy scripture, even though the New Testament testifies unequivocally that Jesus lived and died as a faithful Jew, even though the Apostle Paul, formerly the Rabbi Saul of Tarsus, a messenger of the faith to the Gentiles, said that "there is no distinction between Jew and Greek; the same Lord is Lord of all and is generous to all who call on him" (Rom. 10:13). In Paul's eyes the Jews remained God's chosen people. They were the trunk, of which the faith in the Crucified was nothing but a new shoot. Nevertheless, a sharp break between Judaism and the nascent Christian church occurred already during the generation after Jesus. The New Testament reflects the intensity of this theological controversy, though no one could have fathomed its consequences. The enormity of the crime of the *Shoah* and Christian indifference, complicity or outright hostility may defy human comprehension. The issue becomes clearer if one looks at how this hatred has developed.

Theological roots of Christian anti-Judaism

The history of anti-Judaism and antisemitism within and outside of Christianity has been dealt with extensively by many competent historians, but a short summary may serve as an introduction to this chapter. While Paul said no distinction is to be made between Jews and Greeks, both his letters and the gospels reflect a growing disappointment over the refusal of Abraham's descendents to accept Jesus as God's Messiah (*Christos*). Their lack of receptivity soon developed into mutual hostility between church and synagogue. To the Jews the idea of the Messiah's death on the cross was preposterous. Moreover, they questioned the veracity of the accounts of Jesus' rising from the dead — the very basis of the Christians' central beliefs and for further doctrinal development.

Before the end of the 1st century the synagogue formally broke with the Christian community. The Christians in turn counter-attacked. They called the

Jews a "stiff-necked" and "apostate" race which no longer merited the designation of God's "chosen people". God had hidden his face from them. They would be turned over to damnation. The church had instead become the "new Israel", the "new chosen people". Rome or Constantinople was now the divinely appointed "new Jerusalem". In addition, the church collected a scriptural canon of its own, the *New* (that is the *real*) Testament, through which alone the canonical Hebrew scriptures were to be interpreted. These were reduced in status and renamed the *Old* Testament.

Out of this early theological warfare arose the hate-filled accusation that the Jews had condemned themselves when they had turned Jesus over to Pilate and called out: "His blood be on us and on our children!" (Matt. 27:25). This lay behind the gruesome term "Christ-killers!", which reverberated whenever and wherever Jews were massacred. The idea attributed to Jesus in the gospel of John that the Jews were descended from the devil (John 8:44) led to the accusation, "confirmed" in the torture chambers of the Inquisition, that the Jews were in league with Satan. Not surprisingly, as soon as the Roman emperor Theodosius decreed Christianity the state religion in 380, synagogues were burned in the name of Jesus the Jew.

Throughout the centuries there was no need to search for causes of natural catastrophes, epidemics and other crises: the Jews were obviously guilty. The New Testament "proved" it and the clergy repeated it. Destroying Jewish communities was a good act in the eyes of God.

The Jews were a thorn in the flesh of Christianity. They did not mix socially. They followed different rites and ethical rules. They spoke a language no one else understood and refused to be converted. They were outside all norms, a suspect and accursed race. Still, apart from sporadic outbreaks of violence, there were no systematic persecutions once the Roman empire collapsed. During the early middle ages, relationships between Christians and Jews began to assume a certain precarious normality. The atmosphere took a decisive turn for the worse in 1095 when Pope Urban II called for the Crusades, in order to liberate Christ's tomb from the Muslim "unbelievers". Before setting out on their long journey to Palestine some Christian knights attacked Jews in their own surroundings and burned them at the stake for their "unbelief". Besides seeing this as earning them eternal salvation, some knights used the occasion as a method of liquidating their debts to Jewish money-lenders. In some cases, the Christians imposed the payment of additional ransom, allowing the Jews just to stay alive.

When Jerusalem fell to the Crusaders on 15 July 1099 thousands of Jews were murdered along with the local Muslim and (Orthodox) Christian inhabitants. The blood of the conquered ran down the streets, and at nightfall after the massacre the knights raised their blood-stained hands in the Church of the Holy Sepulchre and thanked God for their victory.

In 1266, during the "century of faith", a church council forced the Jews to live in separate areas. This was the beginning of the ghetto. In 1279 all Jews were ordered to wear special clothes and headgear, making them easily identifiable in a crowd, the antecedent of the yellow star imposed by the Nazis for the same purpose.

The next great catastrophe was the expulsion of the Jews from Spain in 1492, the same year Granada, the last Arab stronghold in Europe, fell and Columbus sailed for America. Since the 8th century a unique Arab-Jewish civilization had flourished in Spain, and its distinctive architecture, philosophy, mathematics and writing made it one of the marvels of mediaeval Europe. This culture was destroyed by the Christians during the so-called *Reconquista*. Both Muslims and Jews were forced to convert, driven out or murdered — usually after being tortured. The clergy called the converted Jews *marranes* (pigs), and they were constantly harassed by the Inquisition and ostracized by their Christian neighbours. Thousands of Jews fled to other European countries and North Africa.

The Protestant Reformation of the 16th century signified no improvement of relations between Christians and Jews. Martin Luther called the Jews "thirsty bloodhounds and murderers of Christendom". His violent tirades may have been downplayed by later Protestants but this did not diminish anti-Jewish prejudice. Deadly bias was deeply ingrained in all of Europe, east and west, north and south, regardless of confessional adherence.

Modern antisemitism

The European Enlightenment in the 18th century seemed at last capable of diminishing anti-Jewish prejudice, and Jews in Central and Eastern Europe looked to Germany with high esteem. But liberation from the ghetto and civic equality brought Jews into direct contact and competition with the bourgeois classes of Christian origin. The vicious circle began to turn again; and by the second half of the 19th century traditional Christian anti-Judaism had turned into modern antisemitism, with fatal consequences.

Developments in Poland and Russia played a key role in this transition. Up to the 17th century both countries generally maintained a positive attitude towards Jews. They willingly received refugees fleeing persecution in Spain and other parts of Europe. The Russian Orthodox clergy were often favourably disposed towards the Jewish people, though at some points they were also the instigators of persecution.

In 1648 the Cossack leader Bogdan Chmielnicki led a revolt against Polish Catholic estate owners who were ruthlessly exploiting Orthodox Russian and Ukrainian peasants. Joined by Tatars from Crimea and Russians living in Poland, Chmielnicki's hordes murdered not only Polish landowners and Roman Catholic priests, but also thousands of Jews; and the carnage spread well beyond Poland into Ukraine, Lithuania and Bielorussia. In Gomel all the Jews were handed over to Chmielnicki and were tortured and killed. After a temporary setback in 1651 at the hands of a Polish army, Chmielnicki resumed his murderous campaign with help from the Russian czar, who saw an opportunity to incorporate Poland into his empire. By 1655 the Cossacks had massacred or driven out the Jews from all major cities in Bielorussia and Lithuania. Half a million Jews had lost their lives, the largest Jewish catastrophe prior to the second world war. [1]

In 1791, after having incorporated new Jewish subjects with the annexation of eastern and central Poland and western Ukraine, Russia restricted Jewish residence to the southwestern part its empire, the so-called "Pale of Settlement". During the

19th century, the east European *shtetl* (small town) culture flourished in this area, home to four million Jews. But Russia was anything but tolerant, and numerous abusive measures were imposed on this minority in terms of dress, education, language and military service. In the 1880s, Czar Alexander III, fearful of the approaching revolution, once again authorized Cossack bands to spread destruction and death in the Jewish settlements of Ukraine and Poland; and the Russian expression *pogrom* ("like thunder") — an organized, officially condoned massacre of helpless people — became part of the modern vocabulary. New restrictions and deportations followed. After Russia's disastrous war with Japan in 1904-1905 the Cossacks struck again throughout the Pale. Hundreds of Jews were murdered in Kishinev, the Romanian-speaking capital of Moldavia, and in Odessa. After the outbreak of the first world war further pogroms took place in Russia and Russian-held Poland. As a result two million Jews left for the United States, 200,000 for Great Britain, 100,000 for Canada and 300,000 for other European countries. [2] Out of this experience of persecution, Zionism (see below, chapter 5) would arise as an instrument of Jewish self-defence.

By the turn of the century this virulent form of antisemitism was seeping westward into Austria-Hungary and France. Between 1894 and 1906 France was shaken by the trial and condemnation of Captain Alfred Dreyfus, a Jewish officer falsely accused of betraying military secrets. Conservative Roman Catholic circles agitated against Dreyfus and Jews in general, feeding on the racist spirit spread by Joseph Arthur Gobineau (1816-82) in his *Essai des inégalités des races humaines*, which justified both antisemitism and European colonialism in Africa on racist grounds. Many European Jews thus came to consider Germany, with its strong government, more than ever the enlightened centre of Europe.

The atmosphere was further poisoned by the publication in 1903 of a vicious piece of anti-Jewish satire, *The Protocols of the Learned Elders of Zion*, probably fabricated by the czarist secret police and translated into many languages. Its insinuations of a Jewish plan for world domination came to influence even well-meaning and well-informed Christians during the decades to come, creating a fertile atmosphere for the later ideas of National Socialism and fascism.

The ideological antisemitism which replaced traditional Christian antisemitism and anti-Judaism became intermingled with the fashionable new racial theories. Jews were no longer seen as adherents of another faith who refused submit to Christian truth, but as members of another race. Germanic and northern European Christians saw themselves as Aryans, descendants of a mystic and superior *Herrenrasse*, a master race. The Jew was a mere *Untermensch*, a subhuman being. Thus the object was no longer to convert Jews but to destroy them, as part of a massive effort to redraw the map of Europe.

Slavic peoples like the Poles and the Russians, even though they were Christians, were also not considered part of the Aryan race; and their land could thus also be taken away to provide new *Lebensraum* (living space) for the Germanic Aryans. They did not necessarily have to be exterminated, because they might be needed as slaves in the new state. These racial-territorial theories were being put in place throughout Europe during the forty years before the Nazis seized power in 1933. Similar attitudes were reflected in the racial theories of all the colonial powers, as well as in the separation of races in the United States and South Africa. [3]

The first world war: the dam breaks

Still, the worst disasters might have been averted had it not been for the first world war, which destroyed the inherited political, social and psychological structures of Europe. The experience of endless trench warfare and the terrifying modern weaponry produced by science and industry sent out shock waves. Moreover, in 1917 a violent revolution replaced the czarist government in Russia with a totalitarian socialist regime. The long-heralded world revolution seemed to be around the corner. The old multi-ethnic Austro-Hungarian and Ottoman empires were destroyed in 1918, to be replaced by a series of national states at war's end. But instead of global revolution, new reactionary forces emerged in many countries. In Italy, Germany and Spain, fed by the great economic crisis, these movements linked up with the most chauvinistic nation-state ideologies and took to the streets. Racist ideologies which had heretofore been debated in small circles spread to the public at large. Antisemitism became accepted and virulent. All that was needed was a messianic demagogue to set the match to this tinderbox.

The emergence of this demagogue was described for the international military tribunal in Nuremberg in 1946 by Hans Frank, who had been a Nazi minister and governor general of occupied Poland. As a student in 1920 Frank had seen Adolf Hitler for the first time addressing the "little people" of Munich, a tense and restless crowd of old men, teenaged boys, discharged soldiers, college and university students and many women, all feeling humiliated and impoverished by the lost war and seeing no future.

> Why fate, why God has sent us someone like Hitler, should be debated at a profound theological level. How is it possible that a person who is endowed with such refined cunning, captivating eloquence, seductive charm and supreme intelligence... can suddenly emerge from among ordinary people, so as literally to seize, lead and electrify them? [4]

Hitler blamed capitalists, nobility, treacherous army officers, communists and above all the Jews for the lost war and the lamentable state of Germany. He fanned centuries-old antisemitism into a white heat, overturning the painful struggle for equality and social justice that had marked European history since the Enlightenment. Hitler had read the *Protocols*, and in his perverted mind "world Jewry" was allied with capitalism and communism in order to dominate the world. His political instrument to break up this domination was the *Nationalsozialistische Deutsche Arbeiterpartei* (National Socialist German Workers' Party), which gained the support of 42 percent of the electorate by 1932. By making a deal with other rightist parties — who thought they could control him — Hitler seized power on 30 January 1933, proclaiming the creation of a thousand-year Reich, an image he took from the biblical book of Revelation.

By the time war broke out in 1939, Hitler had convinced the German people that his repeated aggressions against other countries were preventive and defensive steps taken to prevent Germany from being encircled and annihilated. It was either *them* — the capitalists, the communists and the Jews, who dominated everything — or *us*, he kept shouting.

Helpless churches

Most Christians in Germany were steeped in traditional anti-Judaism when Hitler came to power, but the borderline between this and modern ideological antisemitism was fluid, and neither had been theologically examined. Moreover, neither German Protestant nor Roman Catholic church leaders had generally accepted Enlightenment liberalism (except for scientific biblical scholarship, in which Germans were world leaders). Consequently, most had remained staunch monarchists throughout the Weimar Republic (1919-33). W.A. Visser 't Hooft, the first general secretary of the World Council of Churches, vividly described his difficult discussions with German church representatives after the first world war on whether or not Germany bore major guilt for the outbreak of the war of 1914 (most denied it).[5] These church leaders were thus predisposed to see Hitler as a kind of "redeemer" who would restore the honour of the humiliated fatherland. When the great persecution of Jews broke out in 1933, Christian leaders failed to understand the deadly spirit of totalitarian National Socialist antisemitism. Ingrained religious prejudice prevented the development of a reflective theological critique of the racial contempt of the new regime and of the radicalized street mobs.

Undoubtedly, most Christians in Germany would have recoiled in horror had they realized what the vicious spirit of the Nazi regime would lead to. But to outside ecumenical enquiries and requests that they intervene with the Hitler regime for the sake of the Jews, German church leaders kept replying that they basically agreed with their government that the Jews had to be "put in their place", though they admitted that more "humane" methods could be used. This was the general attitude of the churches which had been incorporated into the *Reichskirche* (imperial church) headed by Bishop Ludwig Müller, an active supporter of the Nazi government. Equally supportive of the regime and its anti-Jewish policies was the leadership of the free churches of evangelical persuasion, who were grateful to the *Führer* for granting them legal recognition.

This uncritical spirit, often coupled with a lack of civic courage, made it difficult for those pastors, priests and laypeople who did see the writing on the wall and began to help the threatened Jews. Many eventually paid for their courage with their lives.[6] Even the famous Barmen Declaration of 1934 by the opposition Confessing Church, inspired by Swiss theologian Karl Barth, which objected vehemently to the totalitarian claims of the *Führer* state, did not mention the persecution of Jews. Nor was Dietrich Bonhoeffer, one of the foremost members of German resistance, able to arouse the attention of like-minded fellow theologians to this question. Later Barth and Martin Niemöller, another major figure in the Confessing Church, admitted to their regret that they had not understood the deadly consequences of Hitler's antisemitic project, even though he had unequivocally spelled it out in his *Mein Kampf* as early as 1923.

Some church leaders in Anglo-Saxon countries, among them archbishop of Canterbury William Temple and Samuel McCrae Cavert, general secretary of the

Federal Council of Churches in the United States, tried in vain to share their concern on the Jewish question with the German churches. But in their own countries their appeals were met with indifference, even if antisemitism in Britain and the US was less virulent than in Germany and other parts of Europe. There was no groundswell of public opinion to compel politicians to open up the borders to Jewish refugees. In 1939 the British government limited Jewish emigration to Palestine to 75,000 during the next five years. While fears of Arab reactions played an important role in setting this policy, the British government did not go out of its way to offer the persecuted Jewish community any viable alternative; and restrictive immigration policies were maintained in both Britain and the US after the outbreak of the war in 1939.

Official US unwillingness to let in Jewish refugees must be seen in relation to the anti-immigrant spirit of the period. A racist quota system introduced in the 1920s excluded Asians and Africans and severely restricted immigration from southern and eastern Europe, partly in order to reduce Jewish immigration to a minimum. In the South and in parts of the Middle West the Ku Klux Klan was demanding a "white America", free of blacks, Jews and even Roman Catholics. While the political tide changed during the liberal Roosevelt era of the 1930s, social attitudes in many small towns and rural areas remained unchanged, and the government did not dare to challenge them. A vigorous antisemitic campaign was promoted over the radio by Charles Coughlin, a Roman Catholic priest in Detroit who was backed up by wealthy Catholics in New York and Boston. Coughlin was neither challenged nor defrocked by Catholic authorities. On the Protestant side, the wealthy automobile pioneer Henry Ford sponsored an English translation of *The Protocols of the Learned Elders of Zion*.[7]

Switzerland at first accepted Jewish refugees from Germany, but changed its policy after the annexation of Austria in 1938, fearful that massive Jewish immigration might revive latent antisemitic feelings among the people and lead to threatening moves by its powerful neighbour to the north. The government proposed to the German authorities that they stamp all passports of German Jewish citizens with the letter "J". In this way would-be Jewish immigrants could be easily recognized and admission refused. There were Swiss immigration officials, however, who disregarded this exclusion and allowed Jewish refugees to cross the border; and by 1942, the Swiss Protestant leadership, cooperating closely with the World Council of Churches "in process of formation" (whose offices were in Geneva) and the French Reformed Church, called on the government to end this ignominious concession to National Socialist Germany. By the end of the war there were 200,000 refugees in Switzerland, out of whom 30,000 were Jewish; but 30,000 if not more Jewish refugees had been rejected at the borders and went to their death.

A high point of this story was the courageous action of French Protestants during the occupation (1940-44). Their minority status and collective memories of persecution during much of their own history fostered a spirit of civic disobedience and resistance. Marc Boegner, president of the French Reformed Church, and Madeleine Barot, director of the aid agency CIMADE, were among the leaders of this struggle against totalitarian nihilism, in which they were supported by like-minded Roman Catholics.[8]

The official Roman Catholic position concerning the persecution of Jews was equally ambivalent. Within weeks of Hitler's seizure of power in 1933, Pope Pius XI approved a concordat with the new National Socialist state, not only to guarantee the legal and financial security of German Catholicism, but also to support the stance of National Socialism against communism. The concordat provided the German dictatorship with an international legitimacy which it at first had lacked; and no attempt was made to use it to support Jews or the political opposition. Even though the Hitler regime later ignored parts of the concordat, the church leaders never criticized either the Nuremberg race laws of 1935 or the burning of synagogues and destruction of Jewish businesses in 1938, both important steps towards the genocide.

Towards the end of his life Pope Pius XI began to have misgivings, and it is said that he was preparing an encyclical against racial persecution when he died in 1939. His successor Pius XII, the former Vatican secretary of state and an admirer of Germany, set the proposed document aside and spoke out against the murder of Jews only once — and then very cautiously — towards the end of the war. The pope even kept silent in 1943 when German occupation forces sent the Jews of Rome to death camps. The only concern the Vatican ever expressed officially was that converted Jews be kept alive or allowed to emigrate. This in no way diminishes the courageous actions taken by many Roman Catholic individuals on behalf of the persecuted; but it was not they who formulated official church policy.

Preparations for the holocaust

When the remnants of German democracy were swept aside in 1933, all parties other than the National Socialists were banned. The press and the radio were brought under government control, to be used as powerful propaganda instruments. A highly efficient security police (Gestapo) imposed a climate of fear. Political opponents such as communists and socialists were brought to concentration camps. The Jews suffered persecution not for divergent political convictions but because of their supposed *race*. For the first time the racial theories which had been spread about since the 19th century were implemented as a matter of government policy. Jewish businesses were boycotted, Jewish civil servants and professionals expelled from their jobs, Jewish students dismissed from institutions of higher learning. For much of the Jewish community this meant economic and financial ruin.

In 1935 the Nuremberg race laws outlawed marriage and sexual relations between Jews and non-Jews and forbade Jews from going to restaurants, cinemas, public parks and swimming pools. "Jewish" books were burned. No Jew was allowed to attend the 1936 Olympic Games in Berlin, where foreign visitors seemed barely to notice the antisemitic posters openly displayed. Neither the International Olympic Committee nor any foreign government protested.

Soon similar antisemitic legislation was introduced in Italy and Hungary; and in Romania the nationalist and racist Iron Guards began to harass and kill Jews. When Hitler annexed Austria in March 1938, the Jews there suffered untold humiliations. They were massively arrested and synagogues were stoned and burned, often with the ready participation of local Christians. The same happened in Czechoslovakia in 1938 and 1939.

Between 1933 and 1937, 130,000 Jews left Germany, especially to Palestine and to North and South America. After the annexation of Austria, 400,000 more Jews tried to get away.[9] With pressures increasing, Western and neutral governments called a world refugee conference in Evian, France, in July 1938, to seek a common solution. The conference was a moral disaster. One national delegation after the other, including that of the United States, professed its inability to accept more refugees. The excuses ranged from overpopulation and unemployment to race problems to the simple desire to "appease" the Germans.

During the night of 9-10 November 1938 the National Socialists unleashed the *Kristallnacht* ("night of the broken glass") on the frightened Jewish community. Throughout Germany, Austria and the annexed German-speaking areas of Czechoslovakia, homes, shops, offices and synagogues were utterly destroyed by security forces, party members and the mob. They broke, looted and burned everything which had any connection with Jews. Thirty-five thousand Jews were arrested and brought to concentration camps. Several thousand died in the process; 8000 committed suicide. Altogether 300,000 Jews were now imprisoned.

When the Germans invaded Poland on 1 September 1939 and thereby triggered the second world war, mass executions of Jews began immediately. The first poison gas experiments were undertaken with the help of scientists, as soon as the executioners realized that "traditional" forms of execution with rifles, pistols or even machine guns were too slow. Hitler, who had suffered in 1917 from a German mustard gas attack on the western front when the wind turned unexpectedly, had long been interested in this method of killing. The mass executions were the speciality of SS task forces, with regular army units often lending a helping hand. They were willingly assisted by local collaborators and allied governments in occupied areas such as France, Croatia, Bosnia, Hungary, Romania, Ukraine, Bielorussia, Lithuania, Latvia, Estonia and Poland. Concentration camps were established wherever Germany extended its domination.

The death camps

In the autumn of 1941, after the Red Army had stopped the German advance within sight of Moscow, Hitler decided on a rapid and coordinated elimination of the Jews in all of German-occupied Europe. He realized that he could no longer win the war and that he had to act quickly if he was to settle the "Jewish question" before he died. Plans for the "final solution" were worked out during a conference at Wannsee near Berlin on 20 January 1942 under the direction of Reinhard Heydrich, deputy chief of German security (who would be killed five months later by the Czech underground, which resulted in the destruction of the village of Lidice and the murder of the Jews in Bohemia and Moravia). The number of European Jews was estimated at eleven million.

Coordination of the "final solution" was entrusted to the SS, which was given authority over all government departments, the army, industry, scientists and the railways. Five special death camps in Poland — Chelmno, Belzec, Maidanek, Sobibor and Treblinka — were chosen as the principal "receiving centres", since most of Europe's Jews lived in Poland, the former Pale of Settlement in western Russia and Hungary. Centrally located was Auschwitz-Birkenau in Upper Silesia, not far from Cracow, where most of Eastern Europe's railway lines came together. Two million Jews died in the five camps mentioned above and two million in Auschwitz. There were other smaller concentration camps within Germany, including Bergen-Belsen, Ravensbrück, Buchenwald and Dachau, as well as in Austria, Estonia, Latvia, France and Yugoslavia. The camps were usually kept away from population centres so as to assure the secret.

The cattle trains rolling towards the death camps were organized by Adolf Eichmann, a lieutenant colonel in the SS, who had been born into a churchgoing Protestant family. Before the prisoners boarded the cattle cars, he and his subordinates told the Jewish councils to inform the Jewish community at large that they were being sent to settle new villages "somewhere in the east", and that they would be well treated and should not panic. To confirm this illusion up to the last moment, when the prisoners arrived at Auschwitz they saw a sign over the main gate proclaiming that *Arbeit macht frei* ("Work liberates"); and on entering the gas chambers each prisoner was handed a towel and a bar of soap to be used in the "shower".

Few if any believed that such a genocide was conceivable in a highly cultured nation of such long Christian tradition, despite Hitler's repeated threats over the years that he would one day destroy the Jews. But Germany was not the only country to murder Jews. In 1941 local ethnic Romanians killed 25,000 Jews in Odessa, supported by the invading Romanian army, one of Hitler's allies. In September of that year the German SS machine-gunned 34,000 Jews in the gorges of Babi-Yar near Kiev. Another 100,000 were murdered just before the Red Army reoccupied the Ukrainian capital in November 1944, and the surviving Jews were subjected to a pogrom by their Ukrainian neighbours *after* the Red Army had liberated them. [10] French police, Croatian Ustasha, the Hungarian Arrow Cross and countless civilian informers shared in this monstrous crime.

Hundreds of thousands if not millions of others also died in the gas chambers, including opposition leaders, Sinti and Roma (Gypsies) from all European nations and many Polish, Yugoslav and Soviet military prisoners. Special task forces, usually composed of Jewish prisoners, removed the bodies to large furnaces where they were burned. The members of the task forces were periodically replaced by new ones, having been subjected to the same death process themselves.

When Hungarian Jews went to their death in May and June 1944, Auschwitz reached its peak capacity of 12,000 to 15,000 a day. In the course of the two months nearly half a million Hungarian Jews died. [11] Although an Allied airman had discovered the location of the Auschwitz death camp in early May 1944, the joint military command refused to destroy the installations or even disrupt the rail lines leading to them; and the grisly furnaces kept smoking until November 1944. The Germans unsuccessfully tried to cover the traces of their momentous geno-cide. Red Army soldiers, arriving in mid-January 1945, were the first outsiders to see the gruesome place.

The history of the holocaust would be incomplete without mentioning some of the "Righteous among the Nations" who helped Jews to survive, often at great

personal risk. For instance, several thousand Jews were hidden by Social Demo-
crats and Christians in Berlin itself. Entire nations resisted Nazi pressure by saving
Jews, notably Finland, Denmark, Bulgaria and Italy. The 1700 Jews of Finland
had already been rounded up by German security forces when the Finnish
government got them back and brought them to safety. King Christian X of
Denmark himself wore the Star of David as a signal to the entire population; and in
1943 the Danish underground, tipped off by a German diplomat, shipped the
country's 7000 Jews to neutral Sweden. Thousands of Hungarian Jews were
helped by simple Hungarian and Romanian peasants and local Catholic, Protestant
and Orthodox clergy to escape into Romania, where they were protected until the
arrival of the Red Army. Bulgaria sabotaged the delivery of its 50,000 Jews to the
German authorities, largely due to the active intervention of the Orthodox church
and King Boris II, who paid with his life for this defiance. Earlier, however, the
Bulgarian government had turned over to the Germans 15,000 Jews from Bulga-
rian-occupied territories in Macedonia and Greece. In Budapest the Swiss consul
Carl Lutz saved no fewer than 62,000 Hungarian Jews from death, the largest
single such action in all of German-occupied Europe. He cooperated closely with
the papal nuncio Angelo Rotta, Friedrich Born of the International Committee of
the Red Cross and Swedish diplomat Raoul Wallenberg — who all undertook
parallel actions — and an underground network of Hungarians and Germans.
There were 125,000 surviving Jews in Budapest at war's end, 250,000 in all of
Hungary. [12]

After the end of the war, in 1946, Jacob Lestchinsky, a Polish Jew who had
escaped the holocaust, tried to explain what had really happened and what it meant
that only three-and-a-half million of Europe's nine-and-a-half million Jews had
survived. For most of the survivors, he said, Europe had become "a vast, terror-
haunted cemetery". The Jews remaining in countries controlled by Germany
during the war had not only witnessed the torture and slaughter of their people, but
had themselves been herded like cattle from concentration camp to concentration
camp.

> They know there is hardly a people in Europe which fell under Hitler's yoke whose
> hands are not stained with Jewish blood... Not only the Germans committed mass
> murder but also Poles, Ukrainians, Bielorussians, Lithuanians, Latvians, Romanians,
> Slovaks, Croatians... Hitler transported hundreds of thousands of Jews to Poland and
> other countries in the east for extermination. But this does not mean that in Western
> Europe there were no elements ready to help the Germans to deport Jews to the gas
> chambers and crematoriums. Here, too, there were collaborators aplenty. [13]

One of the worst aspects for the survivors was indeed coping with memories of
mental and physical torture. Even after decades, these devilish recollections would
re-emerge, causing severe spells of depression and endless painful visions of lost
family members, friends and neighbours. [14] Beyond this personal dimension, the
extent and the depth of the destruction of Jewish identity can scarcely be
fathomed. Europe's centuries-long habits of religious and racial exclusion, which
culminated in the Shoah, have affected every single Jew. Many Jews were
surprised that all their efforts at assimilation following the Enlightenment had

failed to bridge the gap of racial prejudice. Although thousands of Jews had fallen on the battlefields of the first world war for *Kaiser und Vaterland*, Hitler was convinced that they had profited from the war, committed betrayal and were responsible for German defeat. During the second world war, 500,000 Jews fought in the Red Army, of whom 200,000 died. This did not prevent Stalin, an inveterate antisemite, from plotting a pogrom in 1953, which was not carried out only because of his death. Even so the Soviet Union became a difficult place for Jews.

Theological reflection after Auschwitz

The question must be raised as to whether the churches have thought hard enough — if at all — about the implications of the deliberate murder of six million Jews. Surprisingly, the confession of guilt (*Schulderklärung*) made by German churches in Stuttgart in October 1945 did not mention the genocide of Jews. And during the following years, official German church statements, while regretting the excesses of the National Socialist regime, kept avoiding the problem. Perhaps the churches did not wish to face the incomprehensible enormity of the atrocity; perhaps the problems of post-war reconstruction, the influx of German refugees from the east, the division of Europe into east and west and the accompanying cold war rhetoric offered a convenient excuse for sweeping the issue under the rug. It was often noted that thousands of innocents had also perished in the bombardments of Cologne, Berlin and Dresden. Former Nazis were all too often rehabilitated, also within the churches, and they too worked at erasing the memories of the past. Mediaeval theological precepts on the supposed guilt of Jews for the crucifixion of Jesus Christ remained largely unquestioned until the Second Vatican Council, and are still accepted by many conservative and fundamentalist Christians today.

The Eichmann trial of 1960-61 stimulated the first serious reflection among Christians on the holocaust, leading to the creation of Christian-Jewish dialogue groups. Like their Jewish counterparts, many Christians began to wonder if the enormity of the murder of six million people could ever be understood. It became abundantly clear that Christians and churches, in order to remain faithful to themselves and to Jesus Christ, had no other choice but to accept this disturbing event, to move beyond theological dogmatism, old and new, and to be in solidarity with any human being anywhere who is tortured and suffers violence for whatever reason. Especially through the ecumenical movement the churches have gained new insights in the encounter with peoples from developing countries and in the struggle against racism worldwide. How can the churches reflect this commitment biblically and theologically?

Theological reflection on the Shoah has been advanced considerably by Jewish theologians. Apart from the question of guilt, concern began to focus on the fundamental question of God's action or silence: was it possible to believe in God after Auschwitz? Johanna Kohn has identified five types of Jewish reflection which might also help Christians in their own thinking. [15]

1. The idea of suffering as a punishment for sins is deeply rooted in the thought of Israel, and thus some, especially orthodox Jews, have regarded Auschwitz as a

deserved recompense for the unfaithfulness of Jews — whether past assimilation or the idea that Zionism, rather than the Messiah, would restore Israel. Some Jewish theologians equated the Germans with the Babylonians, who destroyed Jerusalem "because of her wickedness". Such ideas are strongly opposed by others, who cannot see Hitler as an instrument of God and ask why, of all the Jews, God would punish above all those from the east, who had been the most faithful and pious and the least assimilated.

2. The US theologian Richard L. Rubenstein has proposed a kind of Jewish "death-of-God" theology. The only proper response to the incredible act of destruction which Auschwitz was, says Rubenstein, is an "intuitive act of unbelief". The God who himself died at the death camps was the God of a meaningful history. Suffering-as-punishment makes no sense. Communities and synagogues may of course continue to exist, but only as sociological entities; it is not clear whether — and if so, how — they should continue to pray.

3. Some theologians set the martyrdom of Jews at Auschwitz in the tradition of the Suffering Servant (Isa. 53), who died *on behalf of* others for the sanctification of God's name and as a warning to other nations. It is to be hoped that Auschwitz will never be repeated, but why no angel came to prevent it, as in the case of Abraham when he was about to sacrifice Isaac (Gen. 22:11-12), remains unanswered. Moreover, it is difficult to assume that the six million victims saw themselves collectively as a sacrifice for others, subjected as they were to all kinds of abominable humiliations. Scarcely any of them, least of all the children (estimated at 1.2 million), knew why they were put to death. Still, some Jewish theologians have argued that the motif of sacrifice merits serious consideration in dialogue with Christians, that through the six million massacred Jews Jesus Christ has been crucified again. For many Christians, according to Ernst Ludwig Ehrlich, Judaism remains a thorn in the flesh, as does the person of Jesus Christ. That is why they have interiorized, dogmatized, absolutized and ultimately killed him.

4. Others would say that in the face of the terrible and unacceptable fact of the death camps, one can only fall back on the biblical theme of the hiddenness of God — that God and his ways can never be fully comprehended. But believers must not fall into a nihilistic vacuum: deep down, against all logic, they retain the faith that God is somehow their Saviour. This conviction was expressed and sustained by the belief that in the newly established state of Israel God visibly kept faith with his people. This historical event should be seen as a new divine revelation, comparable with the Exodus from Egypt and the giving of the law on Sinai. The problem with this approach, from the point of view of Jewish theologians, is that the re-creation of the ancient homeland came at such a horrible price. If the new Jewish state is seen as a form of reconciliation, it must thus be considered sinful, for the sacrifice was simply too great.

5. Taking their distance from a sacrificial interpretation of the Shoah, a growing number of Jewish theologians see the restored Israel as posing not so much the question of the nature of God as the question of the nature of the human being. As far as the history of the people of Israel is concerned, Auschwitz extended an already long suffering to a scope beyond any imagination. But it is

only one step in history, and the challenge to Jews and to all human beings of good will is to prevent such a horror from ever being repeated.

A resurgence of antisemitism has been evident in many countries in recent years, showing that concern about a repetition of the holocaust is not unfounded. Besides acts of vandalism in Jewish cemeteries and bombings of synagogues, openly antisemitic declarations are heard from rightist politicians in France, Russia and the United States, where antisemitic political views are linked with some sectors of Christian fundamentalism. It is as if antisemitism is a barometer of the dysfunctioning of societies, pointing to coming social and political storms.

A disturbing development of the past several years has been the openly antisemitic views expressed by the African-American leader Louis Farrakhan. A convert to Islam, Farrakhan not only argues that the death of six million Jews at Hitler's hands was small by comparison with the holocaust that took the lives of tens of millions of African slaves, but has also republished and distributed the *Protocols of the Learned Elders of Zion*. According to Farrakhan, even though Jewish immigrants to the US were treated with disdain by white Christians, they have managed to work themselves out of poverty to considerable wealth and influence, while the status of blacks has not only not improved but worsened. On similar grounds he has attacked more recently arrived Asian immigrants who are rapidly climbing the social ladder. The racist underpinnings of this bitter argumentation cannot be ignored.

Reflections within the ecumenical movement on global justice, fresh approaches to reading the Bible and better insights into the development of doctrine and into some of the hidden aspects of church history have helped to create new impulses for other ways of "being a Christian", reforming worship, education and outlooks. Only through such a continuing process can the virus of antisemitism be overcome, both within the churches and in society as a whole. Auschwitz need not be repeated, but it could be — which is why this issue must remain high on the ecumenical agenda.

NOTES

[1] Josephine Bacon and Martin Gilbert, *The Illustrated Atlas of Jewish Civilization*, London, André Deutsch, 1990, pp.136f.

[2] *Ibid.*, pp.152-54.

[3] A fascinating study of Hitler's transition from religious to ideological anti-Jewish prejudice is Friedrich Heer, *Der Glaube des Adolf Hitler: Anatomie einer politischen Religiosität*, Munich, Bechtle, 1968.

[4] *Ibid.*, p.200.

[5] W.A. Visser 't Hooft, *Memoirs*, London, SCM Press, 1973, p.30.

[6] Cf. the two-volume study by Armin Boyens, *Kirchenkampf und Ökumene*, Vol. 1 (1933-1939), Vol. 2 (1939-1945), Munich, Kaiser Verlag, 1969, 1973.

[7] On the US record, see David S. Wyman, *Abandonment of the Jews: America and the Holocaust, 1941-1945*, New York, Pantheon, 1984.

[8] Cf. André Jacques, *Madeleine Barot*, Geneva, WCC, 1991, esp. chs 4-7, pp.20-46.

[9] Of these 8000 were admitted to Britain, 40,000 to Palestine, 55,000 to the USA, 8000 to Brazil, 15,000 to France, 2000 to Belgium, 14,000 to Switzerland, 1000 to Sweden, 845 to Denmark and 150 to Norway; cf. Martin Gilbert, *The Holocaust: The Jewish Tragedy*, London, Collins, 1990, p.64.

[10] Cf. Bacon and Gilbert, *op. cit.*, pp.167-69.

[11] Theo Tschuy, *Carl Lutz und die Juden von Budapest*, Zurich, Verlag Neue Zürcher Zeitung, 1995, pp.164-68.

[12] *Ibid.*, pp.333-35.

[13] Lestchinsky, cited in *ibid.*, p.366.

[14] On the psychological problems of children born to surviving deportees, see Helen Epstein, *Children of the Holocaust*, New York, Putnam, 1979.

[15] Johanna Kohn, *Haschoah: Christlich-jüdische Verständigung nach Auschwitz*, Munich and Mainz, Kaiser-Grünewald, 1986, pp.59-92; cf. also the exhaustive study by Christoph Münz, *Der Welt ein Gedächtnis geben: Geschichtstheologisches Denken im Judentum nach Auschwitz*, Gütersloh, Chr. Kaiser Gütersloher Verlagshaus, 1995.

3
Sudan

After assuming power in Sudan through a military coup in 1989, Omar Hassan Ahmad al-Bashir declared at a public rally in Khartoum, "I vow here before you to purge from our ranks the renegades, the hirelings, enemies of the people and enemies of the armed forces... Anyone who betrays this nation does not deserve the honour of living."[1] Clearly it was al-Bashir himself who intended to decide who was a renegade, hireling, enemy of the people or of the armed forces in this largest country of Africa. His goal was to impose ideological, political and religious uniformity, according to the "principles of Islam", on Sudan's multiple and immensely varied ethnic populations, especially the country's southern one-third of black Africans, who had never "obeyed" the government in Khartoum and who surely had no intention of doing so now.

While the absence of international media access to the Sudan means that little is known about the methods used to implement al-Bashir's announced policies, it is estimated that 1.5 million people have perished since 1983, victims of the mad drive for political and religious uniformity — over and above the 500,000 who died during the first phase of the civil war from 1955 to 1972.[2]

Since the time of the *Mahdi* in the 19th century religion has always played an important role in Sudan. But today the conflict is no longer simply one between an Islamic and Arab north and a black animist or Christian south. The onslaught of al-Bashir's uncontrolled security apparatus on all of civil society is tearing a nation of 26 million people and 400 languages to shreds. Human resources and precarious forms of economic subsistence in this partly arid and partly tropical country — one of the world's poorest even before it was overtaken by civil war and oppression four decades ago — are becoming depleted.

As in all such situations of ethnic conflict, the causes do not date from today.

The shift from Christianity to Islam

"Sudan" is a shortened form of the Arabic *Bilad al-Sudan*, the Land of the Blacks, the term originally used by Arabs for all of Africa south of the Sahara. From the time of the Ancient Kingdom, Egypt has shown a constant interest in the peoples and tribes along the life-giving Nile River, and it extended its influence into Nubia and on towards Ethiopia (Blue Nile) and even Uganda (White Nile), without ever fully controlling Sudan until the 19th century. This influence from the north has almost always been dangerous for those living further south. Rich as Sudan was in water and mineral resources, its greatest wealth was the slaves; this memory still animates black Sudanese resistance to Khartoum.

Christianity presumably came to Sudan during the 1st century by way of travellers such as the court official of Queen Candace of Ethiopia to whom Philip preached (Acts 8:26-39). But it was not until the 6th century that Nubia and present-day Sudan were penetrated by Christianity in any substantial way, although the region had long been surrounded by Christianized provinces or states such as Egypt, North Africa and Ethiopia. Mission work was no doubt impeded by the theological-political controversies over the Trinity and the nature of Christ. The fourth ecumenical Council of Chalcedon of 451 more or less ended the Christological controversy within the boundaries of the Roman-Byzantine empire, but most of the Egyptian Copts and church communities outside the empire refused to subscribe to it. During the severe persecution that followed, many Coptic Christians fled to Sudan and proclaimed their faith there. But progress was slow and probably superficial. Only during the latter part of the 6th century was Bishop Longinus sent to Nubia to consolidate Christian missions. However, no local bishops and clergy seem to have been formed, the liturgy was conducted in Coptic and probably also Greek, and Christianity became the religion of the nobles and the ruling families, with the black masses remaining largely untouched. Nevertheless, three Christian kingdoms emerged in Nubia: Nobadia, Makuria and Alwa.

In 640 the Coptic population of Egypt greeted an invading Arab army as liberators from Byzantine oppression, but the process of conversion to the new faith was slow. The Nubian Christian kingdoms did not submit so easily to the Muslim emissaries coming from Egypt. More effective were Arab merchants in the 7th century, who crossed the Red Sea, established outposts south of Nubia from which they proclaimed Islam and intermarried with the local people. Gradually Islam became the religious faith of a newly Arabized black population. The Nubian Christian kingdoms became isolated and lost their vital connections with the Christians of Egypt, where the Copts retained their majority until well into the middle ages, and with Christian Ethiopia. During the 14th century, Egypt, where the majority was now Muslim, extended its influence over Nubia and replaced the old Christian ruling classes with its own appointed governors. The rare travellers from outside reported surviving though dispirited Christian communities in northern Sudan as late as the 16th century. Meanwhile, sustained by scholars from Islamic universities in Egypt and the Arab peninsula, a flourishing Islamic movement was established throughout Sudan and extended its influence as far as Chad and the West African coast. A number of strong Islamic states emerged at the southern edge of the Sahara, ruled by their own caliphs and sultans; and in the 18th century one of the Muslim states in Sudan, the kingdom of Sennar, inflicted a severe defeat on the "infidel" Ethiopians, a victory celebrated throughout the Muslim world.

The trauma of slavery

The modern history of Sudan began with the military campaign initiated in 1820 by Muhammed Ali (1769-1849), the Turkish-Albanian pasha and *khedive* (viceroy) of Egypt. With the approval of the sultan in Constantinople and the British government he ordered his son Ismail to move up the Nile with a small army to subdue the still powerful Arabized kingdom of Fung, with its capital Sennar, to search for gold and ivory and above all to catch black slaves in southern Sudan. Arabs had been capturing blacks in Sudan for centuries, but Muhammed Ali did so on a far more massive scale. He sold many slaves to other parts of the Ottoman empire; others he incorporated into his army, in order to carry out his ambitions of reconquering Greece and subduing the emirates on the Arabian peninsula. During the 19th century an estimated two million slaves were carried off from Sudan's southern provinces. [3]

In retaliation against the barbarity of the Egyptian soldiers, the Sudanese in 1822 set fire to a house in Shendi where Ismail and his staff officers were dining, and all were burned to death. Muhammed Ali then ordered his son-in-law Muhammed Rey to lock the entire population of Shendi in their own houses and burn the city with all its inhabitants. Soon the Egyptians occupied the whole Red Sea coast and controlled all routes to Arabia and Ethiopia. Annual slave raids continued in the southern provinces, and a good part of the Egyptian army came to be composed of black Africans, with the only non-Sudanese being the officers. The governors and most of the leading officials were nearly all Turks, Albanians, Bosnians or Cherkessians, most of whom had come to Africa to enrich themselves. The Sudanese had no part in governing their own country.

European traders did not behave much better than Ottoman officials or Arab merchants. Searching for ivory in southern Sudan, the first permanent British resident in Khartoum, John Petherick, a consular official, discovered the slave trade to be far more profitable than elephant-hunting. Other European merchants became wealthy by selling the privileges awarded to them by the Egyptian government to Arab traders. It was the Egyptian *khedives*, under growing pressure from British abolitionists, who first began to worry about the deplorable conditions in Sudan. Muhammed Ali's successors, Said and later Ismail Pasha, took half-hearted measures to suppress the slave trade and control the Arab traders, though with no practical effect. Around 1870 an Englishman in the service of the Egyptian *khedive*, Sir Samuel Baker, helped to push Egyptian control to the borders of Uganda, but his efforts to stop the slave trade were also largely without success. Arab traders, with the complicity of European merchants, managed to supply the northern provinces of Kordofan and Darfur with 12,000 to 15,000 black slaves annually. [4] Hatred of the slave trade made the black African population virtually immune to Islamic missionary efforts, and the memory of it contributed substantially to the southern provinces' persistent mistrust of the North.

The Mahdist revolt

Until the 19th century Sudanese Islam remained very much a religion of outward forms which did not penetrate deeply into minds of the people. But under the impact of the long struggle against the Egyptians and the British invaders, a particularly combative and nationalist form of Islam arose around the charismatic religious and political leader Muhammed Ahmed Ibn Seyyid 'Abdullah (1843-85). The son of a boat-builder, he received a religious education in his home town Dongola and in 1871 went into religious retreat on the island of Abba in the White Nile. From there he set out to travel throughout the country. Seeing the people's poverty and religious disorientation, Muhammed Ahmed began to criticize the indifference and worldliness of the religious leaders and attracted a large following. Despite his concern for the poor, he also gained support among other social classes who were unhappy about Egyptian and British interference with the slave trade. In due course his perception of Sudan's problems led him to the conviction — which he claimed to receive through divine revelation — that he was the Mahdi, whose coming was foretold in Islamic tradition, the one ordained to bring messianic justice to his people. The Arabic word *mahdi* means "the one who is guided aright". It was a title first assumed by the third Abbasid caliph al-Mahdi, whose short reign in Baghdad (775-785) was marked by religious orthodoxy and cultural and religious development which prepared the brilliant rule of Harun al-Rashid (786-809). According to Muslim tradition the coming of al-Mahdi as the hidden imam of God, who would suddenly appear and fill the world with justice, had been predicted by the prophet himself. Even though al-Mahdi died at 43, the expectation of a coming redeemer remained alive. This tradition must be kept in mind when assessing the role and function of the Sudanese Mahdi.

In March 1881 the Mahdi, as he was now acclaimed, began to speak of his mission and of the need for a *jihad* against the "infidels" — the corrupt Egyptian officials and their foreign allies. With his army of dervishes (religious mendicants) the Mahdi repulsed several military expeditions; and by 1882 the revolt had became general throughout Sudan. The Mahdi occupied El Obeid, the capital of Kordofan province, and in January 1883 he wiped out an army of 10,000 men commanded by the English general Hicks Pasha. In an incredible series of victories, other towns and provinces, including the Red Sea coast, fell to the Mahdi.

Since the British had taken over Egypt, developments in Sudan, which bordered on the Red Sea, Britain's lifeline to India, became a British concern; and General Charles George Gordon (1833-85), an experienced colonial officer of deep evangelical and abolitionist convictions, was dispatched to Khartoum in early 1884 to bring back Egyptian civilians and soldiers besieged by the Mahdi. But Gordon and his small force were themselves surrounded, and after a prolonged siege his fortified camp fell on 26 January 1885 and Gordon was killed. In June of that year both Dongola and Kassala fell to the Mahdi. Then, at the peak of his success and at the very moment he was planning to invade Egypt, he died. For Sudanese Muslims his tomb at Omdurman became an object of devotion as important as Mecca.

The Mahdi's successor Abdullah mismanaged agriculture and led the country to new ruin. Failing in his attempt to conquer Egypt and unable to retain the adherence of various important Arabic-speaking tribes, Abdullah turned south towards Uganda and the borders of the Belgian Congo and tried to impose Islam and legalize slavery. He was strongly resisted both by the local population and by isolated remnants of the Egyptian army still operating near the Ugandan border. The South, which had supported the Mahdist revolt because of its opposition to the Egyptian slave-traders and Ottoman Turks, turned against Abdullah, sowing further seeds of enmity with the modern Islamic state.

The British now undertook various military campaigns in cooperation with the Egyptians to avenge Gordon's death. In 1899 Abdullah was defeated and killed in battle at Kordofan. During the following decade various other Mahdis arose, but they were less fortunate than their famous predecessor and were captured and hanged.

While the Mahdist revolt contributed to the formation of a national consciousness in the Arabized Sudan, including a heritage of strict Islam, its social and economic effects were disastrous. The population dropped from 8.5 million to 1.25 million between 1882 and 1899 due to battle, famine, disease and internecine strife. After that, recovery was rapid.

Having largely financed the conquest of this vast territory and provided most of the superior officers (the foot soldiers were mostly Egyptian), Britain claimed a share in its administration. Thus was formed the Anglo-Egyptian Sudan. Subordinate posts were left in the hands of the Egyptians, while all key positions were held or closely controlled by the British. Government was according to local law, and custom, language and religion were respected. Much attention was devoted to reviving agriculture and commerce, building an educational system to form a new elite and establishing a judiciary. Railway lines were built and vast cotton fields laid out to supply the British textile industry. The slave trade was vigorously repressed, though occasional raids by Ethiopians across the border were reported as late as 1926. But the liberated slaves remained economically dependent, working as unpaid servants or labourers for their former masters. For a half century Sudan was relatively quiet.[5]

Religion in colonial Sudan

After the defeat of the Mahdists, Anglican missionaries from Britain and Presbyterian missionaries from the US began to enter Sudan. They were later joined by interdenominational faith missions, such as the Sudan Inland Mission and the Sudan United Mission. Roman Catholic orders from Italy, which had been in Sudan since 1850, renewed their presence. For a while there was stiff competition among these missions. The colonial administration allowed them to establish educational and medical work in Khartoum, Omdurman and other towns, but not to proselytize openly in the northern Arabized provinces, for fear of Mahdist reaction. Moreover, Copts of Egyptian or Ethiopian origin were equally opposed to conversion attempts. There were no restrictions on missionary activity in the three southern provinces. On the contrary, the colonial authorities encouraged not only the creation of schools and hospitals but also intensive evangelism, hoping thus to set up an effective barrier to Islam's southward advance into the heart of black Africa.

Northern and southern Sudan were virtually governed as two separate political entities. Under the "Closed District Ordinance", any citizen from the north wishing to visit the south had to obtain official permission, which would be granted only after thorough questioning. This measure, considered insulting by the northerners, effectively curtailed Islamic missionary activity and deepened the cultural division of Sudan. Moreover, in the south the fierce competition among missionary societies, particularly between Roman Catholics and Protestants, led the colonial administration to parcel out the region into spheres of influence, which worked against its cohesiveness.

In this connection the problem of education and language requires special mention. Education in the south lay entirely in the hands of the missionaries, who accepted pupils only if they were prepared to convert. Moreover all education was given in English, not in Arabic. Animists who refused to submit to this condition had no chance of obtaining an education.[6] In 1926 the colonial administration tried without success to counteract this discriminatory practice by means of giving or withholding financial subsidies to mission schools. To this day, Christians in the south tend to have a better education than animists, who have become a religious minority. Nevertheless, the educational level in the south remained low, and the missionaries made no attempt to integrate their educational system with that of the Arabized north. The few southerners who wanted a higher education were encouraged to go to Uganda rather than Khartoum. In the north, where pressure for conversion was not permitted and instruction had to be given in Arabic, the influence of the missionaries was much less. The educational system in the north was however superior, and it was mainly from church-related colleges in Khartoum, Omdurman and elsewhere that the new Sudanese elite, which would pursue careers in the colonial administration and later in independent Sudan, was trained. Very few southerners were given this opportunity. Thus in trying to protect the south from Islamic penetration, the missionaries effectively contributed to its further alienation from the north.

With no restrictions on evangelism, the churches in the south grew remarkably. An indigenous leadership emerged, and the Bible, prayer books and liturgies were translated into the main tribal languages. In addition to schools and hospitals, agricultural and technical projects were set up. By 1970 there were an estimated 300,000 Roman Catholics and 150,000 Anglicans in Sudan. The Church of Christ on the Upper Nile (Presbyterian) had an adult membership of 7000. At the outset of the conflict Christianity was well-rooted in Sudan, at least in the south.[7] Under the impact of the war, competition among churches gave way to cooperation, and in 1965 the Sudan Christian Council was founded, composed of ten churches, including Roman Catholics and Copts. It later became affiliated to both the All Africa Conference of Churches (AACC) and the Middle East Council of Churches (MECC). Its creation, signifying that the churches had moved from competition to cooperation in the entire country, was an implicit but clear critique of government policies, by showing political leaders that it was possible for Sudanese from both the north and the south to meet together in a voluntary and peaceful way. But the idea that the building of the nation could be achieved on the basis of mutual respect was one which the post-colonial government never seemed to have quite understood.

Independence and betrayal

In November 1952, several months after the overthrow of the Egyptian monarchy under King Farouk, Egypt's new strong man General Naguib declared Sudan's right to self-determination, which had been denied by the *khedives* and the kings, signifying the end of the Anglo-Egyptian condominium. On New Year's

Day 1956 Sudan became an independent republic. The primary political groupings that had emerged were the pro-Egyptian National Unionist Party (NUP) and the Islamist Umma Party, whose origins were in the Mahdist movement. The bewildered south was left out. A Southern Party was formed, which advocated either separation or at least a political confederation in which the three southern provinces would be on an equal footing with the six northern provinces. In October 1954 the NUP-dominated provisional government issued a stern warning that it would not accept any attempts "to endanger the unity" of Sudan. [8]

The unsettled terms of independence sowed the seeds of the coming tragedy. For reasons of their own, the departing British applied further pressure on the south to remain within the new state. It would have been easy for them to have laid the foundations for post-independence political structures that would guarantee autonomy or even independence to the south. But the chief British concern was to keep undisturbed the passage to India through Suez and the Middle Eastern oil fields, and they did not want to offer the Soviet Union any excuse to upset this. Thus the south was deprived of any protection at the very moment when the new Sudanese nation-state was beginning to extend its control over the entire vast territory of the new Republic of Sudan.

The predictable "civil war" began in mid-1955, six months before independence. The provisional Khartoum government was worried that the southern leadership would formally declare its own independence. The Sudan Defence Forces (SDF), the main military establishment, sent 500 Muslim soldiers to Juba, the capital of Equatoria, to disarm the soldiers of the Southern Corps of the regular Sudanese army, who in turn mutinied and began a reign of terror. While northern troops hunted down mutineers, the latter took revenge, killing not only soldiers but also civilian government officials and their families. The British, whom the southerners had asked for urgent help, replied by insisting that the southern troops surrender to the Khartoum government. The south felt betrayed by its former protector.

War without pity

A short interval of negotiations on a possible federation ended in 1958 when General Ibrahim Abboud disbanded parliament and made himself chief of state, thus bringing to naught all the carefully elaborated preparations for the political structures of Sudan and setting the pattern for the climate of violence which has permanently marked this vast country. The general's programme was tragically simple: "a single language and a single religion for a single country". Arabic was to be the national language also in the south. The southern chiefs were ordered to convert to Islam. Friday would be the nationwide religious day of the week, and mosques and religious Islamic schools were to be built everywhere. Pressure was put on foreign missionaries to withdraw. In 1961 all religious gatherings outside church buildings were outlawed; and in February 1964 all remaining foreign missionaries were expelled and church-related schools nationalized and Arabized.

Within a short time all of the ancient southern fears seemed to have come true. Many Christians were massacred by the Sudanese armed forces in July 1965; and thousands of desperate refugees, including many prominent political leaders and educated southerners, among them clergy and bishops, fled to Uganda, Kenya, Ethiopia, the Central African Republic and Zaire, where the exiled church leaders continued to minister to the spiritual needs of thousands of refugees. A vast international ecumenical aid programme, led by the WCC, was organized. Many Sudanese students were sent to theological schools in other parts of Africa and Lebanon.[9]

Inexorably the classic vicious cycle of mounting violence and counter-violence took hold. The exiles formed several political parties, among them the Sudan African National Union (SANU), which sought external political and military support for guerrilla warfare, waged at first by the 500 members of the former Southern Corps who had mutinied in 1955. In 1963 several scattered groups formed the Anya Nya ("snake poison") under the command of General Taffeng, a former non-commissioned officer in the Sudan Defence Force. The guerrillas' methods became as professional and merciless as those of the regular Sudanese army. Southerners who collaborated with the administration in Khartoum, even under constraint, were executed by the guerrillas; those who refused to collaborate faced the same fate at the hand of the government forces. By May 1964 there were 60,000 refugees abroad. But the atrocities of the Anya Nya did not diminish its popularity, because the Sudan Defence Force initiated ever more severe reprisals on the increasingly disaffected civilian population. Soon the number of refugees fleeing the country numbered in the hundreds of thousands.

The never-ending military expeditions to the south, which cost the lives of thousands, mostly civilians, were a nightmare for the entire country. Government diatribes against "imperialists" and missionaries became less and less credible even among Muslims as the country became increasingly militarized and terrorized. Discontent gave way to demonstrations and strikes; and in October 1964, nine years after the beginning of the southern revolt, General Abboud was ousted.

But the negotiators at a round-table conference held in 1965 were blocked by interference from hardliners from both sides. The radical elements of SANU demanded complete independence for the south, while northern nationalists, both among the military and the Mahdist movement, insisted on the complete submission of the rebellious provinces. Fighting continued all the while. Northern strong men succeeded each other after short periods in office, and by 1967 there were also several rival "governments" in the south. On both sides, political structures seemed to fall apart under the impact of the long war.

On 25 May 1969 Colonel Ga'afar al-Numeiri became Sudan's new strong man. Taking a page from former Egyptian leader Gamal Abdel Nasser's book, he established a "socialist" revolutionary council of military officers, suspended the constitution and abolished all political parties. A communist from the south, Joseph Garang, became minister for southern affairs. He declared himself utterly opposed to southern secession, but promised to grant local autonomy to the region.

For a while nothing new happened, except that the war escalated as a result of massive Soviet military aid to the new "socialist" government. Anya Nya camps were attacked by Soviet fighter planes, troop-carrying helicopters and rockets. Undaunted, the guerrillas counter-attacked with the help of military hardware and advice from the Israelis. A new commander-in-chief, John Lagu, a Sudanese army officer who defected to the guerrillas in 1963, welded Anya Nya into a modern fighting force. Moreover, the southerners began to set up a series of semi-diplomatic representations in other African countries and in the major Western capitals.

Ecumenical involvement in an armistice

By 1970, with the total death toll at 500,000, Numeiri's position had become untenable. Though an army man he had made little military progress; and the Mahdists, considering him "soft" on the south, had nearly succeeded in killing him. In July 1971 Numeiri was temporarily ousted; and when he was reinstated, he was ready to make concessions.

The two warring parties accepted an offer from the World Council of Churches and the All Africa Conference of Churches to negotiate an armistice. Both organizations had a good name in Sudan, having been heavily involved in relief and development work both within the country and among Sudanese refugees. Moreover, the WCC enjoyed considerable prestige throughout Africa because of the support given by its Programme to Combat Racism (PCR) to the struggle against South African apartheid. Neither organization could be suspected of having any partisan preference in Sudan. Also significant was the cooperation of the Sudan Christian Council. [10]

After the southern leaders consented to accept international ecumenical mediation, Numeiri also agreed. Surrounded by enemies, he knew that 15 years of continuous warfare had utterly exhausted his country's already weak economy. Nevertheless, he was aware that many of his officers would have difficulties accepting that southern Sudan would not submit to Islam and to Arab culture. On the other hand, although the southern leaders were militarily unable to reach full independence, they had not relinquished the alternative of a self-governing political entity, even if it was formally attached to Sudan. As a result Numeiri was compelled to engage in cross-current underground negotiations with opposition groups, such as the Muslim Brotherhood and political leaders in exile. From the southern side John Lagu was also faced with the dissent of those who wanted not regional autonomy but full independence. By pointing to the war-weariness of the southern tribes, he was able to overcome this fundamental objection.

One of the most worrisome stipulations for the south was that not only would 6000 southern soldiers be incorporated and controlled by the Sudanese army but also that 6000 northern men were to be permanently stationed in the south. Knowing the suspicious mood of the northern military, what guarantee was there that the soldiers from Khartoum would not once again consider the south as a subject territory?

The peace agreement was nevertheless ratified in Addis Ababa on 27 March 1972 in the presence of Emperor Haile Selassie of Ethiopia, who declared that he himself would guarantee its implementation — even though Ethiopia was in the process of waging a brutal war against independence-seeking Eritreans, who had been receiving Numeiri's support. Exactly how he would guarantee the peace accord was never made clear by the emperor, who had ruled his own country for decades by means of purposeful unclarity. In any case, the aged emperor was overthrown two years later by Colonel Mengistu and murdered. The new military government of Ethiopia, convinced that Western countries were using southern Sudan as a launching pad for its destabilization, became a client of the Soviet Union and called itself socialist. With no one to supervise implementation of the Addis Ababa agreement and neither the AACC nor the WCC in any position to bring back together the extremist and embittered factions, who had inwardly never consented to the compromise of 1972, the armistice began to unravel. The process of "confidence-building" underway globally between the West and the East never reached Sudan.

Under pressure from the Muslim Brothers, Numeiri introduced Islamic law (*shari'ah*) for all of Sudan and declared himself the imam, despite fears among more progressive Muslims that this would irrevocably divide Sudan. The southern Sudanese countered by insisting that unless Sudan became a secular state, with religion relegated to the private sphere, the country would never become stabilized. In 1985 the Muslim Brothers, in conjunction with reactionary army officers, overthrew Numeiri, and the second, more brutal phase of the Sudanese war began.

The unending catastrophe

Religion has not been the only factor in the Sudanese war. For instance, during the second phase of the war government forces devastated the Nuba mountains, an area with a Muslim majority, which had rebelled for economic reasons. Moreover, the discovery of oil in the south in 1978 became an important additional incentive for the government to maintain the region within Sudan and for the southern leadership to keep aiming for full separation. But religion is important for emotive reasons, as bigots on both sides appeal to religious sentiments among their adherents to keep their fighting spirit alive. Many Muslims regard the conversion of the southern black population to Christianity as part of a Western policy to encircle and destroy Arab Islamic countries which has been in effect since the Crusades and the colonial era. [11] Black Africans, on the other hand, resent the degrading expressions and attitudes northerners display towards them. [12] The tension is aggravated by the virtual impossibility of conversion from Islam to Christianity, while there are no obstacles the other way around. A Christian who wants to marry a Muslim is compelled to renounce his or her faith, while Muslims who have converted to Christianity are faced with serious ostracism and, under strict *shari'ah*, the death penalty. The current government does not hesitate to appeal to the religious sentiments of Muslims by describing its oppressive struggle as a *jihad*. [13]

Nevertheless, as the Sudanese war continued into the 1990s, religious specificities have diminished in importance. The theatre of war has partially shifted to the Nuba mountains. The southern Sudan People's Liberation Army (SPLA) has split into two factions, which now fight each other as well as the north. Arbitrary detention, torture and deliberate mass murder of entire communities, solely on the basis of ethnic identity and suspected political allegiance, have virtually dismantled the rest of civil society. The number of deaths since the second phase of the war began over a decade ago has reached

1.5 million. Amnesty International has demanded a thorough investigation of all violations of human rights committed by both the government and the rebel groups, in order to bring the guilty to justice. Clear orders must be given which prohibit all torture, ill-treatment, including rape, beatings and the killing of prisoners.

The protection of human rights must be an integral part of any future peace agreement, to be checked and controlled by the international community.[14] Had such a commitment been demanded from the warring factions that signed the Addis Ababa agreement in 1972, the destruction of an entire nation might have been avoided.

At this writing, time seems to be working against the southern rebels, who are divided more than ever. Government forces are advancing into territories they had never occupied before. On the other hand, prospects for the Khartoum government are grim. The war is costing the government more than a million dollars a day, and in 1995 and 1996 inflation was at the rate of 300 percent. A rebellious mood is growing in the north, whose people are tired of making exorbitant sacrifices for the war and only want to see this ferocious struggle, to which religion has made such a destructive contribution, end. But all debate on the issue is suppressed by the ever-present security forces. All Sudanese nevertheless know that the impoverished country has no other choice but to go the way of reconciliation and human rights as preconditions for the building up of a viable socio-economic life for its people.

Perhaps a sign of hope can be seen in a faraway camp of 150,000 Sudanese refugees outside Dar-es-Salaam, in Tanzania, a thousand kilometres from home. They are a small segment of the three million Sudanese who have fled abroad. The original inhabitants of the camp were Dinka Christians, Catholics and Protestants, from the south. What is interesting is that more and more Muslims are joining them. Ten churches and four mosques now serve their common needs. A dispensary, reservoirs and schools have been created jointly by Christian, Muslim and secular non-governmental organizations. But why did the human costs have to be so exorbitant before this point was reached?[15]

NOTES

[1] Quoted in *Sudan: The Tears of Orphans*, London, Amnesty International, 1995, p.9.

[2] *Ibid.*, p.55.

[3] Hizkias Assefa, *Mediation in Civil Wars: Approaches and Strategies — The Sudan Conflict*, Boulder and London, Westview Press, 1987, p.38. On this history cf. also the entry "Anglo-Egyptian Sudan", in *Encyclopaedia Britannica*, Vol. 21, pp.507ff.

[4] Assefa, *op. cit.*, p.39.

[5] *Ibid.*, p.42.

[6] *Ibid.*, p.43.

[7] "Sudan", in *Concise Dictionary of Christian Missions*, London, Lutterworth, 1971, p.573.

[8] Assefa, *op. cit.*, p.52.

[9] *Ibid.*, p.59; cf. *Concise Dictionary of Christian Missions*, p.574.

[10] For an extended discussion of these negotiations, see Assefa, *op. cit.*, chs 6-7, pp.95-189.

[11] This is the argument of Hassan Makki Mohamed Ahmed, *Sudan: The Christian Design*, Leicester, UK, Islamic Foundation, 1989.

[12] Cf. Alew Damiano Bwolo, "Sudan", in *The Role of Religion in Conflict Situations*, Uppsala, Life & Peace Institute, 1991, p.109.

[13] *Sudan: The Tears of Orphans*, p.57.

[14] *Ibid.*, pp.122-29.

[15] Isabelle Ducret, "A Dar es Salaam, la vie a repris ses droits", in *Le Courrier* (Geneva), 28 March 1996, p.8.

4
Rwanda

The Rwandan massacre of 1994 was the first genocide covered live on television. According to some sources, as many as one million people died within three months, a third of them children. Although it seemed to outsiders that this small country — reputedly "the most Christian in all Africa" — had been seized by utter madness, it is now clear that the mass murder was carefully planned and executed. Like the Jewish people, Rwandans have been traumatically affected by this experience. For Christians it is disturbing to realize that also in the Rwanda genocide, the churches were not innocent.

On 6 April 1994 a surface-to-air rocket brought down the plane of President Juvénal Habyarimana as it approached the airport of Kigali, Rwanda's capital. The president was killed; and within an hour his *garde présidentielle* of 1500 emerged from their barracks into the streets of Kigali. The Rwandan genocide began.

The reporters and television crews from all over the world who roamed the country at will over the next several months could barely understand what they were seeing. Was it a tribal war between Hutus and Tutsis, Rwanda's two main tribes, in which ancient hatreds had reached the boiling point? If so, why did the massacre also take place among the Hutus? Or was it simple savagery, when all human restraints fall? The media could vividly convey the *how* of events but rarely explain the *why*. In retrospect it seems that the explosion was almost foreseeable.

Demography and ecology

When the genocide began Rwanda was probably on the brink of ecological disaster. The overuse and exhaustion of the land was no doubt one of the underlying reasons for the conflict. Year by year the forests were pushed further up the hillsides, the ravines became larger after each downpour, and the once-legendary fertility of the soil diminished. The food situation had become increasingly precarious: during the 1980s, for example, the annual rate of population growth was ten times the rate of increase in agricultural production. Competition for every square metre of land was acute. According to the 1991 census, there were 7.15 million Rwandans — 271 people per square kilometre, 406 people per square kilometre of arable land and, in the most densely populated districts of Ruhondo and Ruhengeri, 820 people per usable square kilometre.

No other country in Africa has such a high population density, obviously far beyond what is sustainable for a country with almost no industry and no tertiary economic sector except government administration and the churches. Of the entire labour force, 93 percent worked on the land, only 3 percent in industry and

4 percent in the service sector. Malnutrition was becoming endemic. In 1982, 9 percent of the population consumed fewer than 1000 calories a day; by 1993 the proportion of the undernourished had risen to 31 percent. There were no land reserves left to lie fallow and regenerate. With careful and sustainable forms of agriculture, Rwanda could have supported a maximum population of 5 million.[1] The situation was made even more desperate during the late 1980s by the drastic decline in the world market prices for coffee and tea, Rwanda's two major export crops.

Three principal factors account for Rwanda's high population. First, the mountainous terrain and the well-organized military structure of the former Tutsi kingdom protected Rwanda's young men and women from being abducted by Arab slave traders. The social system had remained intact. Second, the general medical improvements introduced by the missionaries and continued through rudimentary forms of public health care reduced the death rate. Third, the decisive influence of the Roman Catholic Church in society and government prevented any effective birth control. When Pope John Paul II came to Rwanda in 1990 he roundly condemned all forms of family planning, despite the obvious overpopulation; and the Rwandan clergy followed his line. The Catholic Church dominated education, medical and developmental work. On the eve of the genocide 90 percent of all Rwandans were Christian, 63 percent of them Roman Catholic, 19 percent Protestant and 8 percent Adventist.[2]

The pre-colonial legacy

The problem of land is a key to understanding the relations between Rwanda's two major ethnic groups, the Hutu (85 percent or more) and the Tutsi (slightly over 10 percent). Although no written records are available, it seems that during the 11th century or earlier, the Hutus, an African Bantu people of sedentary farmers, came from the Cameroonian savannahs to what is today Rwanda and Burundi, displacing the original population of Twa hunters and food gatherers (who number only about 2 percent in a few scattered communities today). The Hutus were organized in large families, clans and small kingdoms, ruled by *mwamis* (chieftains and ritual leaders). They cleared the forest by fire and settled in villages.

During the 15th century the Tutsis, a Nilo-Hamite tribe from the Ethiopian highlands, migrated to Rwanda and Burundi in search of grazing grounds for their cattle. The Tutsis, as cattlemen, were engaged in extensive agriculture, while the Hutus lived off the land directly, but there was nevertheless a long and more or less peaceful interaction as long as land was plentiful. Though fewer in numbers, the Tutsis were well-disciplined and better armed and thus able to subdue the various Hutu chieftainships. In the process, however, they were themselves assimilated in terms of language, religion and intermarriage. Ethnic distinctions became less pronounced, and the clan system often encompassed all three ethnic groups, though the *mwami* and principal chiefs were Tutsi. Contrary to the idea that today's ethnic warfare is the simple continuation of an ancient conflict, Rwanda on the eve of European colonialism was well on the way to becoming a fully integrated society.

Colonial racism

The first European visitors, who arrived in Rwanda around 1850, noted — and probably exaggerated — the socio-economic and "ethnic" stratifications between the Hutu farmers and the Tutsi cattlemen. The ongoing amalgamation process seemed to escape the eyes of the Europeans entirely. In effect, they saw in the heart of Africa the same kind of racial and ethnic distinctions on which they had begun to theorize in Europe. They identified the tall and distinguished-looking Tutsis as born soldiers and rulers, the "master race" who leased the land to the others, as the mediaeval feudal lords had done in Europe. The Hutus were the "born servants", short and heavy-set, whose destiny it was to work the land and to obey. The Twa counted for nothing.

No doubt the Tutsi chiefs were quite receptive to the Europeans' admiring opinion of their inborn racial superiority and to the idea that the European concept of a nation-state was suitable for Rwanda. At any rate, the *mwami* Rwabugiri (Kigeri IV), a chief in eastern Rwanda from 1860 to 1895, extended his domain to the present boundaries of the country and created something like a unified nation-state in which Tutsi rule became supreme. The king owned all the land, which he parcelled out to his nobles, who in turn lent it to the Hutu peasants in a feudalistic pattern. Rwabugiri reduced the power of the traditional chiefs and appointed in their place officials from his own region. The army became his own personal instrument, on which his power rested.

This system of royal dictatorship did not change even after the Germans established a protectorate over Rwanda and Burundi in 1899, relating it to their large colony of Tanganyika, but not exerting any direct rule. As in Europe, "pleasing" physical features and tall bodies were taken as a sign of mental superiority, which justified entrusting the protectorate to the Tutsi. In accordance with European racial theories then in vogue, the missionaries considered the Tutsis to be Hamites, a Caucasian race descended from Noah's son Ham. Because of Noah's curse (Gen. 9:20-27), their skin had turned dark, but they were basically European and therefore "superior" to the Bantu races like the Hutus, who were at the bottom of a divinely ordered world racial scale. [3]

The Hutus resented this further disenfranchisement and dispossession. Their animosity against the Tutsis and the colonists — sometimes underground, sometimes overt — runs throughout the colonial and post-colonial era like a continuous thread and would become a powerful contributing factor to the crisis of the 1990s. Hutu resistance to Tutsi rule was strongest in the north, where Ruhengeri and Gisenyi had managed to retain a certain autonomy.

The *mwami* Musinga, who ruled from 1897 to 1931, skilfully used a small but well-armed German military force to submit the region to his absolutist rule. The expedition was accompanied both by Tutsi and Hutu warriors from the south. That Hutu fought against Hutu raised considerable bitterness in the north and contributed to the estrangement between the northern and the southern Hutu.

The Belgian era: a deepening antagonism

Belgium occupied Rwanda and Burundi in 1916 during the Allies' first world war campaign against German East Africa, and at the end of the war it was granted a League of Nations mandate over the two countries, which it attached administratively to the Congo. From 1946 until its independence in 1962, Rwanda was a United Nations trust territory.

The Belgians administered Rwanda far more directly than the Germans. Moreover, they sharpened the ethnic distinctions, introducing the mention of "Tutsi" or "Hutu" on identification papers, with children of "mixed" descent taking on the father's ethnic designation. Although the Belgian colonial administration rested entirely on the Tutsis, the power of the *mwami* was progressively reduced, and he became nothing more than a colonial puppet ruler. Officials were now appointed by the colonial government. To ensure a supply of trained government officials, missionary orders founded schools which were reserved mainly for Tutsi children. When some Belgian officials began to express misgivings about this one-sided preference for the Tutsis, Archbishop Léon-Paul Classe, the apostolic vicar of Rwanda (himself a Frenchman of Alsatian origin), issued a stern warming:

> The greatest harm the government could possibly inflict on itself and on the country would be to do away with the Mututsi caste. Such a revolution would lead the country straight into anarchy and towards a viciously anti-European communism... As a rule, we cannot possibly have chiefs who would be better, more intelligent, more active, more capable of understanding the idea of progress and even more likely to be accepted by the population, than the Batutsi. [4]

From the progressive integration of pre-colonial times, the colonial government, encouraged by the church hierarchy, thus created an apartheid state in which the seeds of "ethnic conflict" lay. By 1958, the Tutsis held 88 percent of all administrative posts, and 95 percent of all chiefs were Tutsi, while 90 percent of Rwanda's population was Hutu. [5]

The Hutus react — independence

As the movement for independence which began in Algeria and Egypt extended into black Africa in the 1950s, a *Bahutu Manifesto* was drafted in 1957, which demanded Hutu emancipation and the democratization of Rwanda. This document claimed that the Hutus were Rwanda's "true nationals" and that the Tutsis were outsiders and foreigners who had usurped power illegitimately and colluded with the Belgian colonialists to retain it. This manifesto was followed in 1960 by a far more radical statement, the "Hutu Ten Commandments", which foreshadowed coming events. Primary loyalty, this document stated openly, was to be given *exclusively* to the Hutu ethnic group. Any Hutu who married a Tutsi woman or was engaged in business together with a Tutsi was a traitor. Most ominously, the eighth "commandment" advised that "the Bahutu should stop having mercy on the Batutsi". [6]

Some of the Tutsis rejected these Hutu demands in equally violent terms. They argued that the Tutsis had assumed power in Rwanda by right of conquest. How could this "natural" right be questioned? At the same time, the Tutsi elite demanded the end of Belgian rule, in order to return to the old system under which they had run Rwanda without having to share power with anyone. [7]

The Hutus and the Tutsis each formed two political parties; and the new Hutu leadership persuaded the Belgians that any new political system should be based on majority rule. As could be expected during the first parliamentary elections in September 1961, the Hutu parties obtained 83 percent of the votes. The monarchy — and with it the Tutsi oligarchy — had come to an end; and Rwanda became a *de facto* one-party Hutu state. Already in 1960, the last *mwami*, Kigeri V, realizing that the Tutsi monarchy no longer had a chance, had left Rwanda, never to return. But in the new republic, the party chief automatically became head of state and as president filled the role of the *mwami*. Power had shifted from the Tutsis to the Hutus with a vengeance; and eight months after the elections, on 1 July 1962, Rwanda (together with Burundi) obtained its independence from Belgium.

How the church played with fire

As in many other places, developments in Rwanda during the colonial era were strongly influenced by the policies of the missions and churches, chiefly the Roman Catholic Church. The first Catholic mission station was founded in Save, in the south; and within a short time a network of 300 mission stations was established around the country, largely through the work of the order of White Fathers. Soon each parish had its own primary school, with secondary schools established in the nascent towns. The country's educational system came largely to be in the hands of clergy, brothers and nuns.

Large numbers of Rwandans converted to Christianity — a phenomenon not unlike the mass conversions of the late Roman empire and the early middle ages in the Mediterranean basin and northern Europe. Baptism and European names became fashionable; masses and worship services resembled popular feasts. From the perspective of the missionaries, this outward show of strength was also intended to discourage Protestant missions, especially the Anglicans and the Presbyterians, as well as the Adventists, who were coming over from Tanzania. From the perspective of the Rwandan converts, accepting Christianity was useful for their standing in society. Indeed, after the first Rwandans graduated in 1923, the church authorities saw to it that they were placed into key posts of the colonial administration. These young men — most of them Tutsis — helped the Belgians to replace the traditional Tutsi chiefs on whom the *mwami* had relied for the exercise of his power.

Many Rwandan converts entered the priesthood and the nunneries, some no doubt to escape the harsh conditions of rural life. Others aspired to the wealth and prestige — symbolized by modern houses and vehicles — to which only whites and priests had access during the colonial era. Moreover, the clergy directed schools and hospitals and had ready access to public authorities.[8]

To counteract the progressive loss of his power, Musinga, the first *mwami* of the Belgian period, tried to reduce the all-pervading power of the colonialists and the Catholic Church. The missionary-dominated hierarchy was especially displeased when the king decreed freedom of religion and allowed Protestant missions to work in Rwanda. Archbishop Classe told the Belgians that Musinga was an "element of discord, suspicion and general embarrassment" and should be removed in favour of one of his sons, Charles Rudahigwa, provided that the latter would be baptized. Accordingly, in November 1931 the Belgian government replaced Musinga by his son, who took the name of Mutura III. During the next twenty years the new *mwami* paid off the debt he had incurred vis-à-vis the Catholic hierarchy, persistently calling on his subjects to convert. In 1946 he consecrated Rwanda to Christ the King.

The demands of the Tutsi elite in the late 1950s for an end to colonial rule were taken as a sign of ingratitude by both the colonial administration and the Roman Catholic hierarchy. Without recognizing that it might be playing with fire, the Catholic hierarchy decided in 1959 that the time had come to switch its support from the Tutsis to the Hutus. In a pastoral letter read out in all parishes and published widely, the apostolic vicar André Perraudin, a Swiss-born White Father who was later archbishop, wrote that the "social revolution" of the Hutus was justified and that continued discrimination against them was inconsistent with an efficient organization of Rwandan society.[9] But rather than fostering a necessary dialogue between the two ethnic groups, the church declaration, coming at this time, was taken by the radical Hutus as decisive political support for overturning all Tutsi power.

In first backing the ruling Tutsis without any critical distance, then switching suddenly to the Hutus, the Catholic Church in Rwanda seemed to be guided more by opportunism than by the quest for justice and equality. The Jesuit director of the Centre Christus in Remera, Octave Ugirashebuja, judges the church in severe terms:

> The triumphalism and the laziness of the church were in part due to the falsely reassuring presence of the missionaries. Their influence, their authority and their material means were not always used with discernment. They have rather contributed to putting asleep the vigilance and the creativity of the indigenous co-workers. Thus, we have become fully caught up within the thorny problem of ethnicism; the missionaries have not really helped us. Quite to the contrary, in taking sides — and history will show that they have taken sides — they have upset our fragile existence. And when the terrible hour of truth came, the missionaries got evacuated. A few became victims, but not many.[10]

Betrayal of the Tutsis — impunity

In November 1959 the crisis worsened when Tutsi youths attacked a Hutu leader. Releasing their pent-up frustrations, the Hutus reacted violently, and several hundred Tutsis were killed. The colonial administration quickly replaced more than half of its Tutsi staff by Hutus, but it took no measures to protect the endangered ethnic group.

The church and the colonial establishment put their faith in a new form of state and a new set of leaders. To justify the change, a new ideological interpretation was given to Rwanda's history, according to which the Tutsis were no longer seen as a divinely ordained ruling class to whom the country was entrusted, but as a foreign minority of usurpers, who had no right to live in Rwanda but had declared themselves as aristocrats — just as the *Bahutu Manifesto* said. Having oppressed the native Hutus and run the country for their own benefit, they deserved the loss of their privileges.

The clerics moreover spread the story that, despite their Christian upbringing, some young Tutsis had become socialist, if not communist sympathizers. [11] Coming as it did at the height of the frenzied anti-communism of the cold war, this accusation had serious implications. Not only were some of the Tutsi intellectuals believed to be dangerous revolutionaries, but by implication they were also considered atheists, which was just as bad. Thus the churches became incapable of serving as a platform for a reasonable discussion on the future of Rwanda, helping the Hutus on one side to assume power responsibly and the Tutsis on the other to form a loyal opposition. The sudden reversal of church policy helped to radicalize Hutu leadership. By the same token, the situation of the Tutsi minority became precarious. Notwithstanding the injustices of the previous system, the betrayal of the Tutsis by the Catholic Church and the colonial state was appalling. In late 1959 the Belgian government airlifted troops to Rwanda, not to protect its former allies but to back up the Hutus. Murders of unprotected Tutsis went unchecked: 335 Tutsi chiefs and subchiefs — more than half — were killed. The Belgians simply replaced them with 300 Hutu chiefs. Later the Hutus executed nearly all of the remaining Tutsi chiefs who had not fled the country. There was no trial of any kind. [12] In 1963, after independence, between five thousand and eight thousand Tutsis were killed in the district of Gikongoro — ten to twenty percent of the Tutsi population there. Traditional ethnic loyalty was such that no one dared to protest when such actions were committed by members of one's own tribe. Nor was there any public stand on behalf of the victims and against their cold-blooded elimination from the Roman Catholic hierarchy or other church leaders. This pattern of silence would continue throughout the coming years. Crimes were committed with unchallenged impunity.

Following independence, Perraudin's protégé Grégoire Kayibanda, leader of the Parmehutu party, became president. An ethnic quota was introduced in the secondary schools and later extended to the universities founded in the 1960s. Loyalty to the new Hutu chief of state counted above all else. Kayibanda surrounded himself with relatives and friends from his own southern district of Gitamara. The *mwami* system continued, but in ethnic reverse and without the former kings. Since the Hutus had been almost entirely excluded from education and politics, the initial years of the so-called first republic under Kayibanda were chaotic. [13]

Between 1959 and 1961 and again during succeeding crises in 1963, 1964 and 1973, large numbers of Tutsis fled from Rwanda, especially to Uganda. By the early 1990s no fewer than 600,000, including families, were in exile. They constituted a strong destabilizing element for Rwanda, because they had not accepted their loss of land and power and did not intend to be integrated into their host countries. Groups of Tutsi refugees executed repeated military forays into their homeland. This unsettled situation contributed substantially to the outbreak of the genocide of 1994.

Habyarimana's second republic: the no-future society

Relying exclusively on a small circle of ministers and advisors, Kayibanda progressively lost touch with the social realities of the country. In 1973 Major

General Juvénal Habyarimana, the national defence minister, overthrew him in a non-violent coup. His second republic lasted until 1994. Habyarimana tried to open Rwanda up to the outside world and to convert the largely rural country into a modern urban society. While Kayibanda had relied on the southern Hutus for his political support, Habyarimana surrounded himself with friends and relatives from his own northern districts of Ruhengeri and Gisenyi, excluding all southerners from government. The army command, most of the soldiers and the members of the notorious *garde présidentielle* created by Habyarimana also came from the north.

Habyarimana dissolved the Parmehutu and created instead the *Mouvement Révolutionnaire pour le Développement et la Démocratie* (MRND), to which all Rwandans — except the Tutsis — had to belong by birth. The party's uplifting title was designed to placate the international community so as to keep aid money and military hardware coming. Habyarimana controlled the party with an iron fist and it became, next to the army, the second pillar of his power. Perraudin's successor as Roman Catholic archbishop, Vincent Nsengiyumva, the Church's first Rwandan primate, was member of the party's central committee until 1990 when the pope ordered him to resign.

Kayibanda and seven other eminent personalities were condemned to death in a secret trial and executed, deepening the rupture between the southern and northern Hutus, which dated back to the time of the German protectorate. Thus Rwanda's internal divisions no longer simply followed the traditional Hutu-Tutsi ethnic split.

The Tutsis abroad continued to wait for a moment to return. Many had escaped to Burundi, where they were supported by their fellow Tutsis. Between 1961 and 1966 the *Forces Patriotiques Rwandaises* (FPR), launched a dozen attacks against the Hutu regime from their base in Uganda. None was successful, even though the Tutsi army was often backed up by the governments of its host countries and helped by mercenaries from Europe and the USA. The Hutus in Rwanda fought back desperately, fearing that the exiles' return would mean not only restoration of Tutsi power but reoccupation of their former land holdings, an increasingly unbearable prospect in view of the rapidly growing population pressure. After one invasion, at the end of 1963, ten thousand Tutsis who had remained in Rwanda were massacred. The Hutu *Forces Armées Rwandaises* (FAR) even crossed the border into Burundi, pursuing and killing Tutsis with the support of their fellow Hutus there.

The outside pressure helped to harden the attitude of Hutu radicals like Alexis Kanyarengwe and Jean Barahinyura. Believing that Habyarimana was being too lenient in an effort to please the international community, they created extremist party militias called *Interahamwe* ("those who work together") and an equally radical political unit, the *Coalition pour la Défense de la République* (CDR), in order to keep the president from introducing possible reforms. Both groups were in close contact with the presidential guard, and most observers believe that Habyarimana was murdered on 6 April 1994 by such extremists, because he refused to boycott completely the reforms being demanded by neighbouring African states. [14]

Between 1990 and 1994 the problems which had increasingly beset Rwanda since the turn of the century began to coalesce. Despite heavy Tutsi emigration, the total population rose above 7 million, exceeding the country's ecological capacity. Farms which had been subdivided again and again with each passing generation were too small, and those who were left landless had no future. The traditional social fabric began to tear apart, with no alternative structures in sight. Young people migrated towards the cities, where they were largely unwelcome, and became easy prey for unscrupulous leaders ready to channel their energies for their own aims. Theft, violence and murder increased.

In the international community until the late 1980s Rwanda's general image was of a poor, but fundamentally economically sound and self-sufficient country. Then the economy collapsed. In 1985 the last tin mine — which had provided 15 percent of the country's foreign currency earnings — closed down, the victim of increasing costs, a fall in world tin prices and mismanagement. Even more serious were the repercussions of the 75 percent drop in world coffee prices between 1986 and 1992. As a result, Rwanda's debt-servicing charges increased fourfold, and farm income, already precarious, virtually disappeared. Severe droughts in 1989-90, 1991 and 1993 produced shortages of two staple crops, cassava and sweet potatoes, resulting in malnutrition.

In 1993, the Tutsi-led FPR staged a large-scale attack across the border from Uganda, trying to recuperate their land. Because Habyarimana's FAR fought badly, the Tutsi army came within 20 kilometres of Kigali, killing many Hutu families along the way and driving no fewer than 950,000 persons into other parts of Rwanda. Away from their own land, they could no longer produce and became an additional social and economic burden for the rest of the impoverished country. Malnutrition increased sharply. Even so, military expenditures, already high when Habyarimana took over in 1973, quadrupled, using up Rwanda's remaining meagre financial resources. In 1990, international lending institutions had imposed a structural adjustment programme on Rwanda, requiring a sharp reduction of state expenditures. This brought the civilian apparatus of the state into mute opposition to Habyarimana, while the military obviously did not suffer. [15]

Preparations for the genocide

To the outside world Habyarimana gave the impression of a moderate, even democratically oriented statesman, anxious to overcome ethnic tensions and to see Rwanda develop socially and economically. Less noticed was the fact that he surrounded himself with his well-disciplined personal presidential guard of 1500 men, backed up by the 30,000 hardline trained killers of the *Interahamwe*, who were used to break up meetings of moderate Hutus (mainly from the south), to orchestrate demonstrations and to harass Tutsis. That ethnicity was no longer the exclusive guideline in these structures is shown by the fact that the president of the *Interahamwe* was Robert Kashuga, the son of a well-known Protestant Tutsi pastor from eastern Rwanda. [16]

Foreign powers seemed to have no compunctions about offering military assistance to Habyarimana. The largest part of the bill was met by France; and French military and civilian advisors sat in nearly every government department.

Belgium and Zaïre also provided support. France supplied 20,000 fragmentation grenades; South Africa exported thousands of landmines; Rwandan army officers were trained in the United States; China contributed simple machetes and nail-studded clubs for use by technically untrained killers. In a single generation, traditional forms of conflict resolution by communal councils or occasional spear fights had given way to a national security state, based on modern weapons. No new political methods of conflict resolution had been developed; and neither Kayibanda nor Habyarimana, both educated in religious schools, had any intention of replacing the colonial system with democratic pluralism.

In 1990, the notorious *Radio Télévision Mille Collines* (RTMC) was created, in a country which until then had hardly known radio and television. Through endless fanatical propaganda, RTMC urged Hutus to hunt down and kill Tutsis, whom it called *inyenzi* (cockroaches) — as Hitler had described the Jews as "vermin". The broadcasts described the most efficient ways to use guns, grenades, clubs, stones, machetes, spears and bows and arrows to kill. Nowhere in Africa had such calls for "ethnic cleansing" ever been heard so openly and brutally. This was premeditated murder, with clearly described objectives and methods. Death squads were organized and address lists of persons to be eliminated were established. [17] However, when the Tutsi-led FPR advanced towards Kigali in 1993, the excited broadcasts of RTMC backfired; and instead of having the intended effect of encouraging the Hutus to resist, it induced large groups of them to flee in terror, first to other parts of Rwanda, then abroad.

The impact of RTMC propaganda was magnified in October 1993, when Melchior Ndadaye, the first democratically elected Hutu president of Burundi, was murdered by Tutsi soldiers of the Burundian army. Tens of thousands of Hutus were killed in Burundi; and another 70,000 fled across the border into Rwanda. Inevitably, perhaps, the Rwandan Hutus concluded that the Tutsis were never to be trusted; and all hope for a settlement seemed lost. [18]

Church leaders remained silent about these dangerous developments. They showed up dutifully at Kigali airport every time President Habyarimana left or arrived. The churches' own ethnic tensions had the same effect as those at the political level. Hutu church leaders often tended to block the appointment of Tutsis to vacant positions. In the deeply ingrained tradition of the vanished monarchy, the church leaders extolled the virtue of obedience and demanded it from both church workers and lay people. Thus they did no more than the political establishment to contribute to the development of a culture of dialogue. [19] The remorseful reflections after the genocide by a Presbyterian pastor, who saw his wife and six children murdered before his eyes, echo in a remarkable way the Stuttgart Declaration of Guilt by the German churches in October 1945:

> We have had killings here since 1959. No one condemned them. During the first republic [under Kayibanda] they killed slowly, slowly, but no one from the churches spoke out. No one spoke on behalf of those killed. During the second republic [Habyarimana] there were more killings and more people were tortured and raped and disappeared; and we did not speak out because we were afraid and because we were comfortable... The Bible does not know Hutu and Tutsi, neither should we. [20]

In fact many Rwandan Christians were uneasy with the collaboration between their churches and the state, but even if they had dared to speak out, few had fully formulated their thoughts. On the very eve of the genocide in April 1994, some of these misgivings were articulated by the Rwanda Association of Christian Workers to the first African synod of Roman Catholic bishops, which the pope had convened in Rome at that precise moment. It was not so much a petition as an angry and desperate outcry against a style of church that never should have existed:

> Do you know the people? Have you visited them? Do you understand their problems, their oppression? Your affluent style of life increases the gap between you and the people. The Christian people feel abandoned. You have to teach the people about democracy, non-violence and human rights. Religious leaders ought to be the first to practise all this. [21]

The United Nations and the Organization for African Unity had long sought to persuade Rwanda's conflicting parties to reach a settlement. As Habyarimana held power personally, the OAU felt it had no other choice than to reach an understanding with him. He was held personally responsible for the murder of at least 2000 persons between October 1990 and January 1993. Nor had he interfered with the increasingly violent language used by his military leaders and civilian administrators against both Tutsis and moderate Hutus. Already in 1992 disturbing evidence had come to light that the government was planning wholesale massacres. [22] With this menace in mind, Tanzania mediated an armistice between the Rwandan government and the FPR, which led to a peace agreement signed at Arusha, Tanzania, on 4 August 1993. It stipulated the introduction of a new system of power-sharing and the dissolution of the presidential guard. A transitional government would be put in place until internationally supervised elections, which would be held no later than 1995. An FPR regiment would be stationed in Kigali to protect the Tutsi minority, backed up by 2500 troops of the United Nations Aid Mission to Rwanda (UNAMIR). [23]

Plagued by the lack of finances and the double-dealing of some foreign powers, especially France, the UN lost precious time in sending the peacekeeping force to Rwanda, and then only in reduced numbers. The recent disaster in Somalia and the ongoing war in Bosnia had diminished the political will of the international community to intervene in another difficult and remote country. France added spectacularly to the confusion by landing 600 paratroopers in Kigali, ostensibly to back up the UNAMIR force but in reality to bar the entry into the capital of the Tutsi forces, thus providing covert support to Habyarimana. The French action and UN inaction encouraged the discredited president to disregard his obligations under the Arusha agreement — as he had intended anyway. Political murders continued with impunity and with the obvious approval of the president. But even though the Arusha agreement had been undermined, Hutu hardliners, especially the presidential guard, which was to have been dissolved, suspected Habyarimana of a sell-out.

Working against time to resolve the impasse, Tanzanian president Ali Hassan Mwinyi, in accord with the Western powers, invited Habyarimana and the presidents of Uganda, Kenya and Burundi to Dar-es-Salaam at the beginning of April 1994 for a new discussion on the Arusha agreement. At the meeting Habyarimana once again promised to implement the recommendations made by the chiefs of state. As his presidential plane, donated by President François Mitterand of France, prepared to land in Kigali on its return flight, the deadly missile struck. With Habyarimana died Burundi's recently elected president Cyprien Ntaryamira, whom Habyarimana had persuaded at the last minute to join him. The death of the latter contributed to destabilizing Burundi as well.

The massacre

Within an hour of the "accident", RTMC announced the news of Habyarimana's death. Immediately, the *garde présidentielle* charged from its barracks with death lists, killing all the Tutsis and moderate Hutus it could find. One of the first to die was Prime Minister Agathe Uwilingiyimana, along with ten Belgian soldiers who were supposed to function as her bodyguard. Entire families were hunted down, women raped, children and babies stabbed to death. People with academic training — priests and nuns, pastors and evangelists, journalists, lawyers, teachers, nurses — were especially targeted. Church buildings seemed to be favoured centres for mass slaughter. Thirty thousand Tutsis who had taken refuge in the Catholic centre of Kabgayi were gunned down, stabbed and clubbed; another 15,000 lost their lives at the Holy Family compound in Nymata, where they had sought shelter as soon as they heard the news of Habyarimana's death. Church members murdered their priests. Parents saw their children die and vice versa. Neighbours were forced to kill neighbours, relatives their kin. Three Roman Catholic bishops were killed, including Archbishop Thadée Nsengiyumva of Kabgayi, along with ten priests.

What seemed at first to be a murderous free-for-all in reprisal for the killing of the president soon gave evidence of long-term and meticulous planning for genocide, as some had already suspected. The killings were coordinated by national and local officials, the presidential guard and the MRND party. According to Joint Evaluation of Emergency Assistance to Rwanda, quoting *African Rights*, the names of the men (and a few women) who were the true organizers of the killings are known; indeed, some were "shamelessly frank about their role and eager to justify genocide".[24] They were from Habyarimana's entourage, and included his wife, his three brothers-in-law and several advisors. Aiming to rid Rwanda of all Tutsis and moderate Hutus, especially those from the south, they spread the slogans of hatred around the country, recruited the killers and placed the guns and machetes into their hands. Besides organizing and directing the presidential guard and the armed forces, they had financed, trained and armed the *Interahamwe*, who did most of the killing or compelled others to do it under their supervision.

The target groups were systematically selected and murdered. The first were moderate and opposition politicians from whose ranks an alternative government might otherwise be formed. Most of these were killed in the first few days, like Agathe Uwilingiyimana, whom the Arusha agreement had imposed on Habyarimana as prime minister as part of the effort to guarantee Rwanda's return to orderly and democratic government. The second target group was the Tutsi population, to be eliminated completely, district by district, men, women, children and babies, even those hiding in churches and hospitals. Rape was extensively used. The third target were those rank-and-file Hutus who had ever expressed any doubts about Habyarimana's exclusivist policies. Hutu clans which had no immediate connection with the late president's northern region were also considered unreliable and "in case of doubt" to be murdered. Finally, there were those Hutus who were married to Tutsis or who tried to protect Tutsi friends and relatives. The Hutu population was to be completely "purified" and transformed. [25]

The murders were carried out with extraordinary cruelty. People were burned alive, thrown into latrines. Canadian writer Hugh McCullum tells the story of Canon Alphonse Karuhije, a Tutsi who was dean of the Anglican Cathedral of St Etienne in Kigali. Even after his archbishop, Augustin Nshamihigo, had fled the country, Karuhije remained at his post, saving the lives of many Hutu families who were being sought by *Interahamwe* patrols and hiding himself in one of the two towers of the cathedral. One day, however, the murderers discovered Karuhije's hideout and hacked him to pieces. He had been betrayed by a fellow priest. [26]

In the face of such murderous folly, the Belgians and the French evacuated their nationals, including most of the missionaries. Among those saved were Agathe Habyarimana, the president's widow, and her children, who became for a while the personal house guests of President Mitterand in Paris. Most foreign embassies in Kigali were closed down, and their local staff, left defenceless, were murdered for the most part. The UN decided to reduce its peacekeeping contingent from 2500 to 270, then rescinded this hasty measure and increased it to 5000 to protect civilians and refugees. But for many they had arrived too late. On 23 June, 2500 French military entered southwestern Rwanda from Zaire, where they planned to create a safe area to stem the disastrous flow of refugees into neighbouring countries.

The Rwandan massacres ended in July, when the Tutsi-led FPR occupied Kigali and installed a Tutsi government, with moderate Hutu participation. Hutu hardliners were pushed back towards Gitamara, Libuyé and Gisenyi. The war turned into a stalemate, but in the countryside and in the refugee camps the hardline Hutus maintained a rule of terror. On 5 July 1994 the International Committee of the Red Cross estimated the number of dead in Rwanda at one million; other sources have put the figure between 500,000 and 850,000. [27]

The war and the slaughter had a devastating impact on the survivors, especially on children. Many were pulled from under heaps of stinking corpses, shuddering with dysentery and diarrhoea. Often they had lost limbs, which had been hacked off, or were suffering from shrapnel wounds or exploding landmines. They were and are haunted by memories of horrors. Many have seen their parents die; some were forced to kill their brothers, sisters or comrades. An entire generation of deeply disturbed children is growing up, bewildered by the physical and emotional violence which has been done to them. The danger is that they too will become violent and anti-social as a result. [28]

The refugees: will they ever return?

According to UN sources, about two million Rwandans, mostly Hutus, have fled to neighbouring countries — 1,322,000 to Zaire, 626,000 to Tanzania, 92,000 to Uganda — while the Tutsis are returning. Another million were displaced within the country. Efforts to persuade the refugees to return to Rwanda are thwarted by rumours, not without foundation, of returnees being murdered by those who have taken over their properties in the meantime. Within the camps, however, many refugees are terrorized by Hutu hardliners. Others are tormented and robbed by the undisciplined Zaïrean military. Meanwhile, the increasingly violent civil war in Burundi has driven more refugees to camps in Zaire and Tanzania. On top of the flow of refugees into these states from southern Sudan, the millions of Rwandans contribute dangerously to the social, political and ecological destabilization of the vast area surrounding Africa's Great Lakes. In 1996 the Tutsi-led Rwandan army attacked camps in Zaire, searching out Hutu hardliners. This, along with the closure of camps by the Zairean authorities, forced hundreds of thousands of refugees to move again.

Against the background of such profound social and psychological upheaval, with no end of the generally hostile climate in sight, constructive reconciliation is extremely difficult. Yet the only alternative is that tensions will erupt again and again, driving Rwanda towards complete self-destruction. Despite its poor showing, the United Nations still has a mission to fulfill, as do leading African statesmen and church leaders. Foreign powers like Belgium and above all France would do best to abstain completely from meddling afresh in these disturbed waters.

The following would seem to be the central elements of such an effort: [29]

1. *The return of the refugees in dignity and security.* The UN should be provided with adequate finances by its member states to enable a sufficient number of peace-keeping forces to protect the camps and the returnees from the *Interahamwe* and, if necessary, from the Tutsis.

2. *A campaign for confidence-building and defusing of supposedly ethnic tensions.* For this, the long-term presence of UN and other international peace-keeping forces is necessary.

3. *Revival and updating of Arusha agreement of 1993.* This would include democratic elections and the redistribution of power in such a way as to protect the legitimate rights of minority groups. Moreover, efficient democratization involves a strict prohibition of parties and political organizations along ethnic or racial lines and of those which incite and commit violence.

4. *Reconciliation at the local level.* Working groups and debates must be organized to help the people to decide how they want live together in the future, mindful of the disastrous past. Ways must be sought to express forgiveness. Community participation and control must become a key feature of the new society, avoiding the domination of unscrupulous local chiefs or powerful families.

5. *New forms of development.* In the face of massive destruction and ecological depletion, national and local policy decisions must be taken in conjunction with the process of reconciliation for rebuilding the infrastructure of the country,

especially in agriculture, education, medical care, industry and family planning. Past international development projects in Rwanda have generally failed, both because they were not directed at the people's real needs and because they tended to reinforce unjust and anti-social power structures. All development must contribute to democratization, human rights and peace.

The role of the churches?

The churches have clearly been part of the problem in Rwanda; and the church institutions are now probably so discredited that they cannot assume a leading role in any process of forgiveness and reconciliation unless they themselves change profoundly. As noted above, church leaders offered neither protests nor warnings when human rights were being violated and murders committed and ethnic tensions were tearing the social fabric apart. Despite many cases of courage, self-sacrifice and martyrdom, the churches have to face up to the problem of Christians killing Christians and of churches and church centres becoming mass graves for thousands. The way the South African church and political leadership is facing the crimes of the apartheid regime could be an example for Rwanda.

But how can the churches be restructured if Rwandans are faced with prominent church leaders, such as (to cite only one example) the Anglican Archbishop Nshamihigo, who, after fleeing to Nairobi in June 1994, refused to denounce the hardline Hutu regime for the massacres and remains, as of this writing, in contact with known mass murderers?[30] Such complicity must be brought to the light of day and dealt with openly. Most of those who have committed murder are still walking around freely at home or abroad, and the church leaders hardly dare to point them out so as to bring them to justice. The churches may no longer be divided along confessional lines, but they are divided over whether the criminals should be brought to justice — something which secular organizations like the OAU and the UN demand.

The problem is not primarily juridical or even political, but theological and ethical. José Chipenda, the general secretary of the All Africa Conference of Churches, who had attempted, together with the WCC, to mediate in the emerging Rwandan crisis in 1992 and 1993, put his finger on the issue when he said that no amount of church activity on behalf of refugees, reconstruction or social and economic development could replace the quest of Christians to become "the salt of the earth" (Matt. 5:13): "We have seen this moral vacuum, this lack of sufficient emphasis on justice in both Burundi and Rwanda. The churches must recover that commitment if they are to play any kind of role in bringing about peace and reconciliation."[31]

In this light, it is surely urgent for the ecumenical community, led by the AACC and the WCC, to take up the theological questions that arise from Rwanda's genocide as intensively as they once took up the challenge of apartheid. In doing so they not only forced the South African churches to face up to this injustice, but also compelled the churches in Europe and North America to examine how the economic and political structures of their own countries had indirectly buttressed the apartheid regime. Unlike South Africa, Rwanda may not be a significant factor for world economy. But the combination of collapsing coffee prices and an irresponsible arms trade — both determined by the north — went a long way to making Rwanda's simmering tensions boil over. This fateful link to the decision-making centres of the world needs to be carefully re-explored. The way in which the power centres of the world dealt with this small nation helped to create a crisis for all of eastern Africa. But the Rwandans too must rediscover their own share of responsibility for the disaster. Their ethnic hatred was homemade. What must they do to ensure that such a tragedy will not recur?

NOTES

[1] Günther Bächler, "Rwanda", in Bächler and Catherine Schiemann Rittri, eds, *Tod durch Bomben: Friedensbericht 1995*, Chur and Zurich, Verlag Rüegger, 1995, pp.141f.
[2] Steering Committee of the Joint Evaluation of Emergency Assistance to Rwanda, *Historical Perspective: Some Explanatory Factors* (1), Uppsala, Nordic Africa Institute, 1996, pp.16f.
[3] *Ibid.*, pp.22-27.
[4] Quoted in *ibid.*, p.27.
[5] *Ibid.*, p.144; cf. Frédéric Fritscher, "Aux origines du conflit rwandais", *Le Monde: Dossiers & Documents* (Paris), no. 242, Apr. 1996, p.1.
[6] The "Ten Commandments" are quoted in full by Hugh McCullum, *The Angels Have Left Us: The Rwanda Tragedy and the Churches*, Geneva, WCC, 1995, pp.114f.
[7] Joint Evaluation, *loc. cit.*, p.28.
[8] On this see Félicien Karege, "L'église catholique avait les moyens d'éviter le génocide", *Le Courrier* (Geneva), 9 Aug. 1996, p.6.
[9] Jean Musy, "L'église rwandaise n'a pas terminé son chemin de croix", *ibid.*, 27-28 Apr. 1996, p.8.
[10] Quoted by Musy, *ibid.*
[11] Karege, *loc. cit.*
[12] Joint Evaluation, *loc. cit.*, p.31.
[13] Fritscher, *loc. cit.*
[14] Joint Evaluation, *loc. cit.*, p.36.
[15] *Ibid.*, pp.35-42.
[16] Rupert Neudeck, "Genozid und Internationale Gerichtsbarkeit", *Orientierung* (Zurich), nos 15-16, 31 Aug. 1995, p.172.
[17] McCullum, *op. cit.*, p.14.
[18] Joint Evaluation, *loc. cit.*, p.45.
[19] *Ibid.*, p.84; cf. also Bächler, *loc. cit.*, p.152.
[20] McCullum, *op. cit.*, p.75.
[21] *Ibid.*, p.63.
[22] Joint Evaluation, *loc. cit.*, p.47.
[23] Bächler, *loc. cit.*, p.152.
[24] Joint Evaluation, *loc. cit.*, p.51.
[25] *Ibid.*, pp.51f.
[26] McCullum, *op. cit.*, pp.70f.
[27] Brigitte Camus-Lazaro, "Les massacres (Rwanda)", *Le Monde Dossiers & Documents*, no. 242, Apr. 1996, p.2.
[28] McCullum, *op. cit.*, p.62.
[29] Bächler, *loc. cit.*, pp.157-59.
[30] McCullum, *op. cit.*, p.80.
[31] Quoted by McCullum, *ibid.*, p.84.

5
Palestine/Israel

Almost continuously since the British government issued the Balfour Declaration in 1917, the bitter conflict between Jews and Arabs over Palestine has been a major world issue. Diplomats do not often debate biblical themes in their encounters, but in this case they sometimes make an exception. The Jews claim this land on the basis of a 4000-year-old promise by God to their ancestor Abraham, an idea which both Muslim and Christian Palestinians consider presumptuous and outdated. They have settled in this country for centuries; they believe the land is theirs. But in the course of the last 80 years, the Jews have occupied most of the country, calling it Israel, obviously not on the strength of a persuasive biblical argument but by other means. This is where biblical theology ends and 20th-century power politics takes over. How should we understand this tragic deadlock, which has brought death to thousands, made millions homeless and upset the fragile balance of the entire Middle East?

The Middle East has been a troubled region since the dawn of history. Not only does it lie at the crossroads of three continents but it also suffers from a harsh desert and semi-desert climate which obliged the inhabitants to be inventive in order to survive, ready to fight those who sought to take away their watering holes or their limited arable land. They learned early how to trade with each other. Observing the celestial bodies — sun, moon and stars — which seemed to decide their fate, they puzzled over the One who appeared to act behind it all, the maker of heaven and earth. At an early period the peoples of the Middle East built up great civilizations and religious systems, which have engendered most civilizations of today.

Some ancient peoples of that region — the Sumerians, the Hittites, the Phoenicians, the Babylonians — have vanished. Others, like the Assyrians, have survived as a small remnant. The Egyptians have preserved their ancient language within the confines of the Coptic church, but their spoken language and outlook are Arabic. The Armenians, Kurds, Iranians (Persians) and Ethiopians have retained their national identity and language, but their religion is different today from what it was in antiquity. They have survived under new religious identities. The one exception to this picture is Israel, which has retained its identity and religious faith without interruption, despite invasions, conquests, destruction, oppression, internal turmoil, exile, dispersion and finally the terrible *Shoah* of the 20th century. After each crisis Israel was still there, beaten, weakened, humiliated, still praying to the same God — even when God did not answer its prayers.

The Jews: "a stubborn race"

This unusual strength seems to defy historical and sociological rationale. Moreover, Israel's notion of being "chosen" is alien to the modern mind. Many peoples throughout history have thought of themselves as a chosen race. But when they encountered difficulties or defeat, they cursed and abandoned their divinities and followed other gods. Not so the Jews. They may have been punished, reduced in numbers or driven from their homes, but they kept their faith and continued to pray to the God who was punishing them, even if they felt abandoned by him.

The Hebrew Scriptures report God as saying to Abraham, "I will establish my covenant between me and you, and your offspring after you throughout their generations" (Gen. 17:7). To be sure, there have always been Jews who tried to disentangle themselves from this "election". Part of God's covenant with Abraham and his descendants was the land promise. The first version of this promise in the Bible must be read carefully for the *obligation* it entails towards other peoples:

> Now the Lord said to Abram: "Go forth from your country and your kindred and your father's house to the land (*Ha'aretz*) that I will show you. I will make of you a great nation, and I will bless you, and make your name great, so that you will be a blessing. I will bless those who bless you, and the one who curses you I will curse; *and in you all the families of the earth shall be blessed*" (Gen. 12:1-3).

It is clear from this that the promised land was to be seen not as an end in itself but as the physical presupposition for sharing God's blessings with others. This "land base" was to be the starting point from which the great gift was to go out to all nations. Only in this way does the land promise make sense as part of the covenant.

The history of ancient Israel as recorded in the Bible need not be repeated in detail here: the life of the patriarchs, Moses and the exodus from Egypt, the wanderings in the desert and the giving of the law code on Sinai, the conquest of Canaan and the period of the judges, the united kingdom under David and Solomon, the building of the first temple, the divided kingdoms of Northern Israel and Judah, the prophets, the capture of Samaria and Jerusalem and the exile, the return under Persian rule, the Hellenistic period, the Maccabean revolt, the Hasmonean dynasty, Roman domination and the Herodian rulers, the second temple, Jesus' life and crucifixion, the Jewish war and the second destruction of Jerusalem in A.D. 70, the revolt of Simon Bar Kokhba and the tragedy of Masada.

In A.D. 132 the Roman emperor Hadrian ordered Jerusalem to be "ploughed up with a yoke of oxen". He renamed the ruins *Aelia Capitolina*, and a temple to Jupiter was built on the site of the destroyed Jewish temple. No Jew was allowed to come near the city on pain of death. The ancient name *Eretz Israel* was replaced by *Syria Palaestina* after the Philistines, Israel's ancient mortal enemies. All Jewish hopes for any form of national existence were dashed.

After Constantine's conversion to Christianity the situation of the Jews became even more difficult. While he fostered a cult of holy places in Palestine, he also planned a severe persecution of the Jews, which was thwarted only by his death. In 361, the emperor Julian, seeking to abolish Christianity, ordered the temple to be rebuilt. But shortly after construction had begun, flames burst out, accompanied by loud explosions. The frightened builders ran away, convinced that this was a sign of divine judgment on the "apostate" emperor, who, they said, had falsified the prophecies of Christ.[1]

Even though their religious centre had disappeared, exiled Jews everywhere daily gathered together in prayer facing Jerusalem, repeating the lament of their ancestors by the Babylonian river Chebar: "If I forget you, O Jerusalem, let my right hand wither! Let my tongue cling to the roof of my mouth, if I do not remember you, if I do not set Jerusalem above my highest joy" (Ps. 137:5-6). Such prayers, repeated generation after generation, created an idealized image of the lost city and land and at the same time nourished the will to return and repossess it. In this stubborn will the modern conflict is rooted.

Not all Jews left their country after the fall of Jerusalem in A.D. 70. A much reduced Jewish community stayed on in Galilee. Withdrawing from politics, they devoted themselves to the study of scripture and law under the guidance of the Pharisees. The priests were replaced by rabbis (teachers), and religious life shifted to synagogues and private homes. These isolated Galilean Jews made significant contributions to the survival of their community. Major synagogues existed in several towns, and the torch was kept alive in the schools, the forerunners of the great religious academies (*yeshivot*) of later periods. *Halakha*, religious law dealing with all aspects of religious life and interpersonal relations, was taught and transmitted from generation to generation. Oral law and Jewish lore were collected, elaborated, codified and written down over the years. A dynamic element of Jewish faith was the continued belief that the Messiah would come and deliver his people from foreign oppression. Rabbi ben Zakkai, who survived the destruction of Jerusalem in A.D. 70, gave the following message of hope to his desperate fellow-believers: "If you are holding a seedling in your hand and the coming of the Messiah is announced, first plant your seedling, then go to greet the Messiah."[2]

By the time Islam arrived during the 7th century, there were large Jewish exile communities along the entire Fertile Crescent, as well as in Yemen, Iran, Bukhara and Samarkand, Egypt, Cyrenaica, Tunisia, Morocco, Spain, Italy, southern France, Greece and Asia Minor. There were also Jewish tribes in Arabia; and in the Black Sea region the Kazars were converted. Despite their minority status and the repeated persecutions, this expansion — which would spread to the Americas after the 16th century — created an impressive network of interpersonal relationships, rooted in a common faith and a stubborn will to survive which kept the land promise alive.

Origins of the Palestinian Arabs

The biblical account of Abraham's two sons Ishmael and Isaac (Gen. 17) testifies to an ancient folk memory of common Semitic ancestry for Arabs and Jews. This link is supported by the close linguistic relationship between Arabic and Hebrew and by similar cultural and religious patterns. Arab civilization dates back to 1000 B.C., roughly the same time as Israelite civilization. A legendary and reputedly wealthy Queen of Sheba, who probably came from what is today Yemen, was said to have visited Solomon in Jerusalem (1 Kings 10). An Arab tribe, the Nabateans, created remarkable irrigation systems which have been excavated and restored in the Israeli Negev desert today.

Today's Palestinian Arabs seem largely to descend from the peoples that entered Palestine after the conquests of the Persians and of the Macedonians and Greeks under Alexander the Great. Besides Jews, these included Arameans, Greeks, Syrians and Samaritans. At the time of Jesus, the rural population in the interior spoke mainly Aramaic — another linguistic cousin of Hebrew — while the urban inhabitants of the coastal cities were Greek-speaking and had adopted Hellenistic life-styles. The New Testament indicates that Jews, the Samaritans and the Hellenized population did not interact much; and there was little social cohesion.

During the 4th century the Christians, whose religion was now recognized by the state, probably became a majority in Palestine as in the rest of the empire. The centre of the Hellenized Christian community was the episcopal see of Caesarea, a place of important theological learning. During the 5th century the patriarchate of Jerusalem was established, formally on a par with those of Alexandria, Antioch and Rome. Under the influence of Egyptian hermits, monasteries and nunneries were created in Jerusalem and Bethlehem.

Under the inspiration of Constantine and the Byzantine imperial court, religious shrines commemorating Christian martyrs and biblical events were constructed, including the Church of the Nativity in Bethlehem, the Church of the Holy Sepulchre in Jerusalem and the basilica over the tomb of the patriarchs in Hebron. These holy places were promoted to counter the attraction of the newly built basilicas over the tombs of Peter and Paul in Rome, which the early popes were seeking to establish as central holy places to bolster Rome's claim to overall episcopal jurisdiction. Jerusalem became a conglomerate of churches, hospices, monasteries, hospitals and homes for the aged. It was surrounded by Christian and Jewish graveyards, particularly on the slopes of the Mount of Olives, for many believers wanted to be present there for the great rising, when the returning Christ or the coming Messiah would set his feet on the mountain to the sound of celestial trumpets. Jerusalem became *the* Holy City and Palestine *the* Holy Land.

During the 7th century a sudden and unexpected movement engulfed the Middle East. Islam, taught by the Prophet Muhammed (c. 570-632), an Arab merchant from Mecca, proclaimed the existence of one single, indivisible God. The Qu'ran and the "Five Pillars of Islam" could be understood by all who were weary of either decadent polytheism or theological infighting over complicated Christian creeds. But Muhammed urged his followers to respect both Jews and Christians as "peoples of the Book".

Jerusalem was captured in 638 by Omar (581-644), one of the Prophet's former companions. Within a few years he drove both the Byzantine and the Persian forces out of the Middle East. One of the first acts of this reportedly ascetic and just ruler was to clean up the temple area, which the Roman and Byzantine occupiers had deliberately desecrated and filled with waste. Both Jews and Christians were allotted a status called "under protection", and there was no persecution. But with the passage of time, pressures increased. Non-Muslims were subject to heavy taxes. Many Christians converted and more Jews left the country.

Conversion from Islam to Judaism or Christianity was however punishable by death. The Jews observed with great dismay the construction on the temple square of the Dome of the Rock mosque by Caliph Abd-el-Malik (687-691), and of the al-Aksa mosque adjacent to it by his son Walid.

Nevertheless, Christians managed to retain a majority in Palestine until well into the middle ages. The Arab conquest was a cultural revolution. Most of the inhabitants, whether Aramaic- or Greek-speaking, adopted the Arabic language and culture, and were influenced by the great centres of learning in Cairo, Damascus and Baghdad. Christian liturgies were translated into the new language. The foundation for a common Palestinian Arab culture had been laid.

From the Crusades to the first world war

The next major historical development to affect Palestine was the Crusades mounted by Western Christians between 1096 and 1291. There were two chief causes: the increasing difficulties created by the Byzantine empire for Western pilgrims travelling to the Holy Land after the schism between Eastern and Western Christianity, and the growing nervousness throughout Europe about the threat of a Muslim invasion. After the Seljuk Turks captured Jerusalem from the Arabs in 1071 and destroyed the Church of the Holy Sepulchre, Pope Urban II appealed to Europe to "free the Lord's tomb of infidels". Taking part in this military campaign would also count as a religious pilgrimage, for which the pope offered generous indulgences. Bad discipline, famine and battle reduced the ranks of the Crusaders; and of the estimated 600,000 who departed for the first Crusade only 40,000 reached the Holy Land. [3]

During the capture of Jerusalem in 1099, Muslims, Christians and Jews were slaughtered indiscriminately. Few events have left a more profound impact on the Arab mind than this brutal invasion and the loss of Jerusalem to the Frankish knights. The Crusades deepened the fundamental mistrust not only between Muslims and Christians, but also between the Eastern and Western churches, already estranged by earlier theological and political power struggles. Later it became evident that the destruction wrought on the Byzantine empire by the Crusaders so weakened it that it no longer had the strength to resist the Ottomans, to whom the empire fell in 1453.

The Crusader kingdoms lasted nearly two hundred years until the Mameluks, a Muslim military class made up of former liberated slaves from Egypt, captured Acre in 1291. The ports of the Holy Land were destroyed to prevent further landings, thus also disrupting international commerce. Most cities lay desolate. The population, including the Jews, was much diminished. A series of earthquakes, followed by more economic and political upheavals, plagues and locust invasions turned Palestine into one of the most desolate countries of the Mediterranean basin. During the 14th century Christian families began to return and rebuild some of the destroyed sanctuaries. When the Ottoman Turks broke up Mameluk rule in 1516, only about a thousand Jewish families lived in Palestine, mainly in Jerusalem, Nablus, Hebron, Gaza, Safed and several villages in Galilee. [4]

The coming of the Ottomans produced little change. Among the few notable events was the rebuilding of the walls of Jerusalem (which surround the old city to the present day) under Suleiman the Magnificent in 1537. By the end of the 18th century much of the land was owned by absentee landlords, the *effendis*, and leased to impoverished tenant farmers. The remaining forests were cut down and the irrigation systems abandoned. Desertification advanced. By 1785, according to a French visitor, the total population of Palestine did not exceed 50,000, of whom 20,000 lived in Jerusalem, 5000 in Hebron, 5000 in Nablus, 3000 in Bethlehem and 2000 in Gaza.[5]

After Napoleon's brief and ill-fated attempt to conquer the Middle East in 1799, the pace of events quickened. In 1831 Palestine fell under the temporary rule of the *khedive* of Egypt, Muhammed Ali. After his defeat in 1840 the Ottoman empire renewed its control, but European interest in Palestine, much of it having to do with plans for constructing the Suez Canal, was growing. Consulates and vice-consulates were established there. Among other things, this heightened attention influenced a dispute between Greek Orthodox and Latin clerics over the Church of the Nativity in Bethlehem, and this local church conflict led to diplomatic complications which contributed to the outbreak of the Crimean War in 1855.

All this stimulated further interest in the Holy Land on the part of European and North American Christians of all confessions. French and Russian monasteries were built. Catholic missionary orders created educational and welfare institutions. Protestant missionaries set up their own schools, hospitals and orphanages and even appointed a common bishop in Jerusalem. Scholars from Europe and North America undertook archaeological excavations, which contributed enormously to the development of modern biblical scholarship. German pietists founded agricultural colonies.

Some of these fervent activities were inspired by millennialist expectations of the Second Coming of Christ and of the end of the world. Old Testament prophecies and the Revelation to St John were understood to predict a number of momentous events which would precede the appearance of Christ "in the clouds", including the "return" of the people of Israel to its ancient homeland and the ultimate battle of Armageddon. Christian missionaries and settlers wanted to be present for these momentous final events. Such beliefs continue to be held by many pietistic and fundamentalist circles within Western Christianity, colouring their view of the State of Israel and bearing striking similarities to the convictions of ultra-orthodox Judaism. These activities coming from the outside eroded Ottoman control over Palestine long before the first World Jewish Congress in Basel, Switzerland, in 1896, when Theodor Herzl issued his appeal for a Jewish state.

Anticipating the demise of the Ottoman empire and worried about the barely disguised colonial interests of European powers, Arab Palestinians began during the second half of the 19th century to think of their own political future. A particular concern was the settlers from abroad, both Jews and non-Jews, who were buying land from the *effendis*. Like other Arab nationalists, the Palestinians disagreed among themselves over whether autonomy should take the form of one large Arab state for the entire Middle East or whether smaller "nation-states" would be more appropriate.

The ideology of Arab nationalism was far less well-defined than Jewish Zionism. "Arab-ness" (*al uruba*) was a mystical concept, as vague in its way as the Germanic mythologies of the time or the later notion of *négritude* of black anti-colonialists. Attempts to fill Arab nationalism with Islamic religious content were not well received by Palestinian Christians, who had been among the earliest promoters of Arab nationalism; but after nationalism failed, the fusion between "Arab-ness" and Islam opened the way to Islamic fundamentalism. [6]

Hardly anyone seemed aware at this stage that two nascent nationalisms were on a collision course: Jewish Zionism, born under the repressive social conditions in Europe, but directed at Palestine, and secular Arab nationalism, seeking liberation from both the decaying Ottoman empire and the threat of European colonialism. The first priority of the Arab nationalists was independence from the Ottoman empire. The latter tried belatedly to turn aside this challenge by introducing administrative reforms, but at almost the same time the idea arose of reversing the disintegration of the empire by converting it into an Islamic state, which was unacceptable to the Palestinians. To counter this opposition, the Young Turk movement proposed a secular democratic society on the Western model, in which Muslims, Christians, Jews and adherents of other religions would all have a legitimate and equal place. But after the Young Turks took power in 1908, it did not take the Arabs long to recognize them as nothing more than ethnic nationalists, seeking to reaffirm the power of the Turkish ruling minority at the expense of other nationalities.

Deceitful colonial policies

The 400-year Ottoman rule of Palestine came to an end in 1917. The Arabs revolted, and a British army commanded by General Edmund Allenby captured Jerusalem with considerable Arab support. The Palestinians suffered a great deal throughout this long and difficult campaign, and they were bitterly disappointed when it became clear that the victory would not bring independence despite the promises that had been made.

The basic problem was the contradictory policies of the British government, which had simultaneously promised independence to the Palestinian Arabs and a "national home" on Palestinian territory to the Jews (Balfour Declaration). At the same time, under the terms of the 1916 Sykes-Picot agreement with France, Palestine was to be placed under an international administration (Britain and France). Nevertheless, in 1918 the British government decided to place Palestine under its own military administration. Then in 1920 the British "received" it back under a League of Nations mandate. Finally, in 1923 Britain decided to separate the territory east of the Jordan from Palestine and create from it a separate emirate under the Hashemite Emir Abdullah, to compensate him and his family for the loss of Mecca to Ibn-Sa'ud and to reward him for his help to the British during the war. On none of these decisions were the Palestinian people consulted. It was at this moment that the seeds for the later confrontation took root, because this sequence of events made large-scale Jewish immigration possible.

Not surprisingly, the peoples concerned saw these conflicting policies and decisions as highly immoral. But they were not necessarily the result of particular deviousness or mental confusion on the part of the British government; rather, they reflected the rapidly evolving power constellations of the day. It must be recalled that in 1916 and 1917 the war was going badly for the Western Allies. It was absolutely essential for the British to ensure the safety of the Suez Canal, without which it would be reduced to status of a medium-size power. Moreover, access to the new oilfields in the Middle East had to be maintained at all costs, since without oil modern battles could not be fought and modern industries and transportation could not be maintained. The weak Arab states could never guarantee such protection, especially now that the revolutionary Soviet Union was turning into a more dangerous and unfriendly rival than Czarist Russia had been. Thus reasons of state were the guiding principle for Britain.

Zionism, the motor for a Jewish state

Unlike the Palestinian Arabs, who had little experience in international diplomacy, the Zionists readily grasped the opportunity offered by Britain's difficulties. When Chaim Weizmann negotiated with Lord Balfour on behalf of the World Jewish Congress in 1917, the Zionist movement represented little political power in Britain and could not even count on majority support among Jews. Moreover, German Jews were just as important to that country's war effort as were Jews in Britain for their country. But Weizmann was convinced that the moment had come for a decisive political move towards the realization of a homeland in Palestine and that even a partial British promise would be better than nothing. Balfour, no doubt overestimating Weizmann's influence, agreed and persuaded the British cabinet to adopt his famous though carefully worded statement:

> His Majesty's government view with favour the establishment in Palestine of a national home for the Jewish people, and will use their best endeavours to facilitate the achievement of this object, it being clearly understood that nothing shall be done which may prejudice the civil and religious rights of existing non-Jewish communities in Palestine, or the rights and political status enjoyed by Jews in any other country.

It is important to understand the transition from biblically and liturgically expressed hopes to the political programme of modern Zionism. During the 19th century European Jews increasingly recognized that the juridical equality granted as a result of the Enlightenment and the French Revolution had not produced social acceptance. On the contrary, emerging nationalisms were leading to ugly new forms of antisemitism and racial prejudice. Long before Hitler and the Nazis, pogroms in Russia and Poland and the Dreyfus affair in France signalled a changing mood. Moses Mendelssohn (1729-86) and Moses Hess (1812-75) in Germany and Hirsch Kalischer (1795-1874), Perez Smolenskin (1842-85) and Leo Pinsker (1821-91) in Eastern Europe introduced the idea that the Jews could overcome antisemitism only by becoming a nation among other nations. Wide — though by no means unanimous — acceptance of the idea came through the writings of Theodor Herzl (1860-1904) of Hungary: *Der Judenstaat* ("The Jewish State") and *Alt-Neuland* ("Old and New Land"). [7]

Systematic plans for the Jewish settlement of Palestine were made by the World Zionist Congress in Basel in 1896 which Herzl convened. The congress envisaged (1) suitable patterns of colonization; (2) creation of local and international institutions to back them up; (3) strengthening of Jewish national sentiment and consciousness; and (4) obtaining the consent of political (Ottoman) authorities.[8] While only a small number of Eastern European Jews responded to the call, with most preferring to emigrate to North America or Western Europe, Zionism nevertheless became for the first time a focal point for Judaism. It was a Jewish version of nationalism, combined with the socialist idealism of the day. Most orthodox Jews, who believed that only the Messiah could restore the "kingdom of Israel", opposed Zionism, because its advocates were assimilated Jews like Herzl, who in their eyes no longer had any "faith".

It was not enough to buy land and get to work on it. A new society had to be created by marginalized individualists, who had rarely been allowed to own land or make their own decisions. The Jewish men and women coming to Palestine were of a different breed from the generations of pious believers who had prayed quietly within their four walls. David Ben-Gurion (1886-1973) offered a striking summary of the hopes that animated these early pioneers, the *chalutzim*:

> The Hebrew worker came here not as a refugee, clutching at any reed offered to him. He came as a representative of the whole people, and as an avant-garde pioneer in the grand enterprise of the Hebrew revolution he captured his position on the labour market, in the economy and in settlement activities. In all his deeds and activities, be they small or large, in his work in village and town, in the creation of his own agricultural and industrial economic structures, in conquering language and culture, in defence..., in all this the Jewish worker was conscious of the historic task destined to be carried out by the working class... The Hebrew worker combined in his life work national redemption and class war, and in his class organization created the content of the historical aims and needs of the Jewish people.[9]

Jewish immigration and Arab resistance

Not surprisingly, such a forthright conception of Zionism met with resistance. But the sultan's refusal of the requested charter did not keep Jewish immigrants from landing on the shores of the Holy Land. Shortly before the outbreak of the first world war, Jewish settlers founded the city of Tel Aviv in the sand dunes north of the Arab city of Jaffa, which did not allow Jews to live within its boundaries. By 1914 the Jewish population in Palestine stood at 90,000.

After the end of the first world war in 1918, Jewish immigration, encouraged by the Balfour Declaration, rose steadily, reaching a peak of 62,000 new immigrants in 1935, the year Jews started to flee Hitler's Germany in large numbers. The makeup of the population of Palestine shifted dramatically: in 1922 Jews were only 12.9 percent; by 1940 one-third of the 1.5 million residents of Palestine were Jews.[10] The new arrivals transformed the countryside with new agricultural techniques, developed new industries, exploited the Dead Sea potash mines, transformed the school system and replaced Yiddish and other European languages with Hebrew. For the first time in history, a "dead" language had come alive again. In 1925 a Hebrew University was established on Mount Scopus. After 1929 the newly created Jewish Agency represented the concerns of all Palestinian Jews before the British high commissioner, functioning to some extent like a government. Public works investments by the British colonial administration — railways, roads, seaports (Haifa), water supplies, electricity, postal services and telephones — facilitated rapid development. The economic growth even attracted Arabs from neighbouring countries, who applied for work with Jewish entrepreneurs, established small businesses themselves or worked as farmhands on the new export-oriented estates.

The spread of Jewish settlements and the rapid transformation of their country bewildered the Palestinian Arabs. The Jewish immigrants did not occupy land by force; and most sought to be on good terms with their Arab neighbours. They were persuaded that they were observing the provision of the Balfour Declaration that they should do nothing against "the civil and religious rights of existing non-Jewish communities". The problem was not one of religious adherence, but rather of a European life-style, modest as it may have been, which inevitably clashed with the ways of the Arabs. One might speculate about how differently modern Israel would have evolved if the first Jewish settlers had not come from Europe but from Arab countries of the Middle East and North Africa or from Ethiopia, most of whose once-large Jewish communities have disappeared. [11]

Not all Jews were indifferent to the fears of the Arabs. The outstanding Zionist leader Nahum Goldman wrote in his autobiography (1970) that "one of the great oversights in the history of Zionism is that when the Jewish homeland in Palestine was founded, sufficient attention was not paid to relations with the Arabs". While the ideological and political leaders of the movement always emphasized the need to establish the Jewish national home in peace and harmony with the Arabs, Goldman wrote:

> Unfortunately these convictions remained in the realm of theory and were not carried over, to any great extent, into actual Zionist practice. Even Theodor Herzl's brilliantly simple formulation of the Jewish question as basically a transportation problem of "moving people without a home into a land without a people" is tinged with disquieting blindness to the Arab claim to Palestine. Palestine was not a land without people, even in Herzl's time; it was inhabited by hundreds of thousands of Arabs, who in the course of events could sooner or later have achieved independent statehood, either alone or as a unit within a larger Arab context. [12]

The first anti-Jewish riots occurred in 1920. Although the Jewish population did not exceed 10 percent, the Arabs were beginning to realize that the projected "national home" could really take the form of a state. There were further riots during the later 1920s, the most serious occurring in 1929 when the Palestinian constitution proposed by the British did not satisfy Arab expectations. During this conflict, a Jewish settlement of 60 inhabitants near Hebron was massacred. But tensions within the Arab community were also acute. Poor peasants rioted against rich Arabs, because the *effendis* had sold land to the Jewish immigrants over the peasants' heads. Dissatisfaction grew when neighbouring countries obtained political independence while Arab Palestine did not. An outright revolt occurred in 1936-38. Jewish settlements were attacked and colonists murdered. The Jews in turn organized military resistance, and some of their radical groups attacked and killed Arab villagers. The British dispatched a large military force to stamp out the civil war, but its proposed territorial division of the country, accepted by the Jews, was refused by the Arabs. The situation remained deadlocked.

Shortly before the second world war broke out in 1939, the British government announced that Jewish immigration would be limited to 75,000 for the next five years — too many for the Arabs, not enough for the Jews. But the outbreak of war interrupted the civil conflicts, and 25,000 Jews and 9500 Arabs volunteered for service in the British armed forces. In response to the European holocaust, the Jewish Agency brought in thousands of new immigrants illegally above the quota imposed by the British. Those caught by the British were sent to camps or to distant islands in the Indian Ocean; those who slipped through British controls but were captured by Arab patrols were usually murdered on the beach.

Israel: the Jewish state

The confused aftermath of the second world war made the Jewish state finally possible. Had it not been for the mass murder of European Jews during the war and the collapse of the British empire shortly thereafter, it is unlikely that Zionism would have been strong enough to achieve its aim of seeing the state of Israel created. But the Western democracies felt guilty once they understood the extent of the Holocaust.

As soon as the armistice was signed in Europe, fighting in Palestine resumed more violently than ever. *Haganah*, the principal military arm of the Jewish settlers, was a well-trained, well-armed and formidable force. After another attempt at a compromise failed in 1947, the British government turned the Palestine question over to the United Nations, which proposed a new division: parts of Galilee, the coastline and most of the Negev would belong to the Jewish state, the rest, especially the Gaza area and the central highlands would remain with the Arabs, while Jerusalem, sacred to the three monotheistic faiths, was to be internationalized. The Jews accepted; once again, the Arabs did not, proposing instead a non-confessional state for all Palestine, which the Jews refused. In retrospect, it is clear that this failure to reach an agreement was an historic lost opportunity, but the internal and external pressures on both sides were such that for either to compromise would have looked like a betrayal.

The civil war became general. Jewish and Arab partisans attacked each other and both attacked the British military establishment, which slowly relinquished control. When Arab fighters from other countries joined, the outnumbered Jewish settlers expected the worst. In late 1947, however, the Arab upper class, the *effendis*, took fright and began to flee. And when nervous Jewish fighters attacked the Arab village of Deir Yasin and killed 250 persons, among them old people, women and children, a large part of the Arab population along the sea coast also fled in panic.

On 14 May 1948 the British high commissioner left Palestine and the colonial administration was pulled out. The Zionist establishment, led by David Ben-Gurion as prime minister and Chaim Weizmann as president, declared the independence of Israel. Jewish immigration was opened up without restriction. Between 1948 and 1951, 702,000 immigrants arrived, not only holocaust survivors from Europe, but also Jews from hostile Arab countries and Turkey.

Although recognized by the United States and the Soviet Union, the new state was immediately attacked both by Palestinian Arab guerrillas and by the armies of the five neighbouring states — Egypt, Transjordan, Iraq, Syria and Lebanon. In this numerically unequal struggle the Israeli soldiers proved to be the better fighters. Step by step they succeeded in removing the enemy from their settlements except for the isolated Jewish communities near Bethlehem and the ancient Jewish quarter of the old city of Jerusalem, whose inhabitants were unable to withstand the siege of the disciplined British-led Bedouin corps under General Sir John Glubb. Two thousand Jerusalem Jews and at least as many attackers died. All of the synagogues in the quarter were razed and Jews were no longer given access to the Wailing Wall. On the slope of the Mount of Olives most Jewish graves were desecrated.

Slowly the Israelis gained the upper hand, and only strong international pressure kept them from a last-minute push to conquer all of Palestine. The armistice line of 1949 has since then become an internationally recognized frontier. The Arab-controlled area of central Palestine, including the old city of Jerusalem and Bethlehem, henceforth called the West Bank (of the Jordan), was administratively attached to the Hashemite Kingdom of Jordan. The Gaza Strip, with its refugee camps along the Mediterranean Sea, was administered by Egypt. The Arabs remaining on the Israeli side of the new line of demarcation became a minority among a predominantly Jewish population. The division of Palestine, which the Arabs had always refused, had become a reality, but under far less favourable conditions than they had earlier been offered.

Armistice without peace

But armistice did not signify peace. Neither the surrounding Arab states whose armies had been defeated nor the Palestinian Arabs who had been expelled were reconciled to the loss of the economically most viable areas of their country. Nor could they accept the creation of the Jewish state which they had fought from the beginning. The principal victims were the 580,000 Palestinian Arabs who had fled their country in 1948 and 1949. Their eviction, together with the massive arrival of Jewish immigrants from Europe and the Arab countries and later from the Soviet Union, resulted in one of the largest population "exchanges" in this century. While Israel, with massive foreign support, provided housing and jobs for the Jewish arrivals, many Palestinians ended up in bleak United Nations refugee camps in the Gaza Strip, on the West Bank, around Jericho and in Lebanon and Syria. Some of the more fortunate found jobs in the booming oil fields of the Gulf states and Saudi Arabia or migrated elsewhere and supported their families from abroad. A new generation grew up in camps and crowded housing. From among these youth without jobs and without a future were recruited young fighters ready to take more and more desperate action. For many years the "Palestinian terrorists", as they were called, were feared not only in Israel but throughout the world. Open conflict between Israel and its neighbours broke out in 1956, 1967 and 1973. In the six-day war of 1967 the Israelis occupied not only the West Bank, the Gaza Strip and the old city of Jerusalem, but also the Syrian Golan Heights. In 1982 and 1996 it pursued Palestinians who were attacking settlers in northern Galilee far into Lebanon. Each time half a million people were displaced.

The unending Israeli-Palestinian conflict radicalized Middle Eastern politics. In quick succession changes occurred in several Arab countries. Old, conservative regimes toppled and were replaced by nationalist or fundamentalist forces, notably in Iraq, Syria, Egypt, Yemen and Libya. In 1952 the Algerians launched their long and bloody war of independence against France, but even 40 years after independence that country has yet to find its inner equilibrium. The pro-Western Shah of Iran was ousted by Ayatollah Khomeini in 1979.

Among the disinherited Arab poor, nationalism associated itself with a revived Islam. At the same time, the entire region became a multi-levelled battleground in the strategic contest between the superpowers of the cold war. At the heart of the game was not only Israel but the oil fields. In Lebanon, as we shall see in the next chapter, ethnic and religious groups engaged in a long and self-destructive civil war. Iraq under Saddam Hussein first fought a long war against Iran, then occupied Kuwait, leading in 1991 to the brief Gulf war and endless subsequent bickering over the future of Iraq.

There is no doubt that the Middle East has become the most heavily armed and least stable region in the world, replete with dictatorships, religious fanaticism and human rights violations. Although Israel's existence is presently ensured by a US military security "guarantee", this may not suffice in the long run. New weapons are making "secure frontiers" obsolete, and security guarantees by great powers depend on the vagaries of their own internal politics, not the needs of their clients. Israel's long-term survival, as Nahum Goldman and others have clearly understood, ultimately depends on how it deals both with the Palestinian Arabs and with the millions of Arabs in the other countries of the region.

"What is happening to us?"

The conservative *Likud* government of Benjamin Netanyahu, elected in 1996, has dangerously threatened the peace process initiated by his predecessors and Yassir Arafat, chief of the Palestine Liberation Organization (PLO) and president of the embryonic Palestinian state. Unless Israel changes its policies, a new *intifada* may well erupt. Even new interstate wars between Israel and its Arab neighbours are possible, unless the United States imposes its *Pax Americana*. But power is in itself a factor of destabilization unless it is permeated with justice. This is precisely the problem with a *Pax Americana* or any similar protective shield: it is a short-term measure, not a solution.

Yet there may be some hopeful pathways from the present confusion and hostility into a more humane future. It would seem that two points should be underscored. First, if Zionism was a valid response to antisemitism and Jewish suffering a century ago, the question must be raised whether it is legitimate to use it as an instrument of eviction of *others* today — especially since those punished, the Palestinian Arabs, were in no way connected with the persecution of Jews in Europe. Second, the holocaust, that experience of so much suffering for the Jewish people, must become an integral part of any rethinking of Israeli relations with the Arabs. Having lost land and hope, it is the Palestinians who now suffer. If there is no adequate response to these two problems, what meaning can a *Jewish* state really have? If this state has neither meaning nor ethics, how can it last? At the root of this way of putting the question lies the ancient biblical quest for the "chosen people" who were mandated to be "a blessing to the nations".

Borrowing from the Semitic tradition of telling stories or parables to illustrate and clarify difficult themes, we can perhaps arrive at some perspective and depth by listening to the voices of some Arabs and Jews.

Nathan Chofsky, a former Russian Jew and long-time settler, speaks of witnessing the side-tracking of the original Zionist vision in the flight of Palestinians from their homeland in 1948 and 1949:

> Here was a people who lived on its own land for 1300 years. We came and turned the native Arabs into tragic refugees. And still we dare to slander and malign them, to besmirch their name. Instead of being deeply ashamed of what we did and trying to undo some of the evil we committed by helping these unfortunate refugees, we justify our terrible acts and even attempt to glorify them. [13]

Fawaz Turki, a Palestinian Arab exiled in France, wrote in 1974:

> The deportations, the blowing up of homes, the expropriation of property, the arrogance on the faces of Israeli soldiers walking into Arab coffee shops in Jerusalem to slap the patrons on the face and demand identity cards, the primitive torture of members of the resistance — all these go on, and to the outside world "the Arabs" have never had it so good. Look at how our standard of living is better than ever. We earn excellent wages under occupation. We drive cars. We watch television. Our health standards have improved. And they show pictures of our West Bank "notables"... shaking hands with Israeli military governors. And nobody seems to realize that, during all this, Palestinians called for and fought for a secular state and not for a struggle to inflict on Israeli society the same devastation they inflicted on us. [14]

A haunting description of the superimposition of modern Israel on a vanished Arab rural society comes from a perhaps surprising source, the brilliant Israeli general Moshe Dayan:

> Jewish villages were built in the place of Arab villages. You don't even know the names of these Arab villages, and I don't blame you, because these geography books no longer exist. Not only do the books not exist, the Arab villages are not there either. Nahalal [Dayan's own village] arose in the place of Mahlul, Gvat in the place of Haneifa, and Kfar-Yehoshua in the place of Tel-Shaman. There is not a single place in this country that did not have a former Arab population. [15]

A comment made in 1991 by the Palestinian Christian Hanna Nasir concludes by formulating the outcry of Palestinians in terms strikingly similar to those of the early Zionists:

> Due to the persecution of the Jewish people in Europe, part of this land was given to them. Now there is no question that the motives behind that were probably correct and good. But the unfortunate thing is that they have come to a land which has people in it... We have sacrificed part of our land. "Sacrificed" is the only word I can use. We have said that we are prepared to accept Israel, a de facto situation which happened to us, but we have to accept and recognize it, and we would like to have part of Palestine only for ourselves and let the problem be settled forever... You cannot fully assert your

identity until you have your land. Until you have your land and can assert your identity *on* your land, it is not a full assertion. [16]

Marc Ellis, a Jewish theologian from the USA who has done considerable reflection on the theological meaning of the holocaust, summarizes the issue between the Israelis and the Palestinians in these terms:

— What Jews have done to the Palestinians since the establishment of the state of Israel in 1948 is wrong.
— In the process of conquering and displacing the Palestinian people, Jews have done what has been done to us for over two millennia.
— In this process Jews have become almost everything we loathe about our oppressors.
— It is only in confrontation with state power in Israel that Jews can move beyond being victim or oppressor.
— The movement beyond victimization and oppression can only come through a solidarity with those whom we as Jews have displaced — the Palestinian people. [17]

Amos Elon, formerly a leading Israeli journalist, has suggested that the weight of the holocaust may slowly be lifting, which may in turn help Israel to see more clearly the nature of its present-day relations with the Arabs:

There is surely a national trauma, but in the meantime there has been a change in generations, and the immigration of hundred thousands of Jews from Arab countries has taken place, who have not gone through National Socialism, not even indirectly through their relatives. All this helps to change the mood of the country. Even if we are not the kingdom of saints to which the early Zionists have aspired, some important segments of their faded dream have remained. [18]

Can Israeli Jews from the Middle East, North Africa and Ethiopia help to build a bridge to their Christian and Muslim Arab neighbours? In a remarkable book called *Justice and the Intifada*, there are some insights from these Oriental Jews, who sometimes are called "the other Israel". By and large Jewish immigrants from Arab countries, who generally belong to the Israeli lower classes, have a more "relaxed" relationship to the Palestinians. They speak the same tongue and understand Arab mentality. An Israeli soldier from such a background, Rami Hassan, who went to prison for refusing to serve in the armed forces, comments:

The obsession with defence in the face of the enemy is expressed much more by the Ashkenazis [Jews of European background]. This is quite understandable in the light of the holocaust. The need for a state in order to exist is much clearer. The Oriental Jews came here more out of religious-messianic motivations. They did not really escape from the Arab countries. Some of them lived very well there. There are few Jews who long for Europe. But there are many Oriental Jews who long for their country of origin. It is common among Moroccan Jews to long for what they call "home" — Morocco. [19]

But even Ashkenazis cannot avoid seeing the holocaust and Israeli actions of today together. Ehud Bandel, an Israeli soldier of Ashkenazi background and a rabbinical student, reflects on serving in the Gaza Strip:

Suddenly you can understand what happened forty-five years ago in a different country. There is a kind of dynamic that develops and you slowly lose your sensitivity.

You stop relating to your enemy as a human being. I am not saying this in a critical way; it is a natural process. In a war you simply cannot relate to the enemy as human beings. Yet you have to stop and ask yourself: "Hey, wait a minute, what is going on here? Where are we headed?" You experience thousands of such incidents during your military reserve duty. You burst into a house to look for somebody who you know is involved in sabotage activity, but can you blame the babies for it? You burst into a house at midnight, and the children wake up and start to cry. And suddenly you see yourself through their eyes. It is as if they are holding up a mirror so that you can see yourself, and your face is suddenly monstrously reflected. What is happening to us?[20]

Ellis puts the dilemma succinctly: the task before Israel and the Jews as a whole is to confront that which threatens the very foundation of Jewishness — the oppression of another people by Jews. Only if the future remembrance of Jewish suffering, the holocaust in particular, and the tradition of dissent also include the sufferings of Palestinian Arabs by the hands of the Jews will "the ethical at the heart of Judaism" be restored. The longer Judaism avoids the confrontation with its own ethical standards, the more insurmountable the task:

If it is true that there was little to celebrate and much to lament at the fortieth anniversary of this community's organization as a state in 1988, the fiftieth anniversary represents a forbidding challenge. For by 1998 the fundamental choice will have already been made: to continue the expansion and militarism and its disastrous results for Palestinians and Jews, or to change radically and embark on a new road.[21]

In the light of the presently disrupted peace process, the choice of a new road will have to be made sooner rather than later.

NOTES

[1] On this see the entry on "Palestine" in *Encyclopaedia Britannica*, Vol. 17, p.130.
[2] Quoted by Josephine Bacon and Martin Gilbert, *The Illustrated Atlas of Jewish Civilization*, London, Andre Deutsch, 1990, p.20.
[3] *Encyclopaedia Britannica, loc. cit.*, p.131.
[4] Cf. *Facts About Israel*, Jerusalem, Israel Information Centre, 1992, p.23.
[5] *Encyclopaedia Britannica, loc. cit.*, p.132.
[6] Shamir Amin, *L'éthnie à l'assaut des nations*, Paris, L'Harmattan, 1994, p.151.
[7] Shlomo Avineri, *The Making of Modern Zionism: The Intellectual Origins of the Jewish State*, New York, Basic Books, 1981, pp.214f.
[8] Cf. the entry on "Zionism" in *Encyclopaedia Britannica*, Vol. 23, p.955.
[9] Quoted by Avineri, *op. cit.*, p.205.
[10] Bacon and Gilbert, *op. cit.*, p.194.
[11] On anti-Jewish measures and pogroms in Arab and other Muslim countries beginning in the 1930s, cf. *ibid.*, pp.207-12.
[12] Quoted by Colin Chapman, *Whose Promised Land?*, Tring, UK, Lion Publishing, 1983, pp.168f.
[13] Quoted in *ibid.*, p.174.
[14] Quoted in *ibid.*, pp.87f.
[15] Quoted in *ibid.*, p.173.
[16] Quoted in *The Role of Religion in Conflict Situations*, pp.75,77.

[17] Marc H. Ellis, *Beyond Innocence and Redemption: Confronting the Holocaust and Israeli Power*, San Francisco, Harper & Row, 1990, p.xv.

[18] Quoted in *Der Nahost-Konflikt: Herausforderung für die Christen*, Basel and Freiburg, Schweizerischer Evangelischer Missionsrat and Schweizerischer Katholischer Missionsrat, 1975, p.80.

[19] Kathy Bergen, David Neuhaus and Ghassan Rubeiz, eds, *Justice and the Intifada: Palestinians and Israelis Speak Out*, New York, Friendship Press, 1991, p.59.

[20] *Ibid.*, p.148; on the critical attitude of many Israeli youths towards the army, cf. also Pierre Heumann, "Das Image der Armee bröckelt ab", *Die Weltwoche* (Zurich), no. 39, 26 Sept. 1996, p.17.

[21] Ellis, *op. cit.*, p.193.

6
Lebanon

The story is told of a Belgian economic advisor some years ago who observed in a conversation with the prime minister of Lebanon that he had been surprised to see how the country's different religious communities were associated with distinct economic activities: "Apple trees in Lebanon are Maronite Christians, orange groves are Sunni Muslims, tobacco plantations are Shi'ite Muslims, olive trees are Orthodox and vineyards are Greek Catholics."[1] Though tongue-in-cheek, this remark by a foreign visitor underscored the delicate balance of intercommunal relationships on which the very existence of that small country depended.

While the different communities in Lebanon did once seem to have established a precarious *modus vivendi*, it is as if a violent storm arose during the last quarter of the 20th century to tear that delicate structure apart. The Lebanese writer Georges Corm places the disaster within the wider context of the Middle East, speaking of the mirage of oil which suddenly arose out of an arid desert of poverty, violence and humiliation:

> From northern Iraq to the far boundaries of Mauritania, the Arabs and their religious and ethnic minorities continue to wander in the purgatory of modern times. Ever since the breakup of the Ottoman empire they have become disjointed societies. "Tradition" is getting lost without the conquest of "modernity". Everything grates in these societies, which are afflicted by all the evils of underdevelopment: overcrowded cities with infrastructures that have often remained at the stage of the beginning of the century, the persistence of illiteracy, inefficient and corrupt bureaucracies, a rural world crushed by the weight of the cities, whimsical and violent elites, for whom the modern state is nothing but a toy in the service of short-sighted egotisms, costly educational systems which produce nothing but unemployed and dissatisfied new generations.[2]

The Lebanese conflict, while growing in part from complicated local roots, does share in the trauma of the entire Middle East, especially the Palestine-Israel conflict, which continuously crosses its own southern borders. But Lebanon has also long been a pawn in a vast international power game, whose major points of orientation are oil and "strategic interests" and whose priorities are determined not in Beirut, but in places like Washington, New York, Brussels, Moscow and Tokyo. The civil war which began in 1975 is in fact composed of a series of different conflicts, fought at different stages, each with different objectives. It is far more complex than the simplistic assumptions often found in the media that Soviet manipulation or Iraqi expansionism or Iranian and other Islamic fundamentalisms or the deep mutual loathing of the ethnic groups within Lebanon are to blame — though there may a kernel of truth in each of these assumptions.

Religion has been one important factor contributing to the Lebanese disaster, especially to the conflict between Christians and Muslims. A careful look at the historic role of religion in Lebanese history is thus necessary, since each religious movement has left behind vital and lively communities, each with its own personality and its own fears. These religious communities have evolved into ethnic groups of sorts, although origins and language are the same. In ever-shifting alliances and antagonisms they have tried through the centuries to come to terms with each other whenever history took a new turn. Such a situation issues a virtual open invitation to outside powers to interfere. Above all, the shock waves caused by the collapse of the centuries-old Ottoman empire and the two world wars prevented this small country from finding its equilibrium. Apart from this context the Lebanese problem cannot be understood.

Ancient memories

What gives all Lebanese a measure of common identity and pride is the glory of ancient Phoenicia. In the light of the vast changes in the Middle East, one may ask whether this claim of ancestry has a realistic basis. In any case, the Phoenicians were a Semitic Canaanite people who presumably migrated from Babylonia in the 16th century B.C. and founded a series of city-states along the eastern Mediterranean coast. For a short period after Egypt's decline in the 10th century, an independent Phoenicia established itself as the Mediterranean's predominant seafaring and trading nation. At different stages the ancient Hyksos, Hittites and "sea peoples" (Philistines) invaded the country. The latter were among the first to forge iron and to manufacture red dye from the purple snail, a secret which the Phoenicians took over and perfected and from which their name is derived (the Greek *phoinikos* means "purple-red"). But the Phoenicians' most important cultural achievement was the invention of the phonetic alphabet. Adapted by the Greeks, it became the basis for most of the writing systems in use today.

The wealth of King Hiram of Tyre and the famed cedars of Mount Lebanon are mentioned several times in the biblical tradition, according to which Solomon's temple was planned and built by Hiram's architects and craftsmen. Hiram and Solomon sent mining expeditions down the Gulf of Aqaba and further into the Red Sea. The extent of Phoenicia's fabulous trading patterns, attested to by several ancient writers, can be inferred from the long prophetic curse against Tyre in Ezekiel 27-28. Throughout the eastern and western Mediterranean they established trading posts and colonial cities, of which the most famous were Tarshish in Spain and Carthage in present-day Tunisia. The Phoenicians kept their trade routes and their knowledge of currents and winds a closely guarded secret, so that conquerors from Sennacherib to Alexander the Great were forced to rely on them to transport their troops.

Despite its enormous economic power, Phoenicia never relied on systematic warfare for its defence and was thus unable to withstand the emerging war-oriented military empires of its time. As a consequence it became subject to a long sequence of foreign rule: Assyrians (876-605 BC), Neo-Babylonians (605-538 BC), Persians (538-333 BC), Macedonians (333-69 BC) and Romans/Byzantines

(64 B.C.-A.D. 636). Under Persian rule the Aramaic language became predominant, and from the Macedonians the conquered country accepted Greek, at least within the coastal cities. Phoenicia-Lebanon thus suffered the same fate as Israel. In contrast to the Jewish people, Phoenicia's ancient religions did not survive. What did survive was the great resilience of the people, who withstood change and oppression to maintain the superb trading capacities inherited from their fabled ancestors.

Church disunity breaks up Lebanese society

According to the New Testament (Matt. 15:21-28; Acts 21), both Jesus and Paul spent time in the area between Tyre and Sidon. The cities of Tyre and Berytos (Beirut) were episcopal sees by the end of the 2nd century. By the 4th century hermits and monks had established themselves on Mount Lebanon. Many Christians were martyred in the Roman era, especially during the violent persecution under the emperor Diocletian (303-313), among them St George, the dragon-slayer.[3]

After Christianity became the religion of the Roman state and the transfer of the capital from Rome to Byzantium, renamed Constantinople, politically confirmed the cultural and linguistic division between the Latin West and the Hellenistic East, the coast of Phoenicia came more fully under the sway of Greek-Byzantine political and cultural life. Mount Lebanon and the large fertile Bekaa Valley east of the mountain ranges facing Syria remained attached to the Semitic world. But the Latin West never lost sight of Lebanon.

The Christian community of Lebanon was affected by the theological confrontations of the day, which centred on Christology, specifically the nature of Jesus Christ as both divine and human. The differences of understanding were not only between East and West, but also, within the East itself, between Byzantine Orthodox Christians and several national Christian communities (Egypt, Assyria, Armenia) at the edges of the empire. Different theological schools and strong personalities tried to outdo the other in debate, but the slowness of communication over vast distances meant that the main protagonists had often never met face to face. Mutual condemnations (*anathemas*) deepened the estrangement. The Trinitarian creeds were formulated against the background of Greek culture and philosophy, which was a strange world to Semites.

The centrifugal forces within the church were stronger than the imperial intention to use Christianity to hold together the crumbling empire. Theological divergences often reflected cultural and social divergences. The rift between the Latin West and the Hellenized East was formalized in 1054 by the mutual excommunications of the Roman pope and the patriarch of Constantinople, and the division was deepened by the Crusades.

The Byzantine empire, as the eastern Roman empire began to be called after the disintegration of the western part, weakened in turn and slowly withdrew from North Africa and the Middle East. Simultaneously, the church structures in the various emerging nations severed their links to Byzantine or Greek Orthodoxy, considering it an instrument of imperial power. In 431 the Assyrian church broke away under their leader Nestorius. Following the Council of

Chalcedon in 451, the Syrian church (sometimes called "Jacobite" after one of its early leaders), the Armenian church and the Coptic church (based mainly in Egypt and Ethiopia) separated from the main church structure. Despite their opposition to the Byzantines, these churches have generally retained Orthodox church structures, liturgy and forms of piety, particularly monasticism. Moreover, the Greek Orthodox church which remained faithful to the Byzantine tradition did maintain a foothold in the Middle East, though its adherents have largely adopted the Arabic language. All of these developments have left their mark on present-day Lebanon in the form of different church organizations or religious communities. Today's "ethnic groups" are the descendants of these divergent religious families.

While all of these churches coming from the outside became established in Lebanon, the one Christian community unique to the country is the Maronites. The historical origins of the Maronites are obscure. Their patron, St Maron, is said to have lived near Antioch, where he died in 410. His followers carried his remains to Apamea on the Orontes and built a monastery there. Breaking off from the Jacobites in the wake of theological controversies, they took refuge in the area of Mount Lebanon, where they became farmers and soldiers. The community resisted attacks by the Byzantines and Arab Muslims. Feeling themselves in the midst of an unfriendly environment, the Maronites welcomed the Crusaders, and they were the only Orthodox Christians to fight on the side of the Frankish knights. Eventually they accepted the primacy of the bishop of Rome; and in 1854 a Maronite college was established in Rome, where its clergy acquired Western theological training. Gradually, although keeping ancient Syriac as its liturgical language and allowing its clergy to marry, the church became Latinized. In the process the Maronites virtually placed themselves under French protection and thus enjoyed considerable autonomy during the Ottoman period. As a tightly knit community, they inevitably set themselves apart from the other Christian communities; and in due course they began to consider themselves as the one authentic core community of Lebanon, which should, by historic right, have a greater say than any of the others.

While the Maronites were the only church community of Orthodox background to accept the primacy of Rome, all the other Orthodox and Ancient Eastern churches were subjected to splits inspired by Roman Catholic initiatives. The breakaway groups — the so-called uniate churches — ranged in size from a few hundred to several thousand adherents. Needless to say, this was profoundly resented by the Orthodox and Ancient Eastern church authorities and deepened the divisions among Lebanese Christians. The existence of uniate churches — not only in the Middle East but also in Europe — continues to be a major obstacle to ecumenical relations between the Orthodox churches and the Roman Catholic Church, although there have been the beginnings of a dialogue on this issue in recent years. Roman Catholic advances among the Greek Orthodox met with considerable success, and about one-third of that community placed itself under papal authority. The Greek Catholics in Lebanon are called Melkites, the "king's men", a designation applied earlier to Byzantine Orthodox Christians, that is, those whose faith was the same as the emperor's.

The scene was further complicated by the formation of a number of small Protestant churches as the result of 19th-century missionary work by Anglo-Saxon churches. Since most of their original converts came from Orthodox and Ancient Eastern churches, the feelings of resentment over alleged "sheep-stealing", already aroused by the uniate churches, heightened — all the more since none of the Lebanese mother churches was large in the first place. The Protestants have contributed to Lebanese religious life with new forms of personal piety and social services. Their middle- and upper-level school system is highly regarded. Moreover, at the time of the Armenian massacres, the work of Protestant orphanages was widely appreciated.

This brief and summary overview of Christianity in Lebanon points to the way in which religion prepared the ground for those social and political divisions which have become so disruptive at the end of the 20th century. Oriented to its own survival, each community tended to isolate itself from its environment. Primary loyalty belonged to the ethnic-religious community, not to Lebanese society as a whole. During the 20th century, the latecomers among Lebanon's churches, the Protestants, made a good contribution to the ecumenical movement. Slowly the churches entered into dialogue with each other across their ancient lines of division; and this did not break off during the civil war. Their critical common reflection on this disastrous event, undertaken within the Middle East Council of Churches, helped the churches to gain new orientations.

A divided Christian community faces Islam

The end of Byzantine rule and the rise of Islam in the 7th century heralded religious and political change in Lebanon as elsewhere, although conversions to the new faith were slow, despite the fact that the protracted Christological controversies had dispirited Christian life and the Muslim belief in God as one and indivisible was much easier to understand than the complicated Trinitarian creeds. The Christians remained a majority in Lebanon until at least the end of the middle ages. The Arab Islamic overlords allowed Christians and Jews to run their own church and communal affairs. Only with the invasions of the recently Islamicized Seljuks and the Ottoman Turks did the situation become more difficult for the Christians.

The central problem was not faith, in the sense of theological convictions, but the social and cultural control exerted by the new authorities. While Christians and Jews were formally tolerated and not overtly pressured to convert, it was clear that they would remain second-class citizens unless they adopted Islam. As conversion from Islam to Christianity was virtually impossible, the churches in the east did not engage in evangelistic work. Their missionary contribution consisted of transmitting the faith from generation to generation within their own communities, which often entailed enormous difficulties and sacrifices. [4]

The significant points of agreement between Christianity and Islam — belief in one God, divine revelation, the existence of a sacred book, strong moral tenets and belief in life after death — could have helped to build bridges between the two religious communities, but little effort was made to form such contacts. Even within the Christian communities, church leaders had never engaged in irenical, ecumenical dialogue. Ever ready to raise charges of heresy against dissenting theologians, they were incapable of listening. The pattern was set by John of Damascus (670-750), one of the great early church fathers of the East, who is perhaps best-known for his decisive shaping of the Orthodox Liturgy. Under admittedly difficult circumstances, he vigorously opposed conversions in his writings and his public speaking, declaring Islam to be a perversion. This negative stance — to which Muslim theologians responded in kind — effectively blocked any interfaith dialogue. The Crusades and later Western colonialism further nurtured this condemnatory spirit. The coming of Islam thus added to the religious and social tensions in Lebanon, making life together more difficult; and surrounded by many other Islamic societies, the Lebanese Christian communities felt ever more beleaguered as each sought to hold on to what it saw as the true faith.

To complicate matters further, Islam itself is far from a monolithic bloc. The first breach occurred already in 657, in conjunction with a power struggle over Muhammed's succession. It is reflected today in the split between the Sunnites (from *sunni*, meaning path or tradition), who make up the majority, and the minority Shi'ites (from *shi'ah*, the party of Ali, Muhammed's son-in-law). Representing more popular forms of Islam, the Shi'ites were generally poorer and more inclined to engage in social revolt than the Sunnites. They awaited the return of the hidden Imam or Mahdi (Messiah), who would restore justice to the world. Shi'ites today are mainly concentrated along the upper Euphrates and in Iran. Lebanese Shi'ites live in the poorer southern areas of the country, while Sunnites are found along the coast, together with the Greek Orthodox, with whom they control a good part of the country's economy.

Another religious community in Lebanon are the Druzes, whose home is in the Shouf Mountains, where they are neighbours of the Maronites (other branches of the Druzes live in Syria). The traditional founder of the movement was the Fatimid caliph al-Hakim bi-Amri-Allah, who disappeared from Cairo in 1021 after declaring himself an incarnation of God. His successor Darazi (from whom the Druzes derive their name) fled to Syria, where he proclaimed al-Hakim's return, gathered a number of followers and complemented Shi'ite convictions with certain Christian and Hindu beliefs, including the migration of the soul. Like the Maronites, the Druzes were often at odds with the empires that dominated the coastline or the Syrian plains. The community is ruled by a small number of feudal families, from one of which the founder of modern Lebanon, Emir Fachr ad-Din II, descended. [5]

During the 11th century the Seljuks, a Turkmen tribe from Central Asia, evicted the Arabs from many of their possessions, capturing Baghdad in 1055 and Damascus in 1075. It was their subsequent entry into Lebanon and Palestine that led to the papal call for the first Crusade in 1095. Crusader ships appeared before the Lebanese coast in 1099. Except for the Maronites, who greeted them as liberators, the Lebanese Christian communities did not welcome these Christian invaders from the West, and the resulting oppression at their hands divided Christians in Lebanon even more deeply. After 200 years of rule, the Crusaders lost Tripoli, their last Lebanese stronghold, to the Egyptian Mameluks in 1298. But the Mameluks' political skill did not match their military prowess; and during this era a number of feudal families emerged from among the various communities in Lebanon as leaders in the struggle for freedom, forging the religious groupings into tightly-controlled political communities. Under the Mameluks the Lebanese economy decayed drastically. Many of the precious cedars were chopped down, with the wood used for building warships (most of those remaining were used by the Germans and the Turks at the beginning of the 20th century to build the Berlin-Baghdad Railway).

In 1516 the powerful Ottoman Turks, who had already taken Constantinople in 1453, defeated the Mameluks in Syria and conquered the rest of the Middle East and North Africa as far as Morocco. The greater part of what is today Lebanon became attached to the *wilayet* (province) of Damascus.

The makings of modern Lebanon

In the early 17th century Emir Fachr ad-Din II (1608-33) of the Druze Maan family emerged as a key figure in the effort to unify the various communities of Lebanon in joint resistance against the Ottomans. Making common cause with the Maronites, he appealed to the Greek Orthodox, Melkites, Sunnites, Shi'ites and the Jews to establish a new state, whose territory extended from Aleppo in the north to Jerusalem in the south. Though formally accepting the suzerainty of the Ottoman sultan, the emir exchanged diplomatic and commercial missions with Venice, Florence and the Holy See. For the first time a certain national feeling developed among the various Lebanese communities. [6]

A second influential personality was Emir Beshir Shehab II (1794-1840). Also of Druze origin, he became a Maronite; and in his palace at Beit Eddine he built three altars — one for the Christians, one for the Muslims, one for the Druzes — to exemplify Lebanon's religious unity. Moreover, anyone who was persecuted anywhere in the Middle East could find refuge in Lebanon. A census in 1820 showed the following religious distribution: Maronites 175,702, Greek Orthodox 68,416, Melkites 38,559, Protestants 3750, Sunnites 121,952, Shi'ites 103,068 and Druzes 39,841. [7]

But Beshir's policies contained the seeds for future trouble. Above all, he attempted to reduce the influence of the feudal families by establishing local and national consultative councils and courts, with judges named by him and not by the feudal lords. In 1822 an uprising occurred, which the Ottomans used to re-establish their authority. Beshir fled to Egypt and concluded an alliance with the Egyptian *khedive* Muhammed Ali, who sent an army up the eastern Mediterranean coast, defeating the Ottomans in 1832 and reinstalling Beshir as emir of Lebanon. Muhammed Ali's son Ibrahim continued the Egyptian advance well into Asia Minor, and for a while it seemed that a generalized Arab revolt would bring an end to the Ottoman empire and even cause a European war, since the British and the French were backing different factions in the struggle. But the European powers ended their rivalry out of the fear that the fall of the Ottoman empire might open the way to Russian expansion in the Middle East.

Although Beshir was back in power, the Egyptians exacted high taxes to finance their military campaign, leading to the economic ruin of thousands of peasants and merchants in all religious groups, who were compelled to sell their properties to monasteries and feudal lords. When the poverty-stricken populace rose against the Egyptians in 1840, the Ottomans again took advantage of the situation to recover the rebellious province. Aided by the Austrian fleet, they bombarded and took Beirut, captured the emir and subjected Lebanon to direct rule from Constantinople. The feudal families were disempowered, and the Ottomans succeeded in destroying the long-time coexistence between the Druzes and Maronites.

Social and political conditions worsened and the confused events of the years from 1840 to 1860 were like a general rehearsal for the great massacres of the late 20th century. The British and French intrigued against each other; and the European powers were never at a loss in inventing pretexts for intervention when they saw their own interests threatened, and setting the different communities against each other. In 1860 agitated Druzes murdered 12,000 Christians in Lebanon; and Muslims in Damascus killed another 5000 Christians there.[8] France sent 8000 soldiers to Beirut as a shield to the Maronites. The Russians threatened to send a fleet to aid the Greek Orthodox. Habsburg Austria helped the (Catholic) Melkites and Great Britain the Druze community.

Nevertheless, this second Ottoman period is significant in that from 1864 to 1914 the *sandjak* (administrative district) of Lebanon was ruled by a Christian *mushir* (governor), assisted by twelve *majlis* (representatives) elected by the different religious communities according to a fixed formula. This arrangement stabilized the country, but it did not result in a more democratic society, despite the influx of Western political ideas. The feudal families and religious leaders continued to demand strict obedience from the members of their communities. Thus while outward peace was maintained, society remained blocked. A major problem was the inability of the various religious-political communities to analyze and understand the growing social and political complexities of their conflicts and the nature of outside interference. Tribalistic forms of confessionalism were reaffirmed and carried over into the 20th century. The various elites, both within the communities and nationally, lacked the *national* civic sense to move the country forward. Politics to them signified constant opportunistic in-fighting in a merciless power struggle.[9]

A multi-ethnic state takes form

As noted in the previous chapter, the Arab nationalism which began to develop in the Middle East towards the end of the 19th century aimed to counteract not only Ottoman domination but also European imperialism. In Lebanon this trend was supported mainly by the Arabic-speaking Greek Orthodox, the only Christian community which kept channels of communication open with the Islamic communities and which was itself open to social concerns. Not surprisingly, given Lebanon's historical development, Arab nationalism too turned out to be divisive. The attempt by its adherents, following the Western model, to separate politics from religion was something for which the Middle East had no tradition. As elsewhere, Arab nationalism remained too weak to establish internal cohesion in Lebanon.

During the two decades preceding the outbreak of the first world war, the influence of the Maronites, who were generally opposed to Arab nationalism, grew considerably. Paradoxically, this was largely due to the emigration of thousands of Maronites from Lebanon to seek a better life in Africa and North and South America. Within a short time large remittances from overseas contributed to the transformation and modernization of Lebanon's economy.

The two world wars helped to shape the political structures of today's Lebanon. The Ottoman empire, which despite its many weaknesses had been a remarkable supranational state, broke apart; and Lebanon, which had structured itself along the Ottoman pattern, was thus incapable of absorbing the nation-state idea. The Western powers, Britain and France, which had alternately tried to prop up or to destroy the empire's decaying structure according to whether their colonial ambitions or their fear of Czarist Russia dominated at any given moment, had no interest in seeing the creation of a unified Arab successor state for the entire Middle East. If necessary, they would divide the Ottoman heritage directly among themselves — which is precisely what happened at the end of the first world war.

Through the intervention of Maronite Patriarch Elias Butros Hoyek with French prime minister Georges Clémenceau in 1920, Lebanon obtained its present frontiers, including Mount Lebanon, the Shouf, the coastal cities and the Bekaa Valley. The connection with France, dating back to the Crusades, was paying off. Syria and Lebanon became short-lived French League of Nations mandates. In 1943, during the second world war, the so-called National Pact, worked out mainly by the Maronite leader Bshara al-Khouri and the Sunnite leader Riad as-Sol, made an independent and neutral Lebanon possible. But the new state basically continued the system of communitarian rule formalized during the last phase of the Ottoman empire. On the basis of a verbal agreement, the chief offices of the state were allocated confessionally: the president was Maronite, the vice president a Sunnite, the president of parliament a Shi'ite, and the deputy president of parliament and deputy prime minister were Greek Orthodox. This framework was based on the 1932 census, which gave the Christian community a 6 to 5 numerical edge over the Muslims. [10] But not enough attention was given to the Druzes, causing resentment among them and reopening the gap between them and the Maronites — who had not forgotten the mass murder committed by the Druzes eighty years earlier.

Flawed though it was, the National Pact provided the minimum stability for an amazing economic boom after the second world war. But it proved too rigid and too fragile to cope with the upheaval caused by the creation of the state of Israel in 1948. In 1948 and 1949 some 300,000 Palestinians fled to Lebanon, where they were housed in what were meant to be temporary camps in the economically weak south. There they remained, year after frustrating year. As 77 percent of the newcomers were Sunnite Muslims, the confessional proportions of Lebanon became upset, rekindling the Christians' ancestral fears of being engulfed by a Muslim human sea. Nevertheless, Lebanon succeeded in providing jobs for 50,000 Palestinians in banking, education, commerce and tourism, temporarily taking the edge off the acute refugee problem. [11] But each succeeding outbreak of conflict brought more refugees, not only from Israel but also from neighbouring Arab countries. The entire Middle East seemed to fall apart, and Lebanon became destabilized.

In 1952 the Egyptian military toppled the monarchy, and shortly thereafter Gamal Abdel Nasser came to power, reviving an all-Arab nationalism, now with a socialist tinge. The Israelis' 1956 Sinai campaign, accompanied by a British and French attack on the Suez Canal, was halted by simultaneous threats from the USA and the USSR. This unexpected success increased Nasser's prestige, and in 1958 he proclaimed the union of Egypt and Syria. Fighting broke out in different parts of Lebanon. Muslim nationalists, supported by the exiled Palestinians, felt their fortunes rising, while the Maronite President Camille Chamoun called for a US military intervention. President Eisenhower, apparently considering a Soviet intervention in the Middle East imminent, dispatched 10,000 US Marines to the beaches of Lebanon, a show of force that ended the civil war.

Over the next decade it seemed that Lebanon had finally found equilibrium, despite the presence of the Palestinian refugees. Government structures were stabilized; intercommunal tensions seemed to ease; and the economic boom resumed, fed by Arab oil millions deposited in Lebanese banks. High-rise buildings altered the appearance of the waterfront of Beirut, whose banks and hotels attracted wealthy foreigners. Lebanon became the "playground of the Middle East". Economically, Lebanon was clearly bound to the Western model. The old clichés were reinforced: Lebanon, the crossroads country, the hospitable land, the land of good community relations, the Switzerland of the Middle East. [12] But it would prove to be the calm before the storm.

The balance is upset

In retrospect a number of factors can be identified as setting the stage for the explosion in April 1975 which led to fifteen years of civil war:

1. Lebanon's economic growth, largely attributable to rising oil prices in the Gulf, resulted in a particularly unrestrained form of capitalism, which benefited only a small minority. While 4 percent of the population could be considered rich and 14 percent as belonging to the middle class, 32 percent had very small revenues and 50 percent of the population lived in absolute poverty. Feeling cheated out of their economic rights, the majority of this last group eked out a meagre existence in the growing rings of poverty around the large cities and in the refugee camps. The harsh economic contrasts rekindled the old ethnic conflicts. [13]

2. The six-day Arab-Israeli war in June 1967 set in motion a chain of events that had a disruptive effect on Lebanon. An expected victory turned into a disastrous rout, with the Arabs losing the West Bank, the Gaza Strip and the Golan Heights. Nasser's role diminished — and with it so did classical Arab nationalism. For the Lebanese as for other Arabs, this was a deep psychological wound; and the collective mental suffering was not alleviated when the temporary Egyptian victory on the Suez Canal in 1973 (Yom Kippur War) turned into another defeat at the hands of the Israelis.

3. Following conflicts with King Hussein of Jordan, more Palestinian refugees were moved to Lebanon in 1969 and 1970, including the headquarters of the Palestine Liberation Organization (PLO), which was then attracting worldwide attention through aeroplane hijackings and other acts of terror. From the strongholds it established in southern Lebanon, the PLO made hit-and-run attacks

against Galilee, invariably eliciting violent reprisals from Israel. Eventually Israel established a "security zone" within southern Lebanon.

4. Lebanon's economic boom not only attracted rich tourists, but also thousands of poor Syrian migrants. Over one million foreigners now lived in this small country which had no more than three million citizens of its own. It became ever clearer that the Lebanese government was losing control and that the carefully balanced National Pact of 1943 was falling to pieces. Even apart from the Palestinians, the number of Christians was probably down to 40 percent or less. There were growing calls for new and more reliable statistics and for a new constitution. Some politicians proposed the division of the country into a Christian state and a Muslim state.

5. In 1973 the major oil-producing countries in the OPEC cartel sharply increased prices. This policy succeeded for several years until the West managed to undercut OPEC power. Prices fell again to low levels. Beirut began to lose its attraction as the principal financial centre for the Middle East. The economic boom fell apart.

6. Simultaneously, Islamic fundamentalism began to develop in force.

7. Throughout 1974 vast supplies of weapons flowed into Lebanon from all kinds of sources. They went to the various ethnic groups and militias as well as to the frustrated Palestinians. Fascist and fundamentalist tendencies became predominant, creating a psychological climate in which future atrocities could be committed in good conscience. [14]

The outbreak of the civil war

What actually happened on 11 April 1975, when the Lebanese cauldron finally boiled over, has never become fully clear. At any rate, a clash occurred near a church in the Ain Rummaneh section of Beirut between members of the Maronite Phalangists under their leader Pierre Gemayel and a small Palestinian group, during which two Phalangists were said to have been killed. In revenge the Phalangists stopped a bus with 26 Palestinians aboard and murdered them.

Like many other cities in the Middle East, Beirut is segregated into religious-ethnic sectors — Maronite, Armenian, Greek Orthodox, Sunnite, Shi'ite, Druze. In normal times interaction between them is no problem. One result of the hostilities that broke out in Beirut in 1975 was that some of these sectors closed themselves off against others whom they considered hostile, leaving only the central business sector freely accessible to all. During most of the war, crossing from one of these sectors to another was a high-risk proposition. Other cities and rural areas were closed off from each other in much the same way.

In reality the Lebanese civil war consisted of countless skirmishes in the form of firefights between neighbouring urban or rural sectors and sniper fire on individuals or groups trying to maintain contacts across hostile lines or simply seeking to go about their normal business. Most of the victims were not battle dead, but simply courageous, mostly unarmed individuals whose lives were put at risk when they went to shop or fetch water or to work along these "death lanes". [15]

The fifteen years of war and terror turned Lebanon into an inferno in which 200,000 people died and twice that number were wounded. There were battles between Christians and Muslims, between Christians and Druzes, between Druzes and Muslims, between Muslims and Muslims, between Christians and Christians, between Israelis and Lebanese, between Lebanese and Palestinians. Two-thirds of all Lebanese were driven from their homes. Each community has in turn felt threatened by the next. Deeply traumatized, they found refuge and protection among their own. An entire generation grew up which has known nothing but fighting and hatred.

Countless peace efforts and armistice arrangements were broken as soon as they were signed. Government leaders were replaced frequently; some were murdered. The authorities lost all control, which in any case would have been difficult to exercise in the light of the help each ethnic group received from its friends abroad. The United States once again sent in the Marines, but unlike 1958 their mere presence did not stop the fighting, especially when it became clear that the Marines would not risk their own security. When more than 200 of them lost their lives in a bomb attack on their barracks, President Reagan called them home. There was also a multinational Arab force — of whom only the Syrians remained permanently in Lebanon — backed for a while by the Soviet Union. Iran supported a reluctant Shi'ite community and the Hezbollah fighters, who in turn cooperated with the Palestinian Hamas. However, the strongest intervention came from Israel in 1982. Israeli military forces pursued the Palestinians as far as Beirut and into the Bekaa Valley. Moreover, at frequent intervals the Israeli air force continued to bomb Palestinian positions and settlements in Lebanon, in response to attacks by Palestinian groups against Israeli settlements in Galilee. Again in 1996, the Israeli army intervened in Lebanon, and, as in 1982, about 400,000 people fled their homes, despite strong objections from the international community, churches and ecumenical bodies.

Without reaching any definite conclusion, the Lebanese war wound down around 1990, not least as a result of the Taïf agreement mediated by several Arab states. The enormous human and material losses were becoming unbearable. The importance of the religious dimension had steadily diminished. While the government perhaps remains little more than a club of regional princes or warlords, all of them more interested in their own religious-political community than in the nation as a whole, the Lebanese political "system" remains basically intact. The Palestinians have not gone away; the Israeli "security zone" remains a festering wound; and Syria retains its military control. But Lebanon has been preserved, which is an important factor; and there is hope that the terrible experience it has gone through might discourage a new generation from taking up arms as easily as their elders — provided that outside powers refrain from interfering.

A religious war?

To the question of whether the war in Lebanon was a religious one, Lebanese sociologist Tarek Mitri responds:

> On both sides of the barricades there are people who do not go to church or to the mosque, who have never read the Qu'ran or the gospel of Jesus Christ. Of course, they are not fighting about the Trinity or the virginity of Mary, nor any other tenet of faith. However, religious feelings have fuelled the war — not in a direct way, but rather in an

indirect manner. Christians were told that they were fighting for their freedom as Christians, that freedom is inherent to their Christian self-understanding and that freedom is threatened if Muslims come to rule them. Muslims were told that they were fighting for justice, that they were the majority and yet they have been disempowered and deprived, and that therefore, if they struggle as Muslims, they struggle for justice. Thus it is through the medium of freedom or justice that religious symbols and sentiments have been fuelling the war. [16]

During the early stages of the war, Mitri notes, the Maronites, the most militant of the Christian communities, used churches and monasteries for arms storage and military training. By 1990, however, the Maronite patriarch had begun to threaten with excommunication all those who took up arms. As a result, the Christians began to fight among themselves. On the Muslim side, some leaders who saw the destruction the war was bringing on their people called for an end to fighting — with similar results. Yet, the fact that Christians and Muslims began to talk together has helped to calm their people down, despite the contrary efforts of fundamentalists on both sides.

But talking together must be filled with more concrete content. Georges Corm suggests four affirmations which could help to counteract the tradition of extreme loyalty to ethnic communities which has bedevilled Lebanon: (1) Each human being has his or her individuality, which is not derived from religious or racial affiliation. (2) Relations between Lebanon's central authority and its various communities must be rethought. Those who govern must be interchangeable according to well-defined procedures without upsetting the life of the entire country. (3) Civil society must be characterized by a balance of powers (legislative, executive, judicial), to which military power is subject. (4) The common national heritage of Lebanon needs to be rediscovered, so that history is seen in common and the education of a new generation can be undertaken jointly. Only then religious freedom can be guaranteed. Corm himself concludes on a hopeful note, looking forward to the day when

> the sons and daughters of this earth will rediscover Lebanon's millennia-old heritage, will abandon the idols and will return to God, the God of Muhammed and of Christ, the God of all the just and of all the wise, to thank him for all the gifts with which he has filled Lebanon, but which their ancestors have refused. [17]

NOTES

[1] This story is told by Tarek Mitri in *The Role of Religions in Conflict Situations*, p.122.

[2] Georges Corm, *Géopolitique du conflit libanais: Etude historique et sociologique*, Paris, La Découverte, and Beirut, FMA, 1986, p.13.

[3] Dorothea Vorländer, *Libanon: Land der Gegensätze*, Erlangen, Ev.-Luth. Mission, 1980, pp.21f.

[4] Paul Löffler, *Arabische Christen im Nahost-Konflikt*, Frankfurt, Lembeck, 1976, p.23.

[5] On the Druze, see Vorländer, *op. cit.*, p.27, and the entries in *Encyclopaedia Britannica* (Vol. 7, pp.681f.) and *Religion in Geschichte und Gegenwart*, Tübingen, J.C.B. Mohr (Paul Siebeck), 1962, Vol. 2, p.271.

[6] Vorländer, *op. cit.*, p.28.

[7] *Ibid.*, p.29.

[8] *Ibid.*, p.32.

[9] Corm, *op. cit.*, pp.69,72,83.

[10] Vorländer, *op. cit.*, pp.33f.

[11] *Ibid.*, p.35.

[12] Corm, *op. cit.*, p.159.

[13] Vorländer, *op. cit.*, p.44.

[14] Corm, *op. cit.*, pp.159,186. While some have questioned the precision of the term "Islamic fundamentalism" (by analogy to the early 20th-century US Protestant movement) for such movements as wahabite puritanism, Khomeinism and the Muslim Brotherhood, the word "fundamentalist" is widely used today for populist nationalist-chauvinist forces among Roman Catholics, Hindus, Jews and others as well as Muslims.

[15] *Ibid.*, p.217; cf. Vorländer, *op. cit.*, p.52.

[16] Mitri, *loc. cit.*, p.125.

[17] Corm, *op. cit.*, pp.230-49.

7
Sri Lanka

Early Islamic traders thought of Sri Lanka, with its exquisitely terraced and contoured hillsides and rice fields whose waters mirrored the sky, as "a second Garden of Eden", where God had placed Adam and Eve for a thousand years after they had been driven from Paradise and where humanity thus began. In *Arabian Nights* Sinbad the seafarer saw a thousand jewels glittering from the battlements of the king of Lanka — "the crystallized tears of the first man". During the past two decades, however, this paradise has been shattered. Sri Lanka's reputed tolerance between religions and races has broken down.

Tensions had already been accumulating for several years when Alfred Durayappah, the mayor of Jaffna, was murdered on 27 July 1975 by an obscure group of four young people who called themselves the "Tamil New Tigers" (TNT). Durayappah, himself a Tamil, was targeted for having cooperated politically with the Sinhalese authorities, which was seen as betraying the Tamils' long and so far fruitless quest to be recognized as a distinct cultural and linguistic community. Sri Lanka was shocked by this first political murder in its modern history. The leader of the TNT was Velupillai Prabhakaran, the 20-year-old son of a government official. He had told his friends that he would not stop until an independent Tamil state by the name of Tamil Eelam had been established in the north and east of the island.

The methods employed by both Prabhakaram and his opponents, the Sinhala-dominated army and security forces, have been incredibly brutal. To give its struggle a political profile, the rebel group changed its name in 1976 to Liberation Tigers of Tamil Eelam (LTTE). Lightly armed and under-financed, it attacked banks and police stations at first. In 1978 it publicly declared its aims and confessed to eleven political murders. The Sri Lankan government issued a prevention of terrorism act, allowing suspects to be jailed for up to 18 months without court orders; and President J.R. Jayawardene ordered the army to stamp out Tamil terrorism by the end of 1979. But the Sri Lankan military was not equipped, psychologically or materially, to fight a civil war, and the LTTE had no difficulty, when necessary, with making its fighters vanish across the narrow Palk Straits, where they became invisible among the 70 million inhabitants of the neighbouring Indian state of Tamil Nadu. Soon the Tamil liberation fighters became one of the world's most proficient guerrilla forces, with some of their fighters going to Lebanon for training and "practical experience" under the guidance of the Palestine Liberation Organization. The first stage of the Sri Lankan "civil war" soon settled into a stalemate.

The stalemate came to an end on 23 August 1983, when LTTE fighters carried out their first large-scale attack on an army convoy, killing 13 of the 15 soldiers. At the news, chauvinist politicians, who had been expecting such an attack, incited the angry Sinhalese population to unleash a pitiless pogrom, which had been planned well in advance. Tamils in Colombo and other cities in the south were sprayed with gasoline and burned to death or hacked to pieces. Together with the angry populace, the Sinhalese Special Task Force (STF), a deadly new unit formed and trained by British mercenaries, went into operation. Thousands of Tamil businesses and homes were destroyed. Hundreds of thousands fled to the north. [1]

Whatever hopes might have remained for a peaceful resolution of the crisis vanished. The Tamil members of parliament resigned. The ranks of the LTTE guerrillas, who had never numbered more than a few dozens, were swelled by countless young recruits, and a spirit of hatred and revenge installed itself on the island.

As in other such situations the causes of the conflict were multiple. Historical memories and religious and political myths — some old, others more recent — all played a role. As Neville Jayaweera points out:

> Religions have been partly responsible for the divisions, conflicts and problems within Sri Lanka today. Whatever might be written and said in textual religion, their concrete historical existence has contributed much to the problems of Sri Lanka. Of course there are many shades of opinions among these religious expressions. However, their more fundamentalist and purist expressions have tended to confine their adherents within a narrow framework, and provide them with reactionary ideologies. [2]

The traditions of peacefulness associated with the two largest religions, Buddhism (Sinhalese) and Hinduism (Tamils) were not as deeply rooted in Sri Lanka as one might expect, and for most churchgoers the Christian concept of justice seemed irrelevant when the contemporary crisis was unmistakeably brewing.

The mystique of the past

Sri Lanka, which the British called Ceylon, was originally inhabited by the Veddas, of whom a few thousand survive in the eastern mountains. It is believed that religious practices such as devil-dancing, belief in ancestral spirits, charms, astrology and fire-walking came from these aboriginal inhabitants. Tamils from southern India may have settled on the island very early. Folk memories of succeeding invasions from India are important for understanding the Sri Lankan psyche. The Hindu epic *Ramayana* tells of the conquest of the greater part of Sri Lanka by the hero Rama at the dawn of time. He came across the island chain at Rama's Bridge (or Adam's Bridge) — which was an isthmus until 1480, when the land passage was breached by a storm. A more reliable historical account comes from the Sinhalese chronicle *Mahavamsa*, which tells of the Aryan king Vijaya, who sailed from northern India by way of the Bay of Bengal and landed on the island in 483 BC. The Sinhalese established themselves in the arid north, building their capital first in Anuradhapura and later in Kandy, in the uplands. Their major achievement was an elaborate system of canals and artificial lakes, which supported a large population and transformed Sri Lanka into the lush paradise so admired by early travellers.

Only with the arrival of Buddhism did Sri Lankan culture reach its classical golden age. Buddhism is said to have been brought to the island by Mahinda, a Buddhist priest and son of the north Indian emperor Ashoka (274-232 BC), himself a convert to Buddhism. A branch of the 2500-year-old sacred Bo tree under which the Buddha is said to have obtained full enlightenment was planted in Anuradhapura, where it can still be seen. Although the tradition that the Buddha himself visited Sri Lanka seems doubtful, a temple in Kandy contains one of his teeth as a relic, and pilgrimages every March and April draw thousands of visitors to Adam's Peak, where they can see the Buddha's footprints (though Hindus consider them the footprints of the god Siva and Muslims believe they are Adam's).

Many splendid temples, monasteries, hospitals, libraries and palaces were constructed during the height of Sinhalese Buddhist civilization, and even the remnants that still exist impress visitors. In the course of time Buddhist monasteries acquired ownership of much fertile land, donated by kings and wealthy individuals. It should be noted that although Buddhism is essentially a tolerant, non-proselytizing philosophical system, its influence did not prevent the Sinhalese kings from engaging in power games and murderous intrigues within their own families and between rival kingdoms, in the process often wasting precious human and economic resources.[3] The last high period of Sinhalese Buddhist civilization came during the reign of King Parakramabahu (1153-86). But his excesses contained the seeds of the succeeding decline. Consciously or unconsciously, the memory and mystique of a "golden age" plays a key role for the Sinhalese of today, who have been trying to re-create it since Sri Lanka's independence in 1948.

Another key feature of the Sinhalese consciousness is the memory of repeated invasions by Hindu Tamils from southern India. Apart from the possible Tamil migrations at the dawn of history mentioned above, these began during the early middle ages. Over centuries of warfare much of the canal and irrigation system fell into ruin and palaces and temples were destroyed. Dutugemunu is remembered by Sinhalese as one of their heroic kings who defended Sri Lanka against the Tamil invaders. But the Tamils eventually gained a permanent foothold in the northern and eastern regions, where they established their own Hindu kingdoms; and the continued incursions were no doubt one of the principal reasons for the loss of vitality of the Sinhalese Buddhist civilization.

After the destruction of the canal and irrigation system the land dried up, and hunger and malaria crept in. The first Portuguese explorers in 1505 found no fewer than seven small Sinhalese and Tamil kingdoms, more or less permanently at war with constantly shifting alliances. Only in 1845 was the vanished splendour of Anuradhapura rediscovered by British archaeologists; and the ruins became a centre for pilgrimages, which helped to awaken Sinhalese Buddhist nationalism against the colonialists. According to Jayaweera, two elements emerged at that time which were to be significant for the 20th-century conflict:

The first was the attempt to link the Sinhala language, Buddhism and the geographical entity called Sri Lanka into a cohesive unit in a very fundamentalist fashion. "Pure"

Buddhism is preserved by the Sinhala people, and Sri Lanka is destined and was chosen by the Buddha for this task. This has the elements of a "chosen race" theory and of an attempt to link the entire island with the identity of Sinhala Buddhists. This mix has been heavily biased against giving power to any ethnic minority over any part of the country. The second element was the argument that Buddhism and Sinhala should be given primacy over other religions and languages and that it is the duty of the state to guarantee it.[4]

Colonial rule

Certainly the experience of the colonial era was another important element that went into the making of Sri Lanka's psyche. In 1517, the Portuguese established a fort in Colombo. Step by step they succeeded in establishing centres for the spice trade and in subduing without destroying the Sri Lankan kingdoms. Catholic religious orders immediately began to make converts among both Sinhalese and Tamil fishermen and other lower castes. The Franciscans arrived in 1543, the Jesuits in 1602, followed by the Oratorians, Augustinians and Dominicans. Force was certainly employed in some cases, but the missionaries made astute use of the resentment of the landless peasants against the large land-holding Buddhist monasteries and the Sinhalese upper classes, who had bound the poor to themselves in a feudal or semi-feudal manner.

The next colonizers were the Dutch. Having just fought off the Spanish occupants, they were anxious to protect their long maritime communications to and from Indonesia. In 1638-39 they destroyed the Portuguese forts on Sri Lanka's east coast, and in 1656 and 1658 they captured Jaffna and Colombo, subjecting most of the lowlands. Only the upland Sinhalese kingdom of Kandy retained its independence. Unlike the Portuguese, the Dutch introduced an efficient, if harsh and rigid, colonial administration, establishing a European legal system, creating a land registry, building roads and clearing debris from canals. Trade and economy were rejuvenated, and despite heavy taxation, Sri Lanka began to prosper again.

The accompanying Dutch Reformed missionaries, backed by their colonial administration, were somewhat tolerant of Buddhism, Hinduism and Islam, but they disestablished the Roman Catholic Church, banished its clergy and tried to convert the Catholics to Protestantism. Some did, though Catholicism was more deeply ingrained among the lowland population than the missionaries had expected, and many prospective converts found the frequently haughty behaviour and dogmatic theology of the Dutch unattractive. In 1707 the Oratorian priest Joseph Vaz entered Sri Lanka covertly and reorganized the Roman Catholic communities, probably helping to save Sri Lankan Catholicism from extinction.[5] Even today the *burghers* (descendants of Dutch colonists) face the prejudices which their ancestors attracted centuries ago, though they have managed to maintain a sturdy self-esteem, high standards of personal conduct and considerable wealth.

Dutch rule ended in 1796 when the British took advantage of the Napoleonic occupation of the Netherlands to take over the colony. When the new masters introduced freedom of religion, some 67,000 members immediately left the Dutch Reformed Church and reverted to Catholicism, despite the difficulties the Roman authorities had, in the wake of the upheavals caused by the French Revolution, with re-establishing a hierarchy. But while the membership of the Dutch Reformed Church dwindled, Protestant missions from Anglo-Saxon countries were founded in quick succession: British Baptists in 1812, Methodists in 1814, the Church Missionary Society (Anglican) in 1818 and US Congregationalists shortly there-after. In spite of considerable efforts, the Protestants were unable to overtake the Roman Catholic Church in numerical terms. By 1967, 8.5 percent of Sri Lanka's population was identified as Christians, the large majority of them Roman Catholic. [6]

The missions not only built up congregations, but created hundreds of schools in the villages and colleges in the larger cities, where English was taught. Until 1920 the churches, although they represented a small minority of the population, were dominant in education. A vast number of local colonial administrators were educated in church schools, and from among them came the first generation of politicians who led Sri Lanka to independence. When the state created its own educational system after independence, the churches lost most of their schools.

In 1803 the British began to invade the hitherto independent Sinhalese kingdom of Kandy. After an insurrection in 1815 against the reputedly tyrannical king, the chiefs handed over control to the colonizers, and all of Sri Lanka was now fully subject to foreign rule. Social and economic change followed, as Sri Lanka was incorporated completely into the colonial system. Roads were built into the newly conquered upland region, bringing in lowland Sinhalese, Muslim and Hindu traders and European planters. Sinhalese villages were destroyed and virgin forest cleared. A small new Sri Lankan upper class came into being, the *karawa* caste.

British tea planters carved out large estates for themselves; and when Sri Lankan Sinhalese and Tamils refused to work for the low wages offered, the British administrators, beginning in 1830, brought several hundred thousand "voluntary" coolies from Tamil Nadu to the highlands of Sri Lanka. Even today their descendants usually include four to five wage-earners per family; the women tend the tea slopes, usually accompanied by children, and the men handle the machines. By 1981 the Plantation Tamils in the central highlands numbered 819,000. Representing only 7 percent of the population, they produced 35 percent of Sri Lanka's annual gross national product but received less than 5 percent of the total income. In 1964 the Sinhalese government declared them stateless. Today, they are enfranchised again, but live entirely apart, ignored by the "older" Tamils in the north and the east. Some observers believe the plantation sector could explode at any time. [7]

Independence: the Sinhalese and the minorities

Thus step by step modern Sri Lanka, with its problems, imbalances and tensions, was put together. By independence, the island had a very heterogeneous population, far more complex than a simple division between the Sinhalese majority and the Tamil minority. The colonial era had added further varieties of populations and created new tensions within the national community. There were tensions between the lowland Sinhalese community and the more rustic Sinhalese around Kandy, who resented the fact that the low-country people had so readily sided with the Portuguese, the Dutch and the British, helping them to destroy the kingdom of Kandy, then moving in to take over the region economically. Tensions also emerged between the members of the traditional Sinhalese and Tamil higher castes, who believed that government should be theirs by divine right, and those who had become wealthy by trading and manufacturing. In addition, Sri Lankan political scientist Jayadeva Uyangoda observes, there is regional segmentation in the Sinhala, Tamil and Muslim societies, "not because people attach much emotional value to their respective regions, but because there are hard social, economic and cultural factors that make people consider their respective regions important". [8] A glance at the marriage proposal columns in the Sunday newspapers shows the extent to which people attach importance to caste, religion and status.

Simply to impose the British model of parliamentary democracy on such a society was bound to spell disaster. To be sure, the Sinhalese establishment considered this highly centralized system very suitable, because their majority would ensure their power in a country which they believed by tradition to be theirs anyway. The counter-proposal of the Tamils and the less privileged Sinhalese to protect their minority status by means of provincial councils found no favour, nor did the idea of the devolution of powers to these provincial councils and to the local communitarian level. The inflexibility of the Sinhalese, strongly supported by the Buddhist higher clergy, was among other things a reaction to the "divide and conquer" rule of the British, which had marginalized the Sinhalese and given the Hindu Tamils a political role far beyond their number. This basic political debate has continued unresolved since 1920. According to Colin R. de Silva, who has participated in the most recent constitutional debates, the process has been hampered all along by lack of foresight, wisdom and, above all, courage. [9]

Between the world wars and shortly after 1945 there were endless debates, but little genuine dialogue, about the mode and share of representation of the different population groups in the new parliament and in the executive cabinet. Each group sought as many advantages as possible for itself. Within these debates the long-dormant tension between the Sinhalese and the Tamils generated its first real sparks, not least because the rapidly increasing population (which has almost trebled since 1946) was making land resources ever scarcer. The religious component, not evident at first, was like oil which helped the flame to spread.

A key problem seems to be the attachment of the Sinhalese community to an idealized version of history, which looks back to a remote past when they and their Buddhist culture were alone on the island — disregarding the fact that the aboriginal Veddas and perhaps earlier Tamil tribes were in fact there before the Sinhalese. This golden age was destroyed, first by the invading Tamils, then by the European colonialists, depriving Sri Lanka of its political independence and upsetting its economy and religious life.

The 19th-century Sinhalese intellectual Anagarika Dharmapala reacted against the humiliation caused by colonialism and the unchecked spread of Christian missions by infusing a fresh spirit into decaying Buddhism, transforming Sri Lanka's ancient religious heritage and theocratic traditions into a political programme which furnished the emerging Sinhalese middle class with an ideology and a new code of ethics. The foundations for Sinhalese nationalism were laid.

This new Buddhism turned against the Hindu Tamils precisely at the moment when the British were bringing in Tamils from India to work on the tea plantations. This fanned the anger of the Sinhalese against the job-seeking intruders, even though they themselves would not have accepted the low plantation wages and harsh working conditions. Although all the Tamils together remain a minority in Sri Lanka, the Sinhalese see neighbouring Tamil Nadu, with its poverty-stricken millions, as perched above them dangerously, "like a giant overhanging boulder" which threatens at any moment to roll down and crush them. The Tamils of Sri Lanka could be the force that dislodged that boulder. [10]

At independence in 1948 the question of how to safeguard the rights of minorities was still unresolved, despite Tamil efforts to obtain constitutional guarantees. But as soon as the restraining hand of the British colonial administration was gone, Sinhalese ideology was applied unhindered. The plantation Tamils were disenfranchised. The *burghers* lost their economic and political rights, and most left for Australia. The departure of this sober and thrifty population was a serious blow to the newly independent country. After the election of 1956, the vindictive and short-sighted nationalist government of S.W.R.D. Bandaranaike decreed that henceforth Sinhala would be the only language of national and local government administration, business and the schools. The government explained this as a corrective to the British colonial imposition of English as the language of government and higher education, which had given the Tamils far more than their share of key positions. The Sinhalese leaders now wanted to rise to the top, even if many of them had no competence in English. Inevitably, the 1956 language law discriminated against the Tamils, who found themselves progressively deprived of access to public services, employment and education.

Instead of strengthening national unity after the colonial era, Sri Lanka entered a period of acute crisis. Communication between Sinhalese and Tamils became difficult. Increasingly, they regarded each other with fear and paranoia. During the following years, Sinhalese violence and Tamil intransigence became stronger. Large-scale violence erupted in 1956 immediately after the introduction of the Sinhala Only Act, and again in 1958, 1960, 1977, 1981 and, most explosively, in 1983 when killings, lootings and rapes of Tamils took place throughout the south, even in the neighbourhood of the presidential palace in Colombo. Some have described these systematic attacks, coordinated by the military and the security forces and aided by the population in general, as a "holocaust". President J.R. Jayawardene did not bother to intervene; and when he finally did speak out, it was to justify the murderous actions, without a word of sympathy for the victims. [11]

Indian intervention and the JVP uprising

The events of 1983 caused consternation not only among Sri Lanka's Tamils but also in the Indian state of Tamil Nadu. To press the Sri Lankan government to come to terms with its rebellious Tamils, India's secret services trained young Sri Lankan Tamils in the use of automatic and semi-automatic rifles, anti-tank weapons, rocket launchers and land mines. Within months the Liberation Tigers of

Tamil Eelam became a superbly trained fighting force, not only attacking Sri Lankan army and police posts at will, but eliminating rival Tamil organizations with unprecedented brutality. In 1986 the LTTE killed 300 fighters of the Tamil Eelam Liberation Organization (TELO), which India had prudently built up as a counterforce to LTTE. The sorcerers' apprentices were getting out of hand, and the rising conflict began to follow its own logic. To India's dismay, peace in Sri Lanka was further off than ever.

The massive influx of modern weaponry was turning insurgency and counter-insurgency into a full-fledged war. To counter the unexpected strength of the LTTE, the Sri Lankan army increased its own efficiency, thanks to assistance from the US and Britain. As the fighting increased in intensity, the political restlessness reached Tamil Nadu itself, a dangerous development for India. The Sri Lankan war was threatening to engulf the entire unstable Indian subcontinent.

India was thus eager to re-establish peace, and the desperate Sri Lankan government agreed. Indian prime minister Rajiv Gandhi proposed that northern and eastern Sri Lanka be granted a certain autonomy, but that the unity of the country be safeguarded. Under this arrangement, the LTTE would turn over its weapons to the Sri Lankan military and obtain the necessary security guarantees. Prabhakaran, who was being held by India, reluctantly consented. To ensure implementation of the agreement, the Sri Lankan government allowed Indian troops to occupy the northern part of Sri Lanka.

As soon as Prabhakaran was free and back in Sri Lanka he denounced the agreement, claiming that the LTTE had been betrayed and that the real objective of the peace agreement was to disarm the Tamil Tigers. He ordered them not to turn over their weapons and instead to attack the Indian "occupiers". In angry "self-defence", the Indian army killed no fewer than 5000 Tamils, but lost between 1200 to 1500 of its own men and sustained 3000 injured. [12]

Suddenly, in a quick turnaround, the Sinhalese-dominated government and the LTTE came to terms and decided to join forces against the Indian "invaders". The Sri Lankan military even equipped their former arch-enemy with fresh arms and ammunition. The LTTE attacked the Indian troops with vigour, and in 1990 a desperate Rajiv Gandhi pulled out his troops from the Sri Lankan quagmire. There was a tragic sequence to this venture. On 21 May 1991 the Indian prime minister was murdered by a woman suicide attacker. Enquiries suggested that it was an LTTE-inspired act.

One reason for seeking at least a temporary truce with the Tamil Tigers was the growing restlessness the government faced among its own Sinhalese rural population in the south, which had been simmering ever since the violent repression of youth demonstrations in April 1971. Young landless Sinhalese, who saw no change and no chance in a society in which large Buddhist landowners — including wealthy monasteries — were blocking all opportunities, attempted a new rebellion in late 1989. Under the Marxist-oriented leadership of the JVP (*Janatha Vimukhti Peramuna* or People's Liberation Front) the revolt spread throughout the south, until even Colombo was encircled. The aim of the JVP was not simply to change the government but to rebuild from the ground up a system whose pillars included the higher Buddhist clergy (the uprising was also supported by younger monks from poorer families), the land-holding class, the educated middle sector, lawyers and merchants — that is, all those whom the poor considered "profiteers".

Suppressing this sudden revolt demanded all of Sri Lanka's strained military resources and made the government more flexible. After some initial hesitation on the part of the common (Sinhalese) soldiers, who had come from these same poor families, the JVP made the mistake of murdering family members of soldiers and officers. The army counter-attacked brutally and put down the uprising. Even more than the ethnic conflict between Sinhalese and Tamils, on which the international community has almost exclusively focussed, the JVP rebellion revealed how Sri Lankan society as a whole had become deformed. [13]

The second and third Eelam wars

Having thwarted the Indian army, the fourth largest in the world, the LTTE broke the armistice with the government a few months later and launched a daring attack by 7000 guerrillas on a strategically important camp. This touched off the so-called second Eelam war, more costly and more bloody than any previous fighting. The guerrilla force was now better organized and better armed, and its several thousand fighters, both men and women, made a personal vow to LTTE leader Velupillai Prabhakaran to abstain from smoking, alcohol and sex. Around the neck each fighter wore a poison capsule to be taken in case of capture. The Tamil civilian population both respected and feared the Tigers for their intransigence and their readiness to die rather than capitulate. While the LTTE often protected the people from the brutalities of the Sri Lankan army, it strictly supervised the civilian population, even in areas occupied by the Sri Lankan army, collecting taxes, holding court, issuing or withholding permits for anyone wanting to leave for the south. Those suspected of treason were executed without mercy. Already in 1984 a number of police informers were hung on lantern poles, and in 1985 a schoolmaster was shot to death, simply because during an armistice he had arranged for a football match between his students and army soldiers.

This phase of the war ended in 1994. The new Sri Lankan president Chandrika Kumaratunga promised changes, saying she wanted to turn her back on Sinhalese chauvinism and bring peace through political decentralization and a new constitution. An armistice was arranged and negotiations with the LTTE initiated. But the hopes of the suffering people were quickly dashed. Under pressure from Sinhalese nationalists, it was clear that Kumaratunga was no longer ready to implement her promises. Decentralization, she said, did not mean a separate state for the Tamils — a point on which the LTTE remained intransigent.

The third Eelam war began. Kumaratunga called the new military campaign a "war for peace". In October 1995 the Sri Lankan army initiated a determined offensive, promising that the war would be over by the end of the year. Jaffna was finally captured, but most of the Tamil population had fled, and the war simply shifted from the north to the east. In fact the LTTE — in a move recalling the evacuation of Phnom Penh by the Khmer Rouge in Cambodia 20 years earlier — had ordered the entire population to leave the city, including the elderly and the sick, mothers and children. Two women teachers were shot when they refused to leave their home.

Despite losing their capital, the LTTE continued to fight. In 1995 and 1996 suicide units blew up most of Sri Lanka's oil reserves. A large bomb detonated in the heart of Colombo killed 90 people and wounded 1200, temporarily putting the nation's business nerve centre out of action. Another LTTE surprise operation destroyed the advanced army camp at Mullaitivu in the northeast, killing an estimated 1400 Sri Lankan soldiers and placing enough ammunition and weapons in the rebels' hands to keep the war going for years to come. Undaunted, the Sri Lankan army attacked again, this time in the direction of Kilinochchi, the new Tamil Eelam capital, but with few results except to produce tens of thousands of new refugees.

Not only has the government of Chandrika Kumaratunga failed to reach its military objectives, but it also seems incapable of progress on the promised constitutional reform. Sinhalese nationalists, led by the higher Buddhist clergy, refuse any concession that would abrogate the unitary Sri Lankan state and jeopardize their absolute power. Meanwhile, the economy continues to disintegrate as the war becomes ever more costly, production, trade and tourism decline, and public debt increases, along with inflation. All this takes a particular toll on the poor of every ethnic group. Even Kumaratunga's dictatorial powers, strict censorship and an overblown security apparatus can no longer induce the necessary number of young men each year to register for military service. [14]

Sri Lanka has become a highly militarized society, in which international arms dealers, including governments, and secret services have a vested interest in maintaining the conflict, and a small number of profiteers are gaining huge revenues from the war. While the poor are systematically pauperized, the rich are getting richer by leaps and bounds. According to Chandra Peiris, the wealthiest 10 percent of Sri Lankans received 30 percent of the country's total earnings in 1973, 39.1 percent in 1978-79, 41.7 percent in 1981-82, and 49.3 percent in 1985. [15] All this makes it evident that the Sri Lankan conflict is unlikely to find an early solution.

The role of religion

The religion of the Tamils has not played an important political role in the conflict in Sri Lanka — in contrast to the importance of Hinduism in the ethnic struggles in neighbouring India. Only on the Buddhist side does the political conflict have a religious superstructure. The question to ponder, as Wesley Ariarajah has pointed out, is why the central teachings of all four major religions in the country have made so little impact on the behaviour of the different ethnic groups:

> The predominant religion is Buddhism, at the heart of which are non-violence and compassion. Hindus make up the second largest religious group; and Hindu *dharma* is based on the concept of harmony, in which the whole created order is seen as the body of the divine and the unity of all beings is affirmed. Also present in Sri Lanka are Christianity, which claims to be the religion of love, and Islam, which cannot be practised without the word *salaam*, peace, permanently on one's lips. [16]

Within these four religious communities many leaders have in fact worked tirelessly for peace and harmony. But they have accomplished little in terms of stopping the violence and bringing about a just peace. What is true in Sri Lanka can be seen to a greater or lesser extent elsewhere in Asia as well; and mere good will on the part of some religious leaders is not enough to stave off conflict. Ariarajah continues:

> Terrible social problems disturb the harmony of people in all Asian nations: abject poverty and deprivation of the masses, repressive rulers and governments, social stratification, oppression of women and exploitation of workers. One would expect religious groups to work towards alleviating this suffering. Instead what we witness today is increasing conflict between religious communities themselves. [17]

But even if the conflict in Sri Lanka and similar ones elsewhere in Asia must be considered social and political, not religious, the use of religious identification "as a symbol and rallying point for political ends... has affected the credibility of all religions", Ariarajah says. Moreover, "the ineffectiveness of religious leaders' attempts to bring about peace and harmony has seriously eroded the appeal of religion for young Asians. Increasing tensions between religious communities can only further damage their credibility as the driving force of the Asian heart and mind." [18]

A significant fact about the Christian churches in Sri Lanka is that they are composed of both Sinhalese and Tamils. During a national consultation in 1991, convened by the Commission on Justice and Peace of the National Christian Council (which includes both Protestants and Roman Catholics), Sri Lankan church leaders took stock of the country's situation and the role of the Christians in it. The picture was a sobering one. Apart from witnessing violence, rape and destruction almost daily, countless local churches have lost members, Tamils and Sinhalese alike. In some places church buildings have been abandoned or destroyed; elsewhere, they exist, but there are no clergy or members left. Nevertheless, many local parishes and congregations have shown signs of great resilience, even though they may be cut off from national headquarters, by offering pastoral care and providing solace and refuge, relief and rehabilitation.

In general, however, the participants noted, Sri Lanka's churches were unprepared for the crisis. Even after the missionaries had left, the local clergy continued to stress personal holiness — abstinence from alcohol, gambling and fornication — rather than social responsibility. Preaching centred on Jesus' sacrificial death rather than on his teachings. The vast school system which the missionaries had established had catered to an elite rather than to the poor. Christians who did take a biblically grounded interest in workers' rights, the land problem, the repression of ethnic minorities or human rights were labelled leftists and marginalized and ran the risk of falling into the hands of the security police.

Theologian Dhyanchand Carr observes that the pro-establishment stance of most Asian churches, their failure to stand up to injustices and their abdication of social responsibility in moments of crisis can be linked with the traditions of the European churches that sent missionaries to Asia, which for centuries not only tolerated but promoted antisemitism, which eventually allowed the holocaust to take place. While "a hidden river of opposition to oppression" has always flowed in the Christian community of Sri Lanka, there was no church protest after independence when the 30,000 *burghers* — fellow Christians — were expelled and left for Australia, or when the hundreds of thousands of plantation Tamils were disenfranchised and threatened with deportation to India. Even when church leaders did timidly dare to voice their concerns to the nation's top politicians about government policies, they informed neither their own members nor the media, probably reasoning that, since the churches still bore the stigma of being a colonialist fifth column, it was prudent to be silent. But as a result no one knew that the church leaders were even engaged in a cautious dialogue with the authorities. And the remarkable consultations and publications of the study centre of the National Christian Council made hardly any impact on the Christian in the pew. [19]

The hesitancy of Sri Lankan churches in the face of social realities has recently been illustrated by the case of Fr Tissa Balasuriya, a member of the Oblate Order. He was among a small group of lay people and theologians who in the wake of the Second Vatican Council (1962-65) helped to initiate a theological renaissance within Sri Lankan Roman Catholicism. He founded the Centre for Society and Religion, with the intention of engaging in social, cultural and economic research and helping to prepare policies for overcoming Sri Lanka's external dependence and internal poverty. Youth problems, the exploitation of workers and Sri Lanka's ethnic tensions received special attention. This reflective process was accompanied by fresh theological and biblical studies. Balasuriya became a highly respected member of the Ecumenical Association of Third World Theologians.

In his book *Mary and Human Liberation*, Balasuriya questioned traditional European patterns of doing theology. Although this book did not exceed the formal limits of Catholic doctrine, its approach and method were not to the liking of the Sri Lankan Bishops' Conference, which had already observed Balasuriya's career with some suspicion. Furthermore, the Sri Lankan government had been putting pressure on the bishops because of Balasuriya. The publication of this new book provided a tool to proceed against him. The Sri Lankan bishops referred the matter to Rome, which examined Balasuriya's writings and found them wanting. His explanations did not satisfy the Congregation for the Doctrine of the Faith; and in May 1995, Cardinal Ratzinger, the head of the Congregation, obtained permission from Pope John Paul II to issue an official declaration that Balasuriya was no longer an approved Roman Catholic theologian. His teaching authority was withdrawn. [20] Subsequently, after further discussions did not resolve the issue, he was abruptly excommunicated at the beginning of 1997.

This sombre description of a divided nation and of its religious communities in distress must nevertheless end with a small sign of hope in the form of a story told by Carr about a Christian community in the Sri Lankan uplands:

> This small congregation of just eight Tamil families near Kandy had been victims of ethnic violence a few years ago. Their houses were burned. They themselves ran into the woods and escaped being killed. During the rioting, to their horror, they had recognized among the maddened crowd a few faces of their neighbours, who had been very friendly up until then. But the next day these very same neighbours sought them

out in their hideouts in the woods and profusely apologized. They expressed their fear in not being able to resist a large group of rioters who had come from elsewhere. They also brought food and looked after them and later helped them to rebuild their houses. [21]

NOTES

[1] Martin Stürzinger, "In Bedrängnis sind die Tiger erst gefährlich", *Die Weltwoche* (Zurich), 8 Feb. 1996, p.5; cf. Neville Jayaweera, *Sri Lanka: Towards a Multi-Ethnic Democracy? Report on a Fact-Finding Mission*, Oslo, International Peace Research Institute, 1990, p.58.

[2] Jayaweera, *ibid.*, p.42.

[3] On the history see the entries on "Ceylon" in *Encyclopaedia Britannica*, Vol. 5, pp.178f. and in *Concise Dictionary of Christian Missions*, pp.95f.; and on "Sri Lanka" in *Religion in Geschichte und Gegenwart*, Vol. 1, pp.1634f.

[4] Jayaweera, *op. cit.*, p.42

[5] "Ceylon", in *Concise Dictionary of Christian Missions*, p.95.

[6] *Ibid.*

[7] Jayaweera, *op. cit.*, pp.55ff.

[8] Jayadeva Uyangoda, "The Political Background of the Provincial Council System", in *Beyond Ethnic Conflict in Sri Lanka?*, Colombo, Centre for Society and Religion, 1992, p.101.

[9] Colin R. de Silva, "The Provincial Councils and Their Significance", *ibid.*, p.105.

[10] Jayaweera, *op. cit.*, p.31.

[11] L. Piyadasa, *Sri Lanka: The Holocaust and After*, London, Marram Books, 1984, p.82.

[12] *Ibid.*, p.81.

[13] *Ibid.*, pp.64f.

[14] This summary of recent developments draws on the article by Stürzinger (note 1 above), as well as his "'Der Krieg für den Frieden' ist keine Lösung", *Die Weltwoche*, 29 Aug. 1996, p.10.

[15] Chandra Peiris, "Disappeared", in *Hopelessness and Challenge: The Mission of the Church in Situations of Conflict*, Hong Kong, Christian Conference of Asia, and Colombo, National Christian Council of Sri Lanka, n.d., p.112.

[16] S. Wesley Ariarajah, "Pluralism and Harmony", *Current Dialogue* (Geneva), Dec. 1993, p.17.

[17] *Ibid.*

[18] *Ibid.*

[19] D. Carr, "Mission", in *Hopelessness and Challenge*, p.10.

[20] Cf. Nikolaus Klein, "Der Fall Tissa Balasuriya", *Orientierung* (Zurich), nos 13-14, 15-31 July 1996, pp.145-147.

[21] Carr, *loc. cit.*, p.26.

8
Bosnia-Herzegovina

Three "snapshots", chosen at random, serve to introduce this ethnic conflict:

• Mostar, the capital of Herzegovina, was one of the fabled ancient cities of the Balkans. Surrounded by rugged mountains and divided by the rushing Neretva River, it has been for centuries the home of Muslims and Catholic Croats, as well as a smaller number of Orthodox Serbs and Jews. They have traded wine, tobacco, fruit, vegetables and walnuts, and worked side by side in nearby coal mines. A web of intricate relations developed among them in ways outsiders could barely comprehend. During the fifty years of communist rule, young people began to ridicule the older generation's insistence on "belonging" to this or that ethnic or religious group. Intermarriage became commonplace.

The very name of the city hints that its essence was to relate peoples and cultures, east and west, north and south, for "Mostar" is derived from the words meaning "old bridge". Indeed, the bridge over the Neretva, built in 1566 by the Turks, perhaps on Roman foundations, was designated by UNESCO as a cultural object of international significance. On 9 November 1993 a Croatian army officer directed his artillery on this historic bridge. Within seconds the ancient "Muslim" monument collapsed into the river below. But the mutual loathing between the Croats and the Muslims, the two principal ethnic groups of Mostar, had been growing for some time before the destruction of the bridge.

• As in all wars, rape has been widespread in the Bosnian war. In this case, however, it became more injurious because most people in these closely-knit communities knew each other personally. In addition to violating the dignity of the victims, it was thus one of the most insidious methods of tearing apart the family life and social fabric of the adversaries. While the rape of Muslim women by Serbian forces was widely publicized, the report of a 1993 team visit to Bosnia made by the World Council of Churches and the French agency CIMADE notes:

> The Serbian officials we met took pains to substantiate their claim that Muslims and Croats have used rape in a systematic manner. In Bosnanski Brod we were shown a room used for rapes by Croats at a concentration camp housed in a high school. We were shown copies of two authorizations by a Muslim police chief for the arrest of two Serb women "for the purpose of sex". The head of Serbian television in Pale gave us a copy of a documentary he produced for Swedish television on rapes carried out against Serbian women. [1]

• In July 1995 the town of Srebrenica in northeastern Bosnia, mostly inhabited by Muslims, was taken by Serb forces under the command of General Ratko Mladic. Srebrenica had been declared one of the "safe areas" in Bosnia, protected by UN peacekeeping forces, and its Muslim defenders had even been persuaded to lay down their arms. The Serbs considered them prisoners of war, and led away an estimated ten to twelve thousand men. Outside of town they were shot dead and buried in mass graves.

These three "snapshots" suggest that the unique thousand-year old European experiment called Bosnia may have been destroyed beyond recuperation between the outbreak of war in April 1992 and the signing of the Dayton Accords in December 1995. The elections in September 1996 merely confirmed the country's division into three highly militarized and mutually hostile mini-dictatorships. Subsequently, a tripartite government has been set up and a parliament has met, but whether this arrangement can last, only time will tell.

In his history of Bosnia, Noel Malcolm comments on a remark by British prime minister John Major in the House of Commons in 1993 that the Bosnian war was the result of the reappearance of "ancient hatreds" after the collapse of communism. If one were to follow — as many have — Mr Major's reasoning, Malcolm continues, France today could also be engaged in bloody civil strife. It could "remember" the religious wars of the 16th century, culminating in the bloody St Bartholomew's day massacre of 1572 when the Catholic authorities attempted to exterminate the Protestant Huguenots. There were many repressions of rural revolts by the monarchy, violence and mass murders during the French revolution, political instability in the 19th century and the conflictive history of collaboration and resistance during the second world war. On the basis of "ancient hatreds" a civil war in France would be virtually inevitable.

Malcolm's point is that historic conflicts do not automatically lead to new ones. There are many cases where true reconciliation and mutual appreciation have followed bloody internal strife. "These animosities were not permanently built into the psyche of the people who lived in Bosnia," Malcolm objects. "The economic causes of hatred were eroded by changes and reforms in the late 19th and early 20th centuries, until they had largely ceased to exist." Only twice — after the first world war, when Yugoslavia was founded, and during the second world war — were there exceptional flare-ups of intercommunal strife, each time "induced and aggravated" from outside Bosnia's borders. [2]

An interesting insight into the culture and psychology of the peoples living in the former Yugoslavia comes from novelist Rebecca West in *Black Lamb and Grey Falcon*. Listening to the vociferous outbreak of a young man over a minor matter, a behaviour which she had often noted during a visit of towns along the eastern coast of the Adriatic, she comments:

> He was simply the product of Dalmatian history: the conquest of Illyria by Rome, of Rome by the barbarians; then three hundred years of conflict between Hungary and Venice; then four hundred years of oppression by Venice, with war against Turkey running concurrently for most of that time; a few years of hope under France, frustrated by the decay of Napoleon; a hundred years of muddling misgovernment by Austria. In such shambles, a man had to shout and rage to survive. [3]

Three communities: same roots

Historic sensitivities have of course contributed to the conflict of the 1990s. All of the former Yugoslavia lies along two critical geographical and political faultlines of Europe: the division between Eastern and Western Christianity and the frontiers between the once-powerful Austro-Hungarian and Ottoman Turkish empires. The different cultures and religions — Orthodoxy, Roman Catholicism and, since the 16th century, Islam — have profoundly shaped the minds of these peoples and remain a part of present-day reality. That is why past events have different meanings for different ethnicities in the Balkans. Their schoolbooks tell different and mutually contradictory stories of unending enemy oppression, battles won and lost, political intrigues and national frustrations. These are histories painted in black and white, good on the one side and evil on the other. There are no shades of grey, no self-doubt.

Over the centuries the peoples of this region have been subject to countless invasions and incompetent governments, unscrupulous princes and dictators, borders drawn without consultation and religions imposed from the outside. Dalmatia, to which some areas of today's Bosnia once belonged, was conquered first by Rome. Later, it was overwhelmed by the Germanic Goths and then by Slavic tribes. The Serbs and the Croats, although both South Slavs, were probably distinct at an early stage, though closely related. How distinct from or related to each other has been hotly debated since the 19th century, usually on the basis of the debaters' present political stance rather than hard evidence. In any case, the Slav invaders seem to have absorbed the earlier populations of Illyrians, Celts, Romans (from all parts of the empire), Goths, Huns and Avars.

As the Roman and the Byzantine empires faded, the Serbs settled in what is today southwestern Serbia and slowly pushed north and west into what are now Montenegro and Herzegovina. The Croats settled on present-day Croatia, Slavonia, Slovenia and parts of Bosnia and Herzegovina. Then came the Germanic Franks, the Venetians and the Hungarians, with their alternatingly enlightened and oppressive rule. They were followed by Ottoman mismanagement, Austro-Hungarian indifference, an unloved and incompetent Yugoslav state and the horrors of German occupation during the second world war. Relations between the different communities in the Balkans tend to be tough because of this rude history, though not necessarily destructive. Community affairs are often run by local autocrats. Pent-up feelings can indeed explode.

Geographically, Bosnia is cut off from the Adriatic Sea and the south by forbidding mountain ranges. Access is easier from the north and the east. Except for short periods, a true Bosnian nationality, with its own language, religion and common historical memory, never really developed. Three nationalities — though all of Slav origin — lived side-by-side in a patchwork-like country. The majority — Serbs and Muslims — spoke the Serbian language; a minority spoke Croatian, which is not much different. As a *lingua franca*, the former Yugoslav state promoted a mixture of the two languages, Serbo-Croat.

The distinctiveness of each group was marked not by language, but by religion. Either Orthodoxy, Islam or Roman Catholicism shaped the group's culture and historical memory. The Bosnian Serbs oriented themselves towards Serbia as their "motherland", and the Bosnian Croats towards the Habsburg empire. Only the Muslims were "nothing but" Bosnians, although historic recollections related them to Ottoman history (and "Turks" is a derogatory term used by

Serbs for Bosnian Muslims). Beyond the confines of Bosnia, each community established a complex set of relationships with the vaster religious-cultural world of the European West, the Byzantine East and the Islamic peoples. Under communist rule the religious traditions were weakened in all three communities, but "religion" still serves the Bosnians as an ideological rallying point.

Each community has cultivated a distinct historic outlook. Neither the Muslims nor the Croats share the collective frustration of the Serbs over their historic defeat at Kosovo Polje in 1389. The ancestors of the Muslims were mainly Bosnian Serbs who adopted Islam when the Turks invaded Bosnia. They retained their land holdings and obtained considerable social and political power as the new upper class. The Croats relied on Austria and Hungary for their protection. During the Turkish invasions, relations with the West were vital to the Croats. They had adopted Christianity during the 9th century through Latin missionaries from the Dalmatian coast and Italy, and became Roman Catholic. Northern Croatia fell under Frankish rule (Charlemagne) and became part of the Holy Roman Empire, developing a distinct identity as Slovenia until 1806, when it was taken over by the Habsburg empire. Croatia and Slovenia were thus related to Western Europe and Western culture at an early stage. Croats were a majority in Herzegovina and a strong minority in Bosnia. At the same time, many Serbs lived in Croatia. The borderline between the Orthodox or Muslim East and the Roman Catholic West was thus not as clear-cut as many historians and politicians represent it to be. Between the three cultures there was the continuous give-and-take of close neighbours.

Throughout this chaotic history the Serbs suffered more than their northern neighbours. After the battle of Kosovo Polje Serbia was occupied by the Ottoman Turks for nearly 500 years. The Serbs had accepted the Orthodox faith in 879 (although Latin missionaries from the Dalmatian coast had evangelized among the Serbs in the 7th and 8th centuries, with the approval of the Byzantine emperors). But as the Byzantine empire weakened, the Serbs were increasingly thrown back on their own resources, and after Constantinople fell in 1453 any hope for relief from Byzantium was dashed. The Roman Catholic Church showed no interest in Orthodox Serbia. The religious conflict between the Roman popes and the Eastern patriarchs intensified as the Ottoman danger grew; and after the Council of Ferrera-Florence in 1438-39 the break in relations between the Roman Catholic West and the Orthodox East was complete. Since the Serbs, even in their hour of distress, refused to recognize the primacy of the bishop of Rome, they could not count on any support from the West.

The democratic traditions developing in Western Europe at the time, such as the limitation and separation of powers, had almost no chance among the Balkan peoples, whose primary goal for much of their history has simply been to survive attack and subjugation. Memories of collective injuries and glories, victories and defeats, were interiorized and turned into all-absorbing myths, interwoven with religious elements. Whenever a crisis occurred, the religious differences were blown up out of all proportion. After independence from the Ottoman empire or from Austria-Hungary, neighbours were both allies and hostile rivals, because more often than not each occupied territory the other wished to recuperate.

Yugoslavia, the common state of the south Slavs, might have been a rational political instrument for the entire troubled Balkan region, because it sought to bring together a number of small, if unstable communities of similar background which had lived side-by-side or mingled together in intricate territorial arrangements. The narrow spirit of ethnic identity deepened by religious antagonisms might have been overcome by a non-religious secular state. With sufficient patience on the part of politicians and mutual ecumenical tolerance on the part of religious leaders, Yugoslavia could perhaps have evolved into a democratic state. But the secularization imposed by force under the communist regime without any preparation was bound to fail. The Yugoslav federation lacked cohesion, and in the economic and political crisis of the late 1980s, the politicians fell back on ancient hatreds to preserve their power, switching their ideology from communism to nationalism. Slobodan Milosevic in Serbia and Franjo Tudjman in Croatia are prime examples of this.

Even with its problems of identity and cohesion, Bosnia probably could have held together were it not for outside interference. While Croatia is certainly not without responsibility for this tragedy, the primary cause was the impact of Serbia. The Serbs have never forgotten the glory of their mediaeval Nemanja kings, who briefly ruled an area from Bosnia to southern Greece and under whose reign Orthodoxy became Serbia's national faith. It was this kingdom which came to an abrupt end in 1389, when the Turkish invaders defeated the Serbs and killed their chieftain Prince Lazar Dusan. The Serbian aristocracy was wiped out. During the succeeding 500 years of Ottoman oppression, the Serbian nation was broken up into various territorial segments. The peasantry was bled mercilessly by the *haratch* tax, and their children were recruited into the Turkish army, thus becoming the instrument of their own subjection. Only the Orthodox church kept the national spirit alive. Out of this traumatic experience grew the notion that some day all Serbs should once again be reassembled and their territory reunited. More than that, Serbia should be wherever Serbians were living.

Among the unfulfilled tasks, as the Serbs see it, is the "recovery" of Serbia's ancient heartland of Kosovo. During the Austro-Turkish war (1683-99), the Habsburg armies drove the Turks out of most of Bosnia and Serbia. The Serbs used this opportunity for an uprising against the Turks, but the latter regained their lost territory in 1690, and 30,000 Serbs, led by their patriarch, left Kosovo with the retreating Austrian troops. This made possible the large-scale entry into Kosovo of Muslim Albanians, who today make up more than 80 percent of its population. Their claims of autonomy, if not unification with Albania, are intolerable to the Serbs. As early as 1968 there were riots between Serbs and Albanians, which after 1980 turned into a permanent crisis. The status of Kosovo as an autonomous region within Serbia was ended, Albanian higher education was suppressed and Kosovo was subjected to military occupation. It became the initial focus for a revival of Serbian nationalism, fomented by Milosevic, without any objection on the Orthodox church's part.

As the Serbs believe themselves to be a "martyred nation", the myth of territorial restoration was transformed into national policy ever since independence in the 19th century. Serbia warred against virtually all of its neighbours and finally defied the Habsburg empire itself, leading directly to the outbreak of the first world war. The war was ignited by the assassination in Sarajevo of Franz Ferdinand, heir to the Austro-Hungarian throne, by the Bosnian Serb nationalist Gavril Princip, at the instigation of Black Hand, an extremist organization closely related to Serbia's secret services. Serbian nationalists still honour the memory of Princip as a national hero.

Bosnia itself has somehow always defied those who sought to rule, divide or absorb it. Invaded by the same succession of peoples as the rest of the Balkans, this mountainous country has survived as a distinct entity since the end of the 12th century, mainly by playing off Croatia and Hungary against Serbia. A third, less powerful pole of attraction was the seafaring republics of Venice and Ragusa (now Dubrovnik), with which much of Bosnia's trade in iron ore and anthracite, metalwork, weapons and sheepskins was carried on. Even after the Ottoman defeat of the Serbs in 1389, Bosnia resisted with reasonable success until after the battle of Mohacs in 1526, when it too, along with Hungary and Croatia, was defeated by the Ottomans.

How religion helped to shape ethnic identity

The upheavals caused by Serbia's defeat and Croatia's discomfiture dispersed refugees into all parts of Bosnia, which is basically how the patchwork of populations throughout its valleys, villages and towns was created. They learned how to live side by side, establishing complicated social and economic relationships. Next to Orthodox and Catholic churches or monasteries, Muslim mosques and prayer houses sprang up, occasionally interspersed with Jewish synagogues. All spoke Serbian or Croatian.

In general the new Ottoman rulers did not force their subjects to convert to Islam outright, although Christian families were compelled to deliver a certain number of four- to eight-year-old boys annually to the sultan in Istanbul in order to have them transformed into Muslim janissaries. Many of the Christians who did convert to Islam seem to have belonged to the land-holding Serbian nobility in Bosnia. Changing religion allowed them to retain their properties and sometimes to obtain high positions in the empire, commercial privileges and large land-holdings. The converted Muslims preferred to live in the towns, which were never large, and kept the Serbian and Croatian peasants in a semi-feudal dependency.

The governing power was in the hands of 48 hereditary *kapetans*, who exercised feudal jurisdiction over their peasants. Thus grew up the institution of the *ciflik*, by which entire villages were turned over to one of these lords, who received one-third of the peasants' annual income. Despite initial difficulties, Bosnia as an Ottoman province acquired a distinctive multicultural flavour and a reputation as a place of peaceful inter-ethnic relations. Herzegovina, the duchy, populated mostly by Croatian Roman Catholics, was administratively attached to it, without depriving it of its identity as a Turkish province.

Why so many Bosnian Slavs converted to Islam — a phenomenon with no parallels in other European countries dominated by the Ottomans: Serbia, Greece, Bulgaria or Cyprus — remains a mystery. There are no reports of Turks from Anatolia settling in Bosnia. Not much is known about the mediaeval Bosnian

Christian church. At the height of 19th-century nationalism, when some Bosnian intellectuals were trying to establish a "national identity", the idea grew that this defunct church was the home of all Bosnians before the Turkish conquest. It was said to have defied both the Orthodox and the Roman Catholics and thus to have been declared heretical by both, presumably due to influence of the Bogomils, the "Friends of God", a dualistic religious movement that arose in Bulgaria during the middle ages and spread as far as southern France, where its adherents were known as the *Cathars*, "the pure ones".

The truth is probably more prosaic. Both papal delegates and Franciscan monks sent to Bosnia to reorganize that church judged it "schismatic", not "heretical". In its isolation it had apparently retained much of the Byzantine liturgy and monastic tradition; and neither the church hierarchy nor the clergy had much contact with other churches and the church was therefore unable to renew itself, particularly because it was fully absorbed with struggling for its own survival. Church liturgies in Bosnia became reduced to popular festivals. The step from folk Christianity to folk Islam was short, and conversion was not necessarily a profound "religious" experience. Even today the same amulets are worn by both Christians and Muslims. The Virgin Mary is as venerated among Muslims as among Christians, as could be observed during the reports of appearances of Mary in Medjugorje in the early 1980s. Christians sometimes invite Muslim dervishes to dance and to read passages from the Qu'ran at their festivals. Moreover, already before the arrival of the Turks, the Franciscan monks had successfully pushed back Orthodox outposts and established Roman Catholic communities, especially in Herzegovina. There is thus good reason to believe that the Bosnian church was largely defunct before the Ottoman conquest. [4]

The rise of modern nationalism

In 1535 the Habsburg authorities created the Krajina, a military frontier in southern Croatia. This mountainous strip of land running alongside the Bosnian border from the Adriatic Sea to the Slavonian plains had been largely abandoned by its population after the Turkish victory at Mohacs in 1526. The Austrian government built a series of forts and brought in Serbian settlers who were seeking protection from the Turks. In 1630 the Krajina received a special status setting it apart from Croatia. Once the Turkish threat ended, the Croatians increasingly came to resent the existence of this territory within its boundaries, especially since the Austrian authorities sometimes used its rugged settler-soldiers against unruly local nobles. Although the Krajina was reincorporated into Croatia (then attached to Hungary) in 1881, it retained its spirit of independence and self-reliance. During the second world war the Krajina Serbs were among the first victims of the savage massacres committed by the Croatian fascists (Ustasha) under Ante Pavelic.

At the beginning of the Bosnian war of the 1990s the Krajina Serbs were radicalized by Serbian nationalists through an intensive campaign of misinformation and fear-mongering. Krajina Serb politicians provoked the Croatian authorities by shelling Dubrovnik and Zagreb and engaging in military action against the Bosnian Muslim enclave of Bihac. [5] In July 1995 the Croatian army overran the Krajina and drove out the Serbs, bringing a 400-year-old regional community to sudden termination.

In 1878 the European powers asked Austria-Hungary to take over the administration of Bosnia, which had reacted sharply to Ottoman plans to modernize and centralize the empire, including land reform. Newly independent Serbia demanded that Bosnia be incorporated into its territory, where "by right" it belonged, but the European powers judged Serbia too unruly and too unreliable. The Habsburg empire was not to annex Bosnia: its juridical status as a Turkish province would be left intact and a final decision taken later. The weakened Ottoman authorities were satisfied, but the Serbs, once again frustrated, were furious. They began to appeal for support to the Czarist government of Russia, which over the following years adopted Serbia's views.

To modernize the backward province, Austria-Hungary built roads, railways, public utilities and industries, created schools and universities and established the rule of law. The administration was entrusted to a joint Austro-Hungarian commission (in which Hungary gained predominance) under the ministry of finance, which was responsible directly to the imperial crown. But despite earlier promises, Bosnia's semi-feudal land-holding system was not reformed, and thousands of Serbian and Croatian peasants remained in virtual serfdom to Muslim landowners. This fanned the spirit of nationalism among the Bosnian Serbs, who began to clamour for self-administration, a demand eagerly supported by Serbia.

The Austro-Hungarian finance ministers were themselves Hungarian magnates with little interest in applying to Bosnia the land reform measures they did not want to see in Hungary itself. Moreover, the Roman Catholic hierarchy, some of whom came from the same Hungarian land-owning class, used all legal and political means to reduce the Serbian Orthodox Church in Bosnia to a state of subservience and thus to counter its political influence as a source of Serbian nationalism. Instead, this policy augmented the bitterness not only among the Bosnian Serbs but also within Serbia itself and among other Orthodox countries. Both the land problem and the treatment of the Orthodox church stirred up Serbian nationalism in Bosnia prior to the first world war, preparing the road to catastrophe. [6]

Parallel to and partially fused with Serbian and Croatian nationalism was the emerging ideology of "Yugoslavism", the unification of all South Slavs. After reforms of the Habsburg empire put Hungary on an equal footing with Austria in 1867, the Slav peoples in the empire began to demand the same rights. The vigorous campaign of Czechs and Slovaks in the north of the empire inspired the Slovenes, the Croats and Bosnia's Serbs, despite the cultural and religious divisions among them. The idea of a common South Slav state gained ground. Serbia and Bulgaria would be included, with the former playing the lead role in establishing the state. The concept of "South Slavia" was based on the idea of the Slav *race*, which reflected the racist concepts popular among European intellectuals of that era and largely ignored the role of culture and religion. While most ordinary people were touched by the latter, they barely understood race. Moreover, the South Slavs were torn apart by rivalries. Serbia and Bulgaria fought a war in 1913 over Macedonia; and Serbs, Muslims and Croats fought over and within Bosnia. South Slavia, founded in 1918 and renamed Yugoslavia in 1929, may have been a convenient instrument for the Western allies to dissolve the Habsburg empire, but it was essentially an empty shell.

In 1908 the Habsburg empire took advantage of the confusion caused by the Young Turk revolt against the Ottoman authorities to annex Bosnia-Herzegovina, hoping this show of strength would impress on the world that it was still a force to be reckoned with. But the Vienna government had not consulted with the other European powers; and now the Western governments were also miffed, as of course were Serbia and Russia, which was pushed by its own vocal Slavophiles to declare openly its sympathy for their Slav "brothers" with whom they shared a common Orthodox faith. The general agitation over the rash act of the Habsburgs contributed to a war psychosis and made conditions ripe for the fateful shot in Sarajevo in 1914 and the outbreak of world war.

The war began catastrophically for Serbia, which was attacked by Bulgaria in an effort to occupy Macedonia. Austria-Hungary pushed Serbia's army down into Greece. Only the intervention of the Western allies prevented Serbia from being wiped off the map. Chancing to be on the side of the winners at war's end, Serbia could at last fulfill its dream of creating South Slavia on its own terms. But because Serbia never understood how to treat as equals the other nations in the new kingdom of the Serbs, Croats and Slovenes, Yugoslavia was too weak to contain the contradictory and often violent ethnic and nationalist spirit of its peoples; and the idealistic concept of uniting the South Slav peoples into a single coherent force was lost.

The new enlarged state extended from Slovenia in the north to Macedonia in the south (but without Bulgaria). In the middle lay Bosnia, where all the political passions of the Balkans clashed together, as if in a nutshell.

The second world war

Unable to come to terms with the nationalist conflicts, King Alexander I established a personal dictatorship in 1929 and imposed unitary Serbian rule on the entire kingdom. On a state visit to France in 1934 he was assassinated in Marseilles by a Croatian nationalist. With Austria-Hungary gone, the Balkans were wide open to outside manipulation, and both Hitler's Germany and Mussolini's Italy meddled very directly in Yugoslavia's internal affairs, using Croatian extremists to break up Yugoslavia from the inside. Accordingly, when Germany attacked in 1941 the disunited state fell apart within days. Croatia was split off and made a state under fascist Ustasha rule, with Bosnia attached to it. Dalmatia was awarded to Italy, part of the Bacska went to Hungary and part of Macedonia to Bulgaria.

Under German occupation Yugoslavia became the scene of an atrocious civil war. The Ustasha, helped by the Germans, fought the Serbs; the Serbian Chetniks, under the royalist Dragomir Mihailovic, fought the Ustasha, the Germans and the communists (though Mihailovic is also said to have collaborated with the Germans); and Josip Broz Tito with his communist partisans fought the Germans, the Ustasha and the Chetniks. Moreover, the Germans also organized an SS division composed of Bosnian Muslims. In the end Tito's partisans won out. He succeeded

— with the help of ferocious repression against his opponents — in uniting adherents from all of Yugoslavia's nations without giving preference to any nationality. Tito saw to it that it was the Red Army and not the Western allies who came to help liberate Yugoslavia; and until 1948 Yugoslavia was firmly attached to the Soviet bloc.

The multiple conflicts cost the Yugoslav peoples, especially the Serbs, the lives of two million human beings; and this civil war within the overall war led directly to the war of 1991-95.

Yugoslavia falls apart

But the massacres of the 1990s were *not* foreordained. Tito's dictatorship was a long and desperate attempt to reduce regional tensions and downgrade the divisive influence of religious culture, which the communists considered retrograde and pernicious. That Yugoslavia fell apart so quickly after he died in 1980 probably had less to do with the resurgence of ethnic tension than with the lack of stature of his successors and the declining economy.

After turning against Soviet domination in 1948, Tito became the strategic and economic favourite of the West, especially the US and Germany. Yugoslavia became an important cold-war pawn, even though its dictator-turned-international-statesman adopted neutralist rhetoric. His gigantic development projects were costly, creating enormous foreign debts, so that the World Bank and International Monetary Fund began to worry about the repayment of their loans after Tito's death and applied pressure. Government bureaucracy had to be cut back massively. Tito's major achievement, the self-administered cooperatives, vanished. The social security system was curtailed. Annual industrial growth declined from 2.8 percent to 0 percent between 1980 and 1988 and to minus 10.6 percent in 1990. [7] Yugoslavia's economy became foreign-determined, the population was impoverished and migration abroad increased sharply — a systemic upheaval almost entirely ignored in international accounts of the explanation of the war in the 1990s.

The deteriorating relations between Albanians and Serbs in Kosovo was the first overt danger signal; the second was the refusal of Slovenia, Yugoslavia's most productive region, to pay any more for the "overblown bureaucracy" in Belgrade and the "inefficiency" and "backwardness" of the southern regions (Serbia, Montenegro and Macedonia). Slovenia declared its independence in 1991, as did Croatia shortly thereafter. The Serbian-dominated "federal" army was unable to subdue the two rebellious republics, though in the process it virtually destroyed the beautiful old Slovenian city of Vukovar, after which the White Tigers brigade and the paramilitary militia of Zeljko "Arkan" Raznatovic and Voislav Seselj "cleaned up" the remaining Croatian population, killing hundreds if not thousands. Later, these semi-official terrorists performed similar acts of "ethnic cleansing" elsewhere in former Yugoslavia.

The population of Bosnia, wedged between Serbia and Croatia, was 4.3 million in 1990: 43 percent Muslims, 33 percent Serbs, 17 percent Croats and 7 percent who refused to identify with any ethnic group and declared themselves Yugoslavs. In the December 1991 elections, the nationalist party of each ethnic group won in its area of predominance; and it became difficult for Bosnia to speak with one voice. The Muslims made a strategic alliance with the Croats, and Muslim leader Alia Izetbegovic was elected president. A referendum in February 1992 favoured independence for Bosnia. But the Bosnian Serb leadership, backed by Serbian president Slobodan Milosevic, refused to negotiate with the Muslim-Croat majority and boycotted the referendum, clearly intending to carve up the country. Milosevic named psychiatrist Radovan Karadzic as his representative in Bosnia and Ratko Mladic as commander-in-chief of the Bosnian Serb "army", which was equipped, financed and partly even manned by Belgrade. [8]

On 6 April 1992, when Bosnia was recognized by the European Union (followed shortly thereafter by the UN General Assembly), between 50,000 and 100,000 Bosnians of all nationalities demonstrated in the streets of Sarajevo protesting against the break-up of their country. But neither mass expressions of the popular will nor diplomatic admonitions from Europe and the international community could move the virulent nationalists.

A century of competition between Serbia and Croatia for dominance among the South Slavs, largely fought on Bosnia's back, made the new country's internal politics more intractable than they might otherwise have been. Moreover, many Serbs in Serbia, Bosnia and the Krajina believed repeated televised propaganda from Belgrade that Ustasha hordes and Islamic jihads from Iran or Afghanistan were about to arrive in masses and cut their throats. Night after night television stations indoctrinated viewers with images of mass murders committed against Serbs in the second world war. [9] The outbreak of the Bosnian war could not be stopped.

The Bosnian war

At first the international community, still relieved by the end of the cold war, seemed to regard the Yugoslav imbroglio as little more than a nuisance. The Council of Europe, the European Union and the UN issued admonitions and gentle threats while offering possibilities for negotiations, as if the Balkan leaders were reasonable and well-meaning gentlemen just looking for a place to sit down and discuss the pros and cons of their respective positions. The nascent civil war in Bosnia was described as "a flareup of violence on both sides". A half-hearted arms embargo was adopted, followed by a general embargo, which took its greatest toll not on Serbia or Croatia but on Bosnia, the government of which had come under attack for trying to preserve the country's unity. [10] European Union negotiators, backed up by the UN, engaged the warring parties in "peace negotiations": Karadzic and others became regular visitors to Geneva.

After many difficult meetings, a territorial subdivision of Bosnia was agreed upon, according to which the Muslims and the Croats would share an area of 51 percent while the Serbs would have 49 percent (despite the fact that the Serbian population did not exceed 33 percent). The fiction of a single country was nevertheless to be preserved. Armistices were signed and broken, and new schemes were debated. Meanwhile, the better-armed Serbs kept advancing until they had conquered 70 percent of Bosnia's area. Their strength lay in the rural areas, while the Muslim population was generally concentrated in the cities. The

Muslims held firmly to the economically vital areas of Bosnia. Thus the Serbs laid siege to Sarajevo, shelling it and killing people but they did not dare to risk open battle and to attack it.

According to Erich Weingärtner, writing in 1993:

It is rarely denied that atrocities are committed during these offensives and counter-offensives. But it is always the other side who started it. When Croat forces pushed south from Brod and Brcko in July and August 1992, they destroyed Orthodox churches and houses belonging to Serbs as far South as Derventa and beyond. In the counter-offensive from August to October, the Serbs destroyed Catholic churches and Croat houses. The result is a devastation of massive proportion. [11]

As is common in civil wars, some of the most destructive actions were committed by ultra-nationalist para-military groups, among them the Serbian Black Eagle, the Croat HOS and fundamentalist Muslim groups supported by extremists from the Middle East, operating partly on their own, partly in collusion with the respective governments. Most of the destruction of churches, mosques and houses of prayer, as well as the worst excesses of "ethnic cleansing" and the establishment of large prison camps, can be attributed to such groups.

Once world public opinion took note, the siege of Sarajevo, which was to last two years, stirred up much human sympathy and concern. Day after day, night after night, Serbian artillery and sniper fire rained down upon the Bosnian capital, which was often blockaded for weeks with food and fuel running low while international negotiators desperately sought to negotiate "armistices". Throughout, images of the endless battle were transmitted around the world by courageous television crews. One-sided as they may have been, it was these pictures that turned international public opinion against the Serbs.

Finally, the international community decided on limited military intervention, and the UN sent lightly armed international forces (IFOR) to Bosnia to keep the warring parties at a distance. Between April and July 1995, NATO bombed some Bosnian Serb positions, though with little effect. The Bosnian Serbs under General Mladic brazenly defied the peace-keeping troops and on 11 and 25 July captured the Muslim cities of Srebrenica and Zepas, which had been declared UN-protected areas. At Srebrenica, the local IFOR refused to dissuade the attackers and did not protest when the Serbs sent as many as 12,000 Muslim men to their execution.

Considering that the European Union had exhausted its possibilities, the United States decided that NATO should intervene massively. In August 1995, after the Croats cleared the Serbs out of the Krajina and together with the Muslims broke the siege of Bihar, recuperating much lost ground, and the Serb stronghold of Banja Luka was about to fall, US mediator Richard Holbrooke took up negotiations. Only then did the fighting slow down. The Serb-held share of Bosnian territory had been reduced to 49 percent and that of the Muslims and Croats to 51 percent — exactly the proportions proposed at the beginning of the conflict — but at a cost of over 200,000 deaths, a million wounded, two million refugees and the deliberate destruction of hundreds of villages, towns, farmsteads, churches, mosques, historic sites and public utilities.

Relatively little has been reported about the enormous ecological damage caused by the Bosnian war. The destruction of the Sisak oil refinery by the Serbian dominated Yugoslav army was a major environmental disaster. Petroleum products soaked into the ground and ended in the Sava river, together with considerable amounts of other chemicals. Chemical industries in Bosnia came under repeated Serb attack, releasing dangerous elements from chlorine storage tanks. Dams were destroyed in both Croatia and Bosnia. At one moment it was even feared that the Yugoslav army would shell the nuclear power plant at Krsko during its campaign against Slovenia. Radioactive material was lost and dispersed, mainly from hospitals. The Yugoslav army also buried dangerous chemicals in the ground. The war damaged parks, virgin forests, vegetation and wildlife reserves. [12]

A peace betrayed

Although the situation is still in flux as this is written, some remarks about recent events may be in order. In the wake of the failure of Europe and the UN to enforce a solution, the armistice negotiations in December 1995 in Dayton, Ohio, were almost entirely dominated by the United States. "Free and fair" elections were agreed upon for 14 September 1996, to be supervised by the Organization for Security and Cooperation in Europe (OSCE). A unified and democratic government was to be installed. Every Bosnian, returning refugees included, would be allowed to live wherever he or she wished. The results of the September vote were as expected: Izetbegovic, the Muslim leader, received 82.2 percent of the votes of the "Muslim" territory; 78.8 percent of the inhabitants of the self-designated Republika Bosna Srspka voted for ultranationalist Momcilo Krajisnik; and 88.3 percent of the Croats voted for their nationalist leader Kreimir Zubac. Izetbegovic became *primus inter pares*.

As time has passed, it has become clear that none of the stipulations of the Dayton agreement is likely to be fulfilled. Instead, three Bosnian republics seem to be emerging, each with its own army, police force, currency, passport and — most absurd — language. The former Serbo-Croat is giving way to Serbian, Croatian and "Bosnian". No one is allowed to cross from one sub-region to another without a visa — and even then only at the risk of his or her life. In none of the three mini-states is there a free press or other democratic institutions. The police of each area has that part of Bosnia firmly in its grip. It remains to be seen whether Bosnia can overcome this division, heal its terrible wounds and grow together again.

This situation, made possible by Western complicity, amounts to a betrayal of those Bosnians who had wanted to keep their country one. It is a breach of trust which reflects not only Western fatigue over Bosnia but also US political considerations in the light of the 1996 elections. An added difficulty has been the unclear role played by Russia, which has often helped to stiffen the resistance of Serbian President Milosevic to Western demands. Serbians in general have tended to portray themselves as the most victimized nation in Europe, which their leaders seem to interpret as giving them the right to make exaggerated demands of their neighbours. This view is generally supported by the Serbian Orthodox Church, even though it formally deplores violence.

The city of Mostar in Herzegovina, where the bitter division is between Croats and Muslims, illustrates that the Bosnian conflict is unlikely to vanish tomorrow. It might have been more reasonable to place Bosnia under outright temporary international occupation and administration, in order to help calm things down, and after due time proceed with setting up a new state. Germany for instance had to wait for three years after the end of the second world war before being allowed — under strict supervision — to organize its federal republic.

The International War Crimes Tribunal in The Hague could offer a means towards reconciliation. On the basis of the 1949 UN genocide convention, the Security Council has empowered it to indict and try individuals accused of war crimes or crimes against humanity; and the tribunal has indicted war criminals from all three ethnic communities. The most prominent are Radovan Karadzic and Ratko Mladic, for whom international arrest warrants have been issued. They have taken refuge within the confines of the non-recognized Republika Bosna Srpska. But again, international cynicism is evident: neither IFOR nor NATO forces has orders to arrest the two, even though the tribunal which has indicted them is a UN institution. The Western governments say they want to avoid unnecessary complications which could endanger the peace process. Nor is Milosevic eager to see the two brought into court, perhaps fearful that they will identify him as the true initiator of the Bosnian war.

The Dayton promises have effectively been jettisoned. NATO was concerned "only with the way out". [13] On the other hand, some have seen in the persistent demonstrations against Milosevic in Belgrade at the end of 1996 and the beginning of 1997 a sign of hope that a spirit of peace and tolerance may develop among younger Serbs.

Disentangling religion from ethnic violence

The voices of the churches and religious communities in the former Yugoslavia have seemed weak and often unconvincing, drowned out by the strident violence of their communities. It is true that outsiders often fail to understand the dilemma of religious leaders whose churches and mosques have faithfully accompanied their communities throughout centuries of oppression and violence. Had it not been for these religious structures, the three communities might have vanished. But the identification (the Orthodox use the term *symphonia*) of religion and people has been such that the churches and mosques have rarely taken a critical stance, even when the disastrous and inhuman consequences of the political decisions of their ethnic communities were clear. However, it could hardly be claimed that the churches of the former Yugoslavia are unique in this respect.

Under the leadership of the Conference of European Churches (CEC), representatives of churches and Islamic communities met in July 1995 to seek some common bases of thought and action for "upholding international laws and conventions" and building up new and responsible forms of community in the future:

In order to build a culture of dialogue and cooperation in place of a culture of violence and hatred, certain deliberate steps should be taken:

1. Humanitarian aid should never be obstructed.
2. People should be helped to help themselves and their neighbours.
3. Propaganda should be counteracted by fair and constructive media.
4. Education should promote tolerance and truthfulness, providing not only an understanding of the past and the present but also a capacity to envision and plan for a common future. [14]

Participants in a more recent encounter, organized by CEC and the theological faculty of the Serbian Orthodox Church, reported that not all members of ethnic communities were filled with hatred. There have also been acts of courage:

Two Serbian boys, forced to flee from their family home in the Krajina, left in their carefully cleaned room their belongings and a letter welcoming the refugees who would soon take their place. A Croat believer in Bosnia risked his life by defending and sheltering his Muslim neighbours. Overcoming distrust, Muslim women in Serbia agreed to work with Christian women in struggling for social justice. [15]

Paul Mojzes, a US theologian of Bosnian background, summarizes the problem succinctly:

This was a religious war, fought by non-religious people, in which all denominations greatly contributed to tension and misunderstanding. We are now left with a series of tiny states, all hating and doing their best to undermine each other.

Mojzes suggests that Bosnia's earlier tradition of tolerance was based only on courtesy, and that the pressing need now is to take this to a deeper level by creating real knowledge and understanding of other religious traditions. In the midst of the ruins of Sarajevo University, Mojzes is assisting Orthodox, Roman Catholic, Muslim and Jewish leaders in creating a department of inter-religious dialogue. [16]

NOTES

[1] Erich Weingärtner and Elizabeth Salter, eds, *The Tragedy of Bosnia: Confronting the New World Disorder*, Geneva, WCC Commission of the Churches on International Affairs, 1994, p.33.
[2] *Ibid.*, pp.xxi-xxii.
[3] Quoted by Cvieto Job in "Yugoslavia's Ethnic Furies", *Foreign Policy* (Washington), no. 92, Fall 1993, p.53.
[4] Noel Malcolm, *Bosnia: A Short History*, New York, New York UP, 1994, pp.27-42, 57f.
[5] *Ibid.*, p.217.
[6] *Ibid.*, pp.140f.
[7] Michel Chossudovsky, "La Bosnie sous l'administration occidentale", *Le Monde diplomatique*, Apr. 1996, p.12.
[8] "Befehl von oben", *Der Spiegel* (Hamburg), no. 28, 8 July 1996, p.118.
[9] Malcolm, *op. cit.*, p.252. On research by Alternativna Informativna Mreza (a network of 70 journalists from all parts of the former Yugoslavia) into the use of history as an instrument for building enemy images, see "Krieg der Bücher: Was die Kinder im ehemaligen Jugoslawien in der Geschichtsstunde lernen", *Die Weltwoche*, no. 25, 22 June 1995, pp.53-57.
[10] Malcolm, *op. cit.*, p.242.
[11] In Weingärtner and Salter, *op. cit.*, p.25.

[12] *Ibid.*

[13] William Pfaff, "War Crimes Panel Could Set a Crucial Precedent", *International Herald Tribune* (Paris), 26 July 1996, p.8.

[14] *Conference of European Churches' Bulletin*, no. 95-02, 12 July 1995.

[15] *Conference of European Churches' Monitor*, no. 15, June 1996, p.6.

[16] Cf. Jonathan Luxmoore, "Sarajevo University to be Home for Interfaith Study", *Ecumenical News International Bulletin* (Geneva), no. 9, 14 May 1996, p.14.

9
Latin America

This chapter will explore the issue of ethnicity in an entire region rather than a single country. Ethnicity in Latin America,[1] the vast region between the Rio Grande and Tierra del Fuego, involves the complicated patchwork of peoples and races created by the sudden and brutal European invasion beginning with the voyage of Christopher Columbus in 1492, a conquest that led to mass extermination and the theft of land and mineral resources on an unprecedented scale.

At the core of the destroyed Indian civilizations were empires reaching from the highlands of Mexico to the South American Altiplano, represented by the largely feudal Aztec, Maya and Inca cultures, class societies with a high degree of political and economic development, which dominated a vast series of subjected peoples. They were surrounded by a number of agricultural, hunting and fishing populations in a delicate fabric of socio-political arrangements, cultures, languages, religions. These peoples often competed with each other and sometimes fought each other. The lack of political cohesion made it relatively easy for the European invaders to conquer the region.

Genocide in the beginning

Not until several years after Columbus landed in the Caribbean did the Spanish monarchy understand that he had not reached the coasts of India but a new continent and grasp the significance of this discovery. With Hispaniola (today Haiti and the Dominican Republic) and Cuba serving as a base, Vasco Nuñez de Balboa in 1509 explored the isthmus of Panama, crossed it and discovered the Pacific Ocean. In 1524 Hernan Cortés effected his monumental conquest of Mexico with a mere handful of men. Shortly thereafter, in 1533, Francisco Pizarro conquered the even larger Inca empire of Peru. By 1536 the Spanish reached what is today the Paraguayan Chaco. Between 1536 and 1538 they marched across the highlands of present-day Venezuela and Colombia. By 1541 they reached Chile. Finally, in 1549, the Portuguese (who were in fact more interested by Africa and India) landed in Brazil and established a few settlements, out of which they built up a gigantic country, almost by default.

The indigenous peoples put up a ferocious resistance once they overcame their shock at the fall of the great empires. The wars against the Caribs, the Pampa Indians, the Araucanians (Mapuche), the Pueblos, the Yaquis and the Apaches lasted for centuries, and repeated uprisings have continued down to our own times. These Indians became superb fighters on horseback and learned the use of firearms.

The *Conquista* was a genocide without which Latin America's subsequent development cannot be understood. The killing took many forms. First there were those who died in battle. The Indians, only on foot and armed with spears and bows and arrows, were no match for the Europeans on horseback with their firearms, artillery and muskets. Those not killed outright were virtually condemned to death from bleeding, infections and lack of medical care if hit by a projectile or cut by a sabre. Far worse were the torture and forced labour inflicted on men in the fields and in the mines and the forced labour and sexual abuse of women, which also resulted in high infant mortality and the destruction of families. Moreover, the Indians had no immunity to many European diseases; and some lowland Indians died because missionaries compelled them to cover up their "sinful flesh" although the warm climate in their regions was not suitable for wearing clothing. [2]

The conquest was also a cultural and religious genocide. The Spanish brutally wiped out the educated classes of the Aztecs, the Mayas and the Incas, the nobility and the priests, destroying temples, palaces and works of art in an effort to eliminate the conquered peoples' historical memory. The cultural shock of the conquest, the social disruption, the loss of land and the sight of multiple deaths all weakened the will of the survivors.

According to Latin American historian Enrique Dussel, the highlands of central Mexico, the heart of the former Aztec empire, had an Indian population of over 11 million in 1532. By 1568 this had shrunk to 2.2 million, by 1580 to 1.6 million and by 1608 to 862,000. The population of the two coastal regions of central Mexico was reduced from nearly 17 million in 1532 to slightly over one million in 1608, again with the largest losses occurring between 1532 and 1568. [3] More recent estimates have suggested that central Mexico originally had a population as high as 25 million, and that what is today called Latin America probably had as many as 100 million Indian inhabitants, a figure which dropped to a mere 10-12 million by 1570 and just over 9 million by 1650. [4] At no other time in recorded history prior to the 20th century had a comparable loss of 90 million humans ever taken place. It exceeds the number of the battle dead of the two world wars of the 20th century *combined*. Entire tribes vanished. Although a remnant of "pure" Indian substance has survived against all odds until today and is numerically even increasing, the lack of top level political and religious leadership remained a fatal handicap.

There was obviously no cultural, religious and theological dialogue between the Iberian Catholic missionaries and Indian priests, such as Matteo Ricci succeeded in establishing in China in the 16th century. Dussel describes the death of the Amerindian way of life as follows:

> The vision of the Hispanic world placed itself in the key positions at the head of the new American civilization, forming the political and cultural elite which no other organized group could confront. Indian civilization — as a living and organic system, capable of evolution — disappeared. The Indian race turned into a social class which the Spaniard did not allow to enter the ruling elite. This is the tragic but real fact — perhaps inevitable: all perception of pre-Hispanic existence was smashed. [5]

It is true that missionary orders such as the Dominicans and the Jesuits did make repeated efforts to stop the enslavement and murder of the Indians, if only to preserve a sufficient number of potential converts. The Dominican friar Bartolomé de Las Casas (1474-1566) was one of the earliest defenders of the Indians. Having witnessed atrocities as a chaplain accompanying explorers, he carried his protest against Indian slavery to Emperor Charles V in 1542, who initiated more humane colonial legislation. But in trying to implement these reforms as bishop of Chiapas, in Mexico, Las Casas was unable to overcome the resistance of the local colonists. Another significant effort to save the Indians from exploitation and destruction was the *reducciones* (reservations) which the Jesuits began among the Guaranis in Paraguay in 1609. They collected the Indians into settlements, where they taught them agriculture, trades and the rudiments of self-defence. A kind of Jesuit "state" came into existence between 1631 and 1767, which built up considerable economic wealth. Despite the benevolent but paternalistic autocracy of the Jesuits, these *reducciones* might have evolved into a viable and self-governing state, had it not been for attacks on them by envious Spanish colonists and roving Portuguese adventurers, as well as church and court intrigues in Madrid and Lisbon. By the time Pope Clement XIV dissolved the Jesuit order in 1773, this hopeful initiative in Paraguay had already been destroyed. [6]

Colonial exploitation of the Indians

For the descendants of the indigenous peoples of Latin America, as of the slaves brought there from Africa (as we shall see in the next section), "colonial exploitation" describes not only the period of formal Iberian colonization from 1492 until 1810, when the Latin American wars for independence were fought, but continues to this day in the form of prejudice and social repression. Perhaps the most recent reminders of this are the 36-year-long Guatemalan "civil war", during which security forces and landowners killed approximately 140,000 Indians who were trying to defend their lands, and the uprising in Chiapas in 1994.

Having destroyed the Aztec and Inca empires, the Spanish put millions of Indians to work in the gold mines of Mexico, Colombia, Ecuador, Peru and Alto Peru (Bolivia). Separated from their homes and families, none of them long survived the cruel conditions underground. The Portuguese discovered equally rich deposits of gold and precious stones in Brazil's Minas Gerais, where they put Indians and African slaves to work. Once the gold deposits were exhausted, it was the turn of silver, symbolized by the incomparable Cerro Rico (Rich Hill) in Alto Peru, at whose foot the city of Villa Real de Potosi was founded. Its population of 160,000 in 1650 exceeded that of any European city. During the first decades of its operation, four out of five miners died within a year of beginning work. Six thousand African slaves died shortly after their arrival, because they could not stand the altitude and the cold of Potosi. [7] Even today, the average life span of a Potosi miner is said to be only 31 years. Between 1503 and 1660, 185,000 kg of gold and a million kg of silver were sent to Spain — three times the reserves of these precious metals available in Europe in 1492. [8]

The rapid depletion of the mines was followed by the establishment of export-oriented monocultures — sugar, cocoa, tea and coffee, cotton, tobacco and rice — as well as production of meat and leather goods. All this was possible only through slave labour. With the military decline of Spain and Portugal, French, Dutch and above all British commercial interests gained control of the trade in these products. Dussel suggests that between 1561 and 1630 the monetary value of the exchange was consistently four to one in favour of Europe; in other words, Europe's world power was built up on the backs of the conquered Indians and of African slaves. [9]

Ordinary people in Spain and Portugal benefitted little from this unprecedented wealth, which aristocrats squandered in lavish life-styles and governments spent on endless wars. When fortunes shifted north, France, the Netherlands and Britain began to build up their colonial empires, develop their economies, advance their scientific knowledge and finance other wars. Mercantile corporations set up in Amsterdam, Liverpool and London became the backbones of the colonial system and the precursors of today's transnational corporations. The division of the world into a small group of the rich (mostly white and Northern) and a vast underclass (mostly non-white and Southern) was starting to open up. This new worldwide imperial system was racist to the core.

The shift from precious metals to agricultural products points to an even more serious problem. In order to produce agricultural goods the European invaders or their descendants took away immense land surfaces from the Indian populations throughout the Americas. During the 19th century, the steamship and cold storage made it possible to move hitherto undreamed-of quantities of farm products, especially grain, beef and cotton. This required the large-scale transfer of European populations to southern Brazil, Uruguay and Argentina, a movement parallelled by the European occupation of the even vaster North American plains. But the great agricultural wealth created by European technology and organizational skill depended on land taken from someone else; and the land-grabbing and European immigration overpowered the native populations of these regions, who were removed or wiped out. Similar land thefts took place in South Africa, Australia and New Zealand at the expense of indigenous peoples.

But an even more subtle exploitation was involved: the acquisition by Europeans of new food products and agricultural techniques from the Indians. Most important were maize (corn) and beans from Mexico and potatoes from Peru. Europeans soon learned that while one hectare of their traditional grain would yield 4.2 million calories, the same surface in potatoes produced 7.5 million calories, without requiring the extensive milling and processing necessary to produce a loaf of bread. Originating in the cool high Andes, the potato plant could be easily adapted to the climates of northern and eastern Europe.

Thus thanks to the (seldom if ever acknowledged) help of the Amerindians, the Europeans for the first time in their history no longer suffered famine. Their health improved. Better food and better health was another important factor in gaining the upper hand over what became known as "underdeveloped" peoples. Between 1650 and 1950 Europe's population (Russia included) increased from just over 100 million to 600 million, enabling European countries to build up the mass armies which fought two murderous world wars in this century. During the same period, Africa's and Latin America's population barely increased. The peoples who so generously "gave" their land and their technical knowledge to their conquerors went hungry. [10]

The Indians nevertheless kept resisting the invaders by rearguard battles and revolts against continuing incursions on their land. A pattern developed: (1) whites occupied formerly Indian land; (2) the Indians counter-attacked, killing a few colonists; (3) to ward off the Indian "threat", the settlers called on the authorities, (4) who initiated a campaign of "revenge", aided by the colonists; (5) the Indians were defeated, and usually massacred; (6) the survivors retreated into more remote and less fertile areas, (7) which were sometimes formally granted to them in the form of "reservations"; (8) but the white settlers advanced again, disregarding the boundaries of the reservations; and (9) the above sequence was repeated. A similar pattern of expropriation and extinction continues today, now often initiated by oil, mining or forestry companies or large-scale cattle ranchers. Occasionally, the Indians became so frustrated that they launched major attacks on the invaders.

One of the most remarkable uprisings was led in the highlands of Peru in the late 18th century by José Gabriel Condorcanqui, who claimed to be a descendant of the Incas and called himself Tupac Amaru II after an Inca noble who had fought against the Spanish during the 16th century. When he was defeated in 1783, the Spanish authorities and local colonists massacred his followers. The struggle for survival of the Yaquis, Navajos, Pueblos and Apaches on both sides of the border between Mexico and the USA towards the end of the 19th century has become part of cinematic legend, thus obscuring the desperation behind these uprisings and ignoring the horrible massacres that often followed the defeat of the Indians.

The most serious Indian attempts to regain control over their destiny were the three major revolutions in Mexico's troubled history: the War of Independence (1810-23), the era of Benito Juarez (1859-72) and the Mexican Revolution (1910-17). Though other factors were also involved, the precarious social situation of the Indians and the return of common lands (*ejidos*) to the Indian communities played a key role in each. After initial successes, the Indians were out-manoeuvred by an ever-shifting combination of powerful enemies consisting of landowners, the military, *caudillos*, the church hierarchy, liberal business interests and large corporations, always with the wary eye of the United States in the background.

To be sure, the USA was not always content with merely observing Mexico; from time to time it intervened directly. In 1836 Mexico lost Texas to North American colonists, and the region was admitted as a new state in 1845. This led to a war between Mexico and the United States (1846-48), at the end of which Mexico was compelled to cede half of its territory. The new national border now ran from the Rio Grande to the Pacific coast of California. This US annexation of northern Mexico heralded a further and very severe loss of Indian lands. Other interventions in Mexico's internal affairs included a military campaign in 1915 during the Mexican Revolution.

Indians also played an important role in the history of modern Paraguay, probably as a result of the never-forgotten influence of the earlier Jesuit "state". Guarani remains the nation's second official tongue to this day. For centuries Paraguay was in danger of being absorbed by its powerful neighbours, especially Brazil, and has therefore developed a strong nationalist spirit, not least out of

Guarani resentment against the many incursions by Brazilian and Argentine colonists. In the 1860s, Paraguayan dictator Francisco Solano López, over-estimating the strength of his well-trained army, attempted to become the arbiter of Brazilian-Argentine rivalries, but his heavy-handed methods led to the war of the Triple Alliance (Brazil, Argentina and Uruguay) against Paraguay (1865-70), in which he himself was killed. Paraguay lost four-fifths of its population in this war, one of the bloodiest in the modern history of Latin America. Of 1.3 million people at the beginning of the war, fewer than 250,000 remained — only 29,000 of them men. Nearly all of the dead were Guarani. From 1932 to 1935 Paraguay fought the so-called Chaco war against Bolivia, instigated by rival oil firms. Although Paraguay won the war, both countries were left economically exhausted. Again, most of the fighting men on both sides had been Indians.

In general, however, the Indians did not easily resort to armed struggle. They realized that violence on their part always gave the colonizers or white ruling class a pretext for further dispossession and genocide. Gonzalo Castillo Cardenas from Colombia speaks of three methods of Indian self-defence:

(1) geographical flight to the periphery, (2) psychological flight to the interior world of the mind, shutting the gates of the soul against the invader from the outer world, and finally (3) the cultivation of profound indifference to everything that happened among the whites. The combination of these three attitudes, which someone once called "passivity without heroics", is what ultimately enabled them to survive. [11]

By and large the attitude of racial superiority which the Iberian colonists left among their descendants in Latin America has been shared by later European immigrants. The relative ease of the conquest made Europeans believe that they were beings of a higher order, divinely mandated to spread their version of civilization, by the sword and the cross and by their "efficiency" and "enlighten-ment". Harmony required integrating the Indians into Iberian civilization, teaching them Spanish or Portuguese, getting them to adopt the history of the conquerors, according to which Latin America's history began in 1492. Well into the second half of the 20th century the day of Columbus's landfall, 12 October, was celebrated as *el dia de la raza*, the day of the (Iberian) race. German theologian Hans-Jürgen Prien, who has spent many years in Central America, describes white Latin American attitudes as follows:

Human rights are accorded only if the person in question is regarded as a fully human being. The first step in the Indian struggle for human rights therefore consists in obtaining recognition as a fully human being. But until today this recognition has not yet been granted, either in the mentality of the average Latin American or in that of the legislators. Both consider Indians as underage children. [12]

Ana Maria, one of the top *comandantes* of the Chiapas uprising of 1994, has some bitter words about the prejudice which has led her and her fellow Indians into open rebellion:

Down there, on the haciendas, we did not exist. Our lives had less value than the machines and the animals. We were like blocks of stones, like plants by the roadside. Without language. Without name. Without face. Without a tomorrow. For the "neo-liberal" power holders — those of today — we didn't count. We didn't produce, we didn't buy, we didn't sell anything, we were simply a cipher in the great capitalist system. [13]

Brazil's formally democratic government treats the existence of Indian tribes in Amazonia as an obstacle to the country's development. While it is officially the task of the National Indian Foundation FUNAI, which is attached to the ministry of the interior, to protect the Indians, a local observer say its real goal is not "the independence and self-determination of the Indian nations" but a "technocratic vision" which "reduces the pluralistic culture of the various ethnic groups into a 'generic Indianism' in a clear attempt to integrate them into the market economy". [14]

The complete lack of any inter-religious or inter-cultural dialogue such as Ricci attempted in China is not surprising given the Spanish and Portuguese mentality at the time of the *Conquista*. During the same year that Columbus set sail, Granada, the last Arab stronghold in Spain, fell to the armies of their "Catholic Majesties" Ferdinand and Isabella. The long struggle against Moors and Jews, backed up by the Inquisition, had produced a type of Iberian messianism which was incapable of conceiving any peaceful co-existence with another civilization and a different faith. And the superior military technology of the Iberian conquerors meant that they did not have to come to terms with the culture and religion of their American enemies.

Accordingly, the representatives of the Catholic Church were as ruthless as the soldiers under whose protection they arrived. Claiming a universal faith, they made no attempt to comprehend the religion of the Indians nor the rationale of their cultic acts. Their art and science were condemned as works of the devil. The Indians were thereby deprived of their humanity — all the more since they believed that their gods had lost a cosmic war against the gods of the Christians. A psychology developed among conquerors and conquered alike that the Indians were the foreigners on a continent which by right belonged to the newcomers.

From the perspective of the Indians, the colonial state and the Christian church formed one brutal religious-secular system, which was a curious extension of the mediaeval *corpus christianum* long after the Middle Ages had given way to the mercantile era. The Council of the Indies, composed of both clergy and laity, decided on the secular and spiritual affairs of Spanish America. This arrangement was based on the *patronato*, the patronate, through which the Spanish and Portuguese monarchy assumed papal prerogatives in establishing bishoprics, supervising missionary orders and controlling church revenues. Already in 1496, in the Treaty of Tordesillas, Pope Alexander IV divided the newly discovered regions between Portugal and Spain and granted patronates to the Iberian kingdoms. Thus the king became the virtual head of the colonial church. When the *criollo* republics of the white colonists became independent in the wake of Napoleon's occupation of the Iberian peninsula in the early 19th century, a three-sided power struggle emerged between the Spanish monarchy, which tried to retain control over the *patronato*, the new republican governments, which as heirs of the monarchy wanted to assume this privilege, and the papacy, which wanted to abolish the *patronato* and establish Roman predominance over the church in Latin

America. This long struggle weakened the position of Latin American Catholicism. With the advent of political liberalism during the middle of the 19th century, Protestantism gained a foothold, first through immigrants from northern Europe, then by way of missionaries from the United States, further eroding traditional Latin American Catholicism.

Colonial exploitation of the African slaves

The second dimension of colonial exploitation, with equally serious consequences down to the present, was slavery. As the Indian population died off or proved "unsuitable" for forced agricultural labour, the colonial enterprise risked foundering. Since it was unthinkable that Europeans would expose themselves to the rigours of hard work under the tropical sun, the solution was sought in Africa.

Slavery and serfdom, largely banished from Europe by the end of the Middle Ages, gained new life with the colonization of the Americas. Not since antiquity, if then, were so many human beings subjected to such degradation — tolerated by the churches and promoted by Christian monarchs and their officials. Economic factors proved more decisive than religious ethics, which had slowly evolved in opposition to the idea of the ownership of human beings. Ironically, it was Bartolomé de Las Casas who suggested — in his concern to protect the Indians — that slaves from Africa might be physically more suited for the labour required (an idea of which he later repented, when he saw the masses of slaves arriving and realized the subhuman treatment to which they were subjected).

The resurgence of slavery had been underway for several decades before the establishment of the American colonies. When Prince Henry the Navigator and other Portuguese explorers sailed down the west coast of Africa in 1442 to seek a passage to India, they noticed that domestic slavery was practised throughout the large savannah and forest kingdoms of western Africa. Local chieftains and Arab traders were willing to capture young men and women, including their own family members, and sell them to the passing Europeans. Mandinkas and Mandingos, the Europeans were told, were especially commendable, since they were believed docile. Later, when the Portuguese and Spanish realized their need of vast labour forces, they dispatched their fleets to West Africa once again — followed by French, Dutch and British colonial merchants.

Most slaves were taken from regions near the west African coast from the Cape Verde Islands at the westernmost tip of Africa to Angola. The principal slave coast ran from Ivory Coast to the Bay of Biafra, the most heavily populated region of West Africa. Here the European powers established many slave forts, vast concentration camps into which the captured slaves were driven to await the voyage to the Americas.

A highly profitable three-way trade, favoured by the prevailing winds on the Atlantic, grew up along the "Black Triangle" between European ports, West Africa and the Americas. On the first leg, European ships carried manufactured goods and especially weapons to West Africa, where the ships were unloaded and filled with slaves for the "middle passage" to the Americas. On the third leg of the journey the ships transported sugar, rum and later cotton from the American mainland or Caribbean ports back to Europe. This threefold movement took about one year.

The largest number of slaves were sent to the Caribbean islands to work in the sugar cane fields. Another substantial group was shipped to Brazil. Others were transported to the Spanish American mainland and the French and British colonies in North America. There was also a subsidiary slave traffic from the Caribbean to the North American mainland.

Recent research in the Caribbean suggests that the slave traffic began slowly, first to Europe, then to the Spanish colonies and Brazil. Between 1451 and 1600, 200,000 people were transported from west Africa. Then it increased rapidly. From 1601 to 1700 three million slaves were carried across the ocean, mainly to Brazil and to Spanish America. Between 1701 and 1810 six million more were shipped, principally to the newly established British and French colonies in the Caribbean and again to Brazil, though Spanish America and North America also received a considerable number. The years from 1811 to 1870, when the slave trade and slavery were progressively abolished, saw another three million transported, mainly to Brazil and Cuba. [15]

Estimates of the total number of Africans transported into slavery range from twelve to fifteen to twenty million. In any case, the number arriving in the Americas and the Caribbean does not reflect the full extent of the tragedy. Total losses due to the slave trade are estimated by some at forty million. The forced marches from the interior of Africa to the slave forts killed perhaps a third of those captured. Of those placed on board ship, 30 to 40 percent are reported to have died. Furthermore, in the process of disembarking on American shores some slaves jumped into the water and drowned. Others were killed when they tried to escape on land. The average life-span of slaves after landing seems to have been only six to eight years. They were literally worked to death, although their treatment improved somewhat as the price of slaves increased. [16] Conditions seem to have been especially brutal in Brazil. Although ten times as many slaves were shipped there as to British North America, the black population of Brazil in 1860 was only half that of North America. [17] Other factors contributing to this particular form of genocide were the absence of African women, demoralization due to homesickness and lack of freedom, and the mixing together of different tribes, nations, cultures and languages, which prevented effective communication.

Forcible abduction and the inhuman working and living conditions never completely subdued the African slaves. They almost always expressed their resentment in one form or another and some were driven to passive resistance and open revolt. Passive resistance could take the form of refusal to work, general inefficiency and deliberate laziness, theft, satire at the expense of the slave owner, running away and suicide. [18] Dancing, singing and music, inspired by new and creative forms of religious syncretism, were means of overcoming sadness and expressing the hope for freedom. Samba, jazz and spirituals are forms of religious expression which originated in Africa and were reshaped during slavery, and have been recognized in the 20th century as an authentic part of world culture.

In the eyes of the white owners, one of the most troublesome forms of resistance was the flight of slaves to inaccessible forest or mountain regions, where they formed the so-called "maroon" communities. These communities, whose name is derived from the Spanish *cimarron*, a term for domestic cattle that had taken to the wild in the hills of Hispaniola, often defended themselves desperately against military expeditions sent out by the planters and the colonial authorities. Most large plantation areas from Argentina to British North America were surrounded by entire archipelagos of such communities:

> Individual fugitives banding together to create independent communities of their own... struck directly at the foundations of the plantation system, presenting military and economic threats that often taxed the colonists to their very limits. In a remarkable number of cases... the whites were forced to bring themselves to sue their former slaves for peace... Such treaties — which we know from Brazil, Colombia, Cuba, Ecuador, Hispaniola, Jamaica, Mexico and Surinam — offered maroon communities their freedom, recognized their territorial integrity and made provision for meeting their economic needs, demanding in return to end all hostilities toward the plantations, to return all future runaways and, often, to aid the whites in hunting them down ... Of course, many maroon communities never reached this stage, being crushed by massive force of arms... Nevertheless, new maroon communities seemed to appear almost as quickly as the old ones were exterminated, and they remained the "chronic plague", the "gangrene", of many plantation societies right up to final emancipation. [19]

On other occasions, African slaves killed their masters outright, often by poisoning them. [20] The most fearful collective murder of white plantation owners took place in 1804 in the French Caribbean colony of Saint-Domingue (former Hispaniola), after Jean-Jacques Dessalines had declared the country's independence and renamed the island by its ancient Indian name Haiti. The problem was that the mixed-race sons of French planters and slaves had assumed power and wealth at the expense of the black population, which remained economically deprived. This ethnic tension turned out to be a constant source of friction and political upheaval. Thus the relative ease in which the slave-owners lived was accompanied by a constant fear of dangerous acts and revolts.

The Roman Catholic Church was ambivalent towards slavery. There were outright papal condemnations of the slave trade in 1462, 1537, 1639, 1741 and 1839 — about once each century. [21] But having strongly condemned the enslavement of the Indians, the papacy was surprisingly tolerant of the colonists' economic argument that without African slavery the American possessions would be worth next to nothing. The church nevertheless pushed for legislation concerning baptism of slaves, recognition of marriage between them and non-separation of family members. Illegal unions between landowners and female slaves were frequently censured, but these condemnations were little heeded, probably because so many priests kept concubines.

Even the Jesuits owned several thousand slaves on their estates in various countries, although they tried to treat them more decently than the colonists did theirs. In their pastoral work in colonial America, the Jesuits attempted to inculcate a spirit of peace into the slaves, in order to render them more "useful" to their owners. Although some individual Spanish theologians rejected both African and Indian slavery outright, their voices were not heard. [22]

The situation was no different on the Protestant side. Zwingli's exceptional theological objection to slavery and the slave trade went unheeded. Indeed, the major share of slave shipping was firmly in Protestant hands: French Huguenots, Dutch, British and even Swedish. After the British and the French occupied several Caribbean islands, most of the estate owners were Anglican and Protestant, as were the slave-holding colonists in British North America.

The centuries-long drainage of their strongest and fittest people caused irreparable damage to the socio-economic structures and psyche of West Africa while placing in the Americas a humiliated, resentful and basically rejected population. For the countries most directly concerned, the unresolved heritage of slavery remains explosive; and the destructiveness of such a collective memory has been shown during our own era in Sudan (see chapter 3 above). At the same time, the positive cultural, religious and human contributions to these countries of the people of African descent has been and can be enormous if society at large is capable of opening itself up to cross-fertilization instead of sterile apartheid.

The disinherited

Despite the formal political independence of the *criollo* republics in the 19th century and modernization in the 20th century, there has been no fundamental break in the historical development of Latin America; and the colonial system remains intact. Indeed, it seems to be strengthening as Latin America is drawn into the global economic system. The issue can be formulated simply. Within Latin America ethnicity or race determines economic and political power. Wealth and power are basically concentrated in the hands of a few white families of European descent, who have the political system at their disposal and preserve their dominance with a well-developed internal security apparatus. This elite is linked with the global power centres in the North. The majority, who are non-white, are disinherited.

To be sure, there are local variations, in which persons of colour or non-Europeans play important roles. From time to time attempts are made to break into the system of white domination. And occasionally there are politicians of European descent who try to open up the rigid power systems of their own class. But these attempts are usually short-lived, because the basic ethnic power structure remains unusually strong.

But the disinherited today are no longer only Indians and Afro-Americans. Colonialism produced new ethnic populations through the forced mixing of races: the sexual violence of the European masters towards Indian and black women. The children born of a white-Indian relationship are called *mestizos* and those of a white-black relationship *mulattos*. Over the years, these originally pejorative and insulting terms have gained a certain measure of currency; and it is thus helpful to remember their derivation. In the eyes of the *criollo*, a *mestizo* is a half-breed, in whom the "purity" of the white "race" has virtually been lost; in other words, he or she is no longer quite a fully human being. The term *mulatto* comes from the Spanish *mulo*, mule, the cross between a donkey and a horse — again implying a diminished humanity.

Mestizos and *mulattos* no doubt make up the majority of Latin Americans today, although no reliable statistics exist, since many people try to conceal from the census-taker what is considered a "less desirable" ancestry. To a large extent, Latin American society could be classified as a three-layer society: The dominant white minority; a middle group of *mestizos* and *mulattos*; and the Indians and the blacks at the bottom. This does not mean that the *mestizos* and *mulattos* constitute a middle class in the European or North American sense; their poverty and lack of power put them much closer to the Indians and blacks, against whom they often nevertheless exert subtle forms of oppression. They, too, belong to the disinherited. Lacking recognition by the whites, they tend to overemphasize their white ancestry while refusing to identify themselves with the Indians or the Afro-Americans. Their feelings of insecurity are often exploited by rightist political parties. While the problem is evident, there has never been in Latin America the kind of open debate on the race question that has taken place in the United States; instead, the claim is often heard that Latin America has no racial barriers as compared with the North.

The presence of *mestizos* and *mulattos* in Latin America goes back to the Iberian conquest of Latin America. The *encomienda* system, by which the crown apportioned vast tracts of land to the colonists and their successors, implied that the Indians living on that land also became the property of the new masters. They were reduced either slaves or *peones*, landless day-labourers. The communal Indian *ejido* lands became privatized. This is how the *haciendas* (*fazendas* in Brazil) came into being. Even a legally free peon, who was allowed to work a small plot of land accorded to him by the landowner, had to pay for this right by giving one-third or even one-half of its produce to his master. So limited was his income that he was usually indebted to his master for life in order to buy seeds and other goods. Thus the Indians were in fact as disinherited as the slaves, who had been forcibly removed from Africa. The abolition of slavery meant little change, because those who were freed and their descendants had scarcely any economic means or skills to escape poverty, least of all to buy their own piece of property. Only rarely has an *ejido* been returned to an Indian community. The large landed estate has remained part of the system of social and political exploitation until today. As representatives from indigenous communities in both North and South America said in an ecumenical declaration in 1977:

> The main form taken by the physical domination is the expropriation of our land. This plundering began with the European invasion and has continued right up to the present time. Along with our land they also snatched our natural resources, the forests, the water, the minerals, the oil. What land has been left to us has been further divided, national and international frontiers have been drawn, our peoples have been isolated and divided, attempts have been made to sow conflict among us. [23]

Linked to this land theft and the system of landed estates was another obnoxious aspect of disinheritance — the sexual subjugation of Indian and African women to the *hacienda/fazenda* owner, on whom they depended for their livelihood. The European colonist could thus demonstrate the *machismo* on which his self-esteem depended, as well as sire new slaves. Moreover, in earlier years, the abuse of Indian and black women made up for the lack of white women in the Americas. Although sexual abuse of non-white women was socially acceptable, marriage to them was out of the question. While the Catholic Church objected to this disrespect for matrimony, its declarations carried little weight, since, as stated above, many priests themselves carried on liaisons with women of different colour.

Modern Latin American authors such as Gabriel García Márquez (Colombia) and Isabel Allende (Chile) have told how this practice, including rape, continues unabated to this day. The resentment such sexual exploitation elicits is illustrated by the story of Pancho Villa, a young Indian peon who wounded the son of his *hacienda* owner whom he discovered raping Villa's sister. Fleeing for his life, he became one of the leaders of the Mexican Revolution (1910-17).

As long as the *hacienda/fazenda* represented the central economic structure, most Latin Americans except the white patriarchal families (not counting tribally organized Indians) did not enjoy a stable family upbringing. The resulting lack of social stability, coupled with general poverty, is one of the serious problems of today's Latin America. The harshness of the patriarchal way of life was somewhat softened by the *compadrazgo* system, in which the landowner became the godfather of most children born on his estate, whether or not they were his own natural children. By means of favours, the *compadre* saw to it that his godchildren received a minimum of sustenance and protection, in return for unconditional loyalty. Much of Latin America's political and social system functions on the basis of such loyalties.

The ethnic picture became more complicated by the arrival of new immigrants beginning with the middle of the 19th century, but especially between 1890 and 1914. Several million white immigrants from the Mediterranean countries of Europe and Germany settled in southern Brazil, Uruguay and Argentina, becoming the majority in the River Plate area, though the large estates generally remained in the hands of the older *criollo* families of Spanish origin. They were followed around 1908 by the arrival of about 200,000 Japanese immigrants, most of whom settled in Brazil. In admitting European immigrants the Latin American governments hoped to benefit from their skills and technical knowledge, but also to enlarge what they saw as the narrow base of the white population. These industrious immigrants set themselves up as small farmers, estate administrators, tradesmen and craftsmen; and their descendants branched out into nearly every area of economic and political life. But many of them did not succeed in climbing the economic ladder, whether because their land was too poor to make a living by farming or because their income as factory workers or day-labourers was too low or because they simply found no jobs at all. Thus thousands of poor whites have joined the ranks of the rural or urban proletariat, sharing the poverty of the Indian peons or of the Afro-Americans.

In the Caribbean, white planters promoted another line of immigration to replace the freed slaves. Between 1835 and 1917 they arranged for the coming of indentured labourers. The planters advanced the money, and the immigrants were obliged to work on their estates for seven years or as long as they needed to repay their debts. After a first attempt of bringing indentured labour from Europe and North America had failed, workers were recruited from overcrowded countries in

Africa and Asia: 36,000 from Madeira, 36,000 from the former Slave Coast in West Africa, 150,000 from China and 500,000 from India. After the decline of the sugar plantations during the early 20th century, the Chinese and the Indians (from India) emerged as a new middle class, to the envy of the black majority. [24]

The modernization of a semi-feudal society: a time bomb?

While ethnic and racial distinctions in Latin America often run along horizontal rather than vertical lines, the divisions are no less real and conflictive and are sharpening as a result of the breakdown of the rural socio-economic system due to population growth, impoverishment of the soil, new farming techniques, falling commodity prices and the like. Sometimes — as happens in northeastern Brazil — farm labourers rebel and occupy land, only to be massacred by *fazendeiro* killers operating in conjunction with the police and the military. Or an Indian peon and his family walk away from an oppressive master and head for the big city. Or the estate is sold to a transnational corporation, whose administrators lack the patriarchal feeling of the former owner for "his" employees and hire professional thugs to keep the workers under control. Quite a different situation exists in Chiapas, where Mexican army units systematically criss-cross areas held by Zapatista rebels, even though "negotiations" are going on, impeding the Indians from planting and harvesting their corn and coffee. [25]

For most of the rural poor migration turns out to be a nightmare. Despite their shiny symbols of progress, abundance and modernity, the cities offer no escape from poverty and hunger. Instead of a better life, joblessness, epidemics, crime, environmental damage and despair await the newcomers. During the last four or five decades, ring after ring of zones of misery have grown up around the great Latin American capitals. Thus, "white" Buenos Aires is surrounded by suburban belts densely populated by thousands of rural Argentinians, Paraguayans and Chileans. By 1995 the Argentine capital had 11 million inhabitants, São Paulo and Rio de Janeiro in Brazil 16.4 million and 9.9 million respectively, Mexico City 15.6 million. By 2015, it is estimated, the population of Buenos Aires will have increased to 13 million, São Paulo to 20.8 million, Mexico City to 18.8 million. [26] As these cities are becoming hopelessly congested, the new migrants are heading towards smaller towns nearby or to provincial urban centres, where the nightmare is repeated.

These situations cry out for heavy investments in essential infrastructures: public transportation, utilities, health care and education. However, it is impossible to see how this can be done with government treasuries empty and foreign debts accumulating. Every Latin American government is under pressure from the World Bank and International Monetary Fund to reduce government spending, with predictable consequences: health hazards threaten life, children and young people remain illiterate and become unemployable. City planning is nearly impossible as speculation drives up the commercial value of properties beyond the range of public treasuries. As governments weaken, they succumb to lobbies and pressure groups, opening the way to corruption. Thus, despite all kinds of regulations, industrial smog and motor vehicle emissions have placed Mexico City, São Paulo and Santiago de Chile among the world's most polluted cities.

Again, the heaviest toll falls on the poor, who usually live near the great thoroughfares and in the shadow of industrial chimneys or next to polluted waterways and garbage dumps. Their often undernourished children suffer from asthma and lung infections. Not long ago, the Peruvian government had great difficulties ending a cholera epidemic which had sprung up in the slums of Lima. Nevertheless, the economic power of some of these megacities is stupendous. São Paulo alone has a greater economic production than all of Poland. [27] The rural poor know that enormous wealth is being created in these cities, which is why they keep coming. In effect, Latin America's megacities are the even more powerful heirs of the semi-feudal colonial estates.

The sudden explosion of these vast cities is obviously the result of five centuries of colonial and semi-colonial misdevelopment. Some of the more reflective political leaders know that something has to be done to tackle the root causes of the problem. This is perhaps why Guatemalan president Alvaro Arzu has made peace with the *comandantes* of the Indian guerrilla army, the *Unidad Revolucionaria Nacional Guatemalteca* (URNG), promising land reform and a reduction of the security forces. In December 1996 a treaty was signed in the presence of tens of thousands of Indians, who celebrated with dancing and music, as well as chiefs of state and diplomats from thirty countries. But the Indians, mindful of the 36 long years of fighting, which cost 150,000 lives and resulted in 50,000 "disappearances", know that the struggle for the land is just beginning. Rigoberta Menchu, who received the Nobel Prize for Peace for her courageous involvement in the human rights struggle of the indigenous people, insists that with peace justice must also come. A special court should be created, in which all survivors have the opportunity to lodge complaints against their torturers and human rights violations against the civilian population are punished. Above all, guarantees must be given that the military and the business community do not retaliate against former guerrillas who have laid down their arms and are in the process of organizing political parties.

Brazilian president Fernando Henrique Cardoso also knows that land reform has to be undertaken, but he is threatened from below by the social explosion of the hungry landless and from above by the powerful landowners allied with the neo-liberal economic forces, who want to preserve the old system. Elias Araujo of the *Movimento dos Campesinos Sêm Terra* (Movement of Landless Farmers) spells out the problem:

> The large landowners, many of whom possess each over 100,000 hectares, control the means of production, bank credits, the means of information and propaganda and many other kinds of resources. These landowners are at the heart of the neo-liberal project. It is clear that if we succeed in introducing a land reform, we shall give a strong blow to one of the pillars of that system. [28]

Religion: blockage and liberation

Religion has played a different role in ethnic conflicts in Latin America from the way it has functioned in the situations explored in previous chapters. There is no ethnic group of one religion fighting a group of another faith. Catholicism is the religion of the majority, with Protestantism becoming a strong minority. This has created tensions in some cases, but nowhere does the division between the two confessions follow ethnic lines. The issue which divides religious people in Latin America is one of ethical content rather than formal confession. The divisions run deeply *within* the two faiths.

During the time of the Spanish conquerors, it was believed that the Christian faith had to replace the "false religions" of the Indians or the African slaves. This attitude accompanied oppression. Today there is far greater comprehension of the folk religion of the Indians or of the *mestizos*, who combined Christian insights with elements from the pre-Columbian religions, or of the blacks, whose West African beliefs became intertwined on American soil with Christian ideas. This may be questioned from the point of view of formal Christian dogma, but these "syncretistic" religions have given comfort and meaning in a situation in which formal Christianity was the faith of the oppressor.

The issue is whether Christianity itself can overcome its own internal block-ages and help the peoples of Latin America to take decisive steps to free themselves from five centuries of internal and external subjection. This is a fundamentally spiritual process with great social, economic and political conse-quences. Before the Second Vatican Council (1962-65) restlessness had been growing in Latin America over the state of the church and social conditions. This became acute in 1959, when the Cuban Revolution touched off a broad debate on whether the cold war ideology of the US and other rich countries adequately explained the causes of the revolution, or whether the real reason was not poverty and neo-colonialism. If the former, the answer lay in military defence, national security and fighting subversion; if the latter, it was at the level of social and economic questions. While Latin America's ruling class and many church leaders opted for the former explanation, there were also for the first time Roman Catholics who questioned the system and the theology that supported it. Similar questioning of the adequacy of traditional missionary theology began within Protestantism, leading in 1961 to the formation of ISAL (*Iglesia y Sociedad en America Latina*). This small ecumenical organization made a substantial contribu-tion to the renewal of social and theological thought.

Dussel divides this period of upheaval into three phases:[29]

1. *Prior to 1962*. During this "pre-conciliar era", the established order was generally accepted (except by liberals, secularists, socialists and Marxists). Church people could be classified into "traditional Catholics", who defended the rights of the powerful classes, and "popular Catholics", who tended to accept the status quo as God-given.

2. *From 1962 to 1968*. During these years the ideology of "development" came into its own, inspired by the fall of colonialism in Asia and Africa. It saw the solution in technical and economic progress without structural changes. Its basic orientation centred on the US-sponsored Alliance for Progress of the Kennedy era.

3. *From 1968 to 1972*. At the Medellín Conference of Latin American Catholic bishops, insights from the Second Vatican Council were to be "transmitted" to Latin America. Medellín went further and formulated a theological "option for the poor". Soon, this concept gained further content through what came to be

called the theology of liberation, which saw the gospel of Jesus as proclaiming in the first place good news for the poor and liberty for the oppressed, and only in the second place comfort for the rich. This fundamental reversal of the traditional theology which had dominated Latin America since 1492 had immediate repercussions. The dysfunctional socio-economic system was criti- cally examined. Similar concerns were taken up within Protestant churches. Ecumenically, the Programme to Combat Racism of the WCC, founded in 1969, made possible a new look at the situation of Latin America's Indians.

The Latin American political right immediately sensed the threat to its traditional privileges signalled by the "option for the poor", and recognized that the theology of liberation removed all religious sanction for its domination. The coup by the Chilean military under General Pinochet in 1973, as well as what came to be called "low-intensity military actions", revealed the nervousness of the privileged classes. Both Catholics and Protestants became sharply divided. Perse- cutions and "security" murders affected many church members. Pope Paul VI, who had a prominent influence at Medellín, died in 1978, and his successor, the more traditionalist John Paul II, did not favour "liberation theology" and indeed moved against certain liberation theologians. The testimony of the church was handicapped, but the new ideas could not be stopped.

For churches and missionaries, work among the Indians has begun to have a new meaning. Formerly, converted Indians left their communities in order to "live their faith". They learned Spanish, became de facto *mestizos* and entered the white world of competition and possession. Losing all sense of solidarity, many became in effect "neo-pagans". Now it was the turn of the churches to convert themselves. They had to learn to take the Indians seriously as persons in their own right, within their own community and with their own language. In advocating the Indians' right to their own land, the churches are learning how to act politically in fighting the powers of this world. In Prien's words, "the old presupposition that God wants the salvation of all people remains. But there is a new emphasis: that God's saving grace is mediated not only through the institution 'church', but that it is already tentatively apparent in other religions."[30] Such an approach can save Christians from falling into the ancient trap of absolutism and disregard of the others.

The German theologian Heinrich Schäfer, who studied ethnic prejudices among Protestant churches in Guatemala, tells a fascinating story of a young Protestant of *mestizo* background, who underwent a genuine conversion when he discovered the social reality of the Indians. One day he heard that some priests and pastors were submitting a petition to the minister of the interior regarding injustices done to the Indians. He met one of those priests:

We began to talk about the Bible and about Christ, and he said: "Look, I am working in a church, where we all read the Bible together. Why don't you join us sometime and we can read together and discuss?" I went there with a few others, intending only to participate in the Bible studies. But when we were there with the poor peasants of the countryside, we began to understand the needs of these people and how they were exploited by the landowners. We saw their undernourishment, their lack of education, of medicine, of everything else. My conscience awoke, and the knowledge was born in me that I could not be a Christian and simply go to church, while our brothers and sisters out there were dying of hunger. At this moment I began to go my own way. I feel that I began my faith afresh, that Christ is present even among those small, dirty children, that he is present among all and not only among those who come together in church. I believe that my real conversion took place only there, with them.[31]

NOTES

[1] "Latin America" is technically a misnomer which has gained currency over all suggested alternatives and is thus used in this chapter for the geographical region covering South America, Central America (including Mexico) and the Caribbean. The term, introduced in the 19th century to distinguish the region from Anglo-Saxon North America and to link it to "Latin Europe" (the Iberian peninsula, Italy and France), ignores the substantial indigenous Indian and African heritage, implying that these peoples are to be culturally integrated and to disappear. Nor does it take account of the English-, French- and Dutch-speaking Caribbean islands, former colonies of largely African (slave) background. Historian Enrique Dussel remarks: "In 1492 the history of Latin America begins. It is neither 'Father Spain' nor 'Mother India', but an offspring that is neither Amerindia nor Europe, but something different"; *Historia de la Iglesia en América Latina*, Barcelona, Editorial Nova Terra, 3d ed., 1974, p.370.

[2] Hans-Jürgen Prien, *Die Geschichte des Christentums in Lateinamerika*, Göttingen, Vandenhoeck & Ruprecht, 1978, p.81.

[3] Dussel, *op. cit.*, p.85, citing research by S. Cook and W. Borah published in 1960.

[4] Prien, *op. cit.*, p.82, citing research by Richard Konetzke.

[5] Dussel, *op. cit.*, p.86.

[6] Cf. Prien, *op. cit.*, pp.262-90; *Religion in Geschichte und Gegenwart*, Vol. 3, p.614, Vol. 4, p.235, Vol. 5, p.102.

[7] See Jack M. Weatherford, *Indian Givers: How the Indians of the Americas Transformed the World*, New York, Crown, 1988, p.17.

[8] Prien, *op. cit.*, pp.104f., citing Eduardo H. Galeano, *Las venas abiertas de America Latina* (1971).

[9] Dussel, *op. cit.*, p.28.

[10] Weatherford, *op. cit.*, p.17.

[11] Gonzalo Castillo Cardenas, "The Indian Struggle for Freedom in Colombia", in Walter Dostal, ed., *The Situation of the Indian in South America* (Barbados Consultation 1971), p.77.

[12] Prien, *op. cit.*, p.165.

[13] Quoted by Pierrette Iselin, "Des menaces de mort ont été faites à nos responsables à San Cristobal", *Le Courrier* (Geneva), 18 Sept. 1996, p.8.

[14] Marco Antonio Mendes, "O Indio e a Segurança Nacional", quoted in *Land Rights for Indigenous People*, PCR Information, no. 16, 1983, p.23.

[15] Peter Ashdown, *Caribbean History in Maps*, Trinidad, Longman Caribbean, 1979, pp.14-18.

[16] Cf. Prien, *op. cit.*, pp.81f., who estimates on the basis of official lists that 3 million Africans were brought to Spanish America and 4 million to Brazil.

[17] Cf. *Ecumenical News International Bulletin*, no. 25, 13 Dec. 1996, p.19.

[18] Orlando Patterson, *The Sociology of Slavery*, London, Granada, 1973, pp.260-83. According to Patterson, the Ashanti slaves from the Gold Coast were the most prone to rebellion.

[19] Richard Price, *Maroon Societies*, Garden City NY, Doubleday, 1973, pp.3f.

[20] Cf. Patterson, *op. cit.*, p.260.

[21] Prien, *op. cit.*, p.194.

[22] *Ibid.*, pp.196-98.

[23] "Barbados II Declaration", in *Land Rights for Indigenous People*.

[24] Ashdown, *op. cit.*, p.31.

[25] Michel Roy, "Un melting-pot de cultures politiques", *Le Courrier* (Geneva), 10-11 Aug. 1996, p.4.

[26] Estimates from the UN Habitat II conference in Istanbul, June 1996, reported by *Der Spiegel*, no. 23, 3 June 1996, p.157.

[27] Ignacio Ramonet, "Mégavilles", *Le Monde diplomatique* (Paris), no. 507, June 1996, p.1.

[28] Quoted in *Le Courrier* (Geneva), 30 Dec. 1996, p.8.

[29] Dussel, *op. cit.*, pp.355-56.

[30] Prien, *op. cit.*, p.175.

[31] Heinrich Schäfer, *Befreiung vom Fundamentalismus: Entstehung einer neuen kirchlichen Praxis im Protestantismus Guatemalas*, Münster, Edición Liberación, 1988, p.166.

10
Focal Points for Further Reflection

The Little Prince in Saint-Exupéry's famous tale speaks of seeing "with the inner eye". It is such vision which came to the young Guatemalan mentioned in the previous chapter who *saw* the oppression of his Indian brothers and sisters: "My conscience awoke!" His conversion — as he called it — resembles the sudden flash of awareness that came to Moses by the burning bush on Mount Horeb when God spoke to him: "I have observed the misery of my people who are in Egypt; I have heard their cry on account of their taskmasters. *Indeed, I know their sufferings*" (Exodus 3:7).

Understanding the intricate maze of today's ethnic conflicts — whose complexities are amply illustrated, though not exhausted, by the nine case situations we have looked at in the preceding chapters — does indeed require an "inner eye" and a "conversion" in the direction of the suffering ones whose life resembles one long and cruel punishment, who are subjected to others or driven away, who are tortured and put to death by hard "taskmasters" or ill-intentioned neighbours.

A list of general conclusions would not do justice to the complexity of ethnic conflict and religion. In this chapter, therefore, I shall suggest four focal points for concentration, which may help readers to decide on a path of further reflection and action to follow.

1. From murderous governments to the "survival of the fittest"?
At the threshold of a new millennium this appears be the prospect confronting humanity. It is surprising that religious organizations, including churches and ecumenical bodies, have had relatively little to say about the terrible global problem of murder by government, even though the painful evidence has been visible throughout the 20th century. There is a moral obligation to remember the 170 million dead counted by Professor Rummel (see above, Introduction), among whom the victims of ethnic conflicts are found. If they are forgotten or the importance of this issue is downgraded, it is likely that these mass murders will be repeated during the 21st century. With the decline of the nation-state, it may be that it will be the global economy which continues this grisly job. The ferocious competition of worldwide business corporations over diminishing natural resources is already producing a fierce struggle of "the survival of the fittest". The logic of this kind of economy will inexorably lead to the abandonment of the weaker, that is the majority. It will not be necessary to *kill* them. They will starve to death by themselves, without a bullet being fired or a landmine exploding. In some countries this process of elimination is already underway.

How society remembers its dead is inseparably related to how it treats those who are still alive. Not many of the 170 million who were murdered by their own governments during the 20th century are remembered today. By contrast, those who lost their lives in interstate wars on the "fields of honour" receive considerable public attention. Nationalistic cults commemorate the "unknown soldier". One suggestive example is Argentina, where the 900 fallen of the South Atlantic war with Britain in 1982 are still remembered in daily flag ceremonies, though the military regime which caused that war has long since been driven from power in disgrace. Under the present democratically elected government these ceremonies for the dead continue unchanged. These public commemorations are an instrument for reminding the people that some day the islands which they call the Malvinas and the British call the Falklands will "return" to Argentina. A psychosis is thereby maintained which is conditioning the people not only to accept another war with more victims, but also to maintain — and pay for — an unsuccessful, essentially undemocratic and therefore politically risky military establishment. What is seldom said is that the same generals and admirals who launched Argentina into this disastrous war were the ones who conducted the "dirty war" against "leftist subversives" which caused many times more victims — as many as 30,000, according to some sources. Were it not for the courageous "Mothers of the Plaza de Mayo" — who have inspired similar groups of women elsewhere — the victims of this "dirty war" would be completely forgotten. There are no flag ceremonies and speeches for them; they are not mentioned as heroic defenders of the fatherland; their deeds are not eulogized in schoolbooks.

Few in the military have ever had the courage to admit their involvement in these "murders by government". The pattern of secrecy, embarrassed silence and impunity is repeated the world over. Church communities, not only in Argentina but elsewhere around the world, have given direct or indirect moral support to manifestations of patriotism, while leaving unchallenged human rights violations within their own societies. Such churches must ask themselves whether they are still part of the one church of Jesus Christ.

Governments responsible for mass murders have one common desire: to cover up. Nazi Germany dismissed the Jewish holocaust as enemy propaganda until the very end of the second world war. Official Turkey is still denying the Armenian genocide after more than 80 years. The Soviet Union and communist China described reports of mass deaths as bourgeois propaganda. The Indonesian government denies that it killed 400,000 "communists" in 1965; and if it admits that there were some killings it justifies these for reasons of state, just as it absolves itself from what is going on today in East Timor. As long as the military regimes of the 1970s were in power in Latin America, they told the world that rumours about a "dirty war" were leftist distortions. Sudan still imposes a rigorous news blackout on the murder of two million of its citizens. In most ethnic conflicts, each side will permit reporting as long as it is the misdeeds of its *opponents* which are highlighted. Rwanda seems to have been an exception. In 1994 reporters and television crews were allowed to roam the country at will, perhaps because those in power wanted to inspire fear. But in general, governments are *not* proud to have their misdeeds become known. Thus they will either deny that atrocities have taken place, blame the victims for them or argue that "national security" had overriding priority. The UN Human Rights Commission may be useful as an international forum for collecting and disseminating information about such misdeeds by the authorities, but it is usually incapable of effective action because of the political interplay among its members. Were it not for the precise details supplied by non-governmental organizations (NGOs), among them the World Council of Churches and Amnesty International, which are reluctantly accepted, its work would be next to useless.

Problematic as the nation-state has been, it can at its best offer the possibility of protection for weaker ethnic and social communities. During the period of "decolonization" in the 1950s and 1960s, the WCC in fact encouraged the churches in the newly independent countries of Asia and Africa to help fill political independence with specific meaning, urging the importance of the task of "nation-building". But as we have seen, the globalization of the economy in recent years has begun a process, which, if unchecked, could end any hope that the nation-state could recover the task which it has in fact often performed so poorly during the 20th century, namely to protect and to be at the service of its people. The preceding chapter on Latin America suggests that this process may already be further advanced than most people realize.

Participants in an ecumenical consultation on international affairs in Seoul in July 1996 spoke in this connection of the fears they had for the 21st century:

> The role and authority of the state is... under siege as global financial institutions usurp the function of shaping and defining our world. Indeed, it has been suggested that one of the characteristics which distinguish the present period... is the dominance of capital and the idealization of neo-liberal conceptualizations of the market... While the supporters of the process of globalization argue that it promotes social, political, cultural and, in particular, economic integration (which should perhaps be called homogenization), it is noteworthy that it is characterized more by fragmentation and alienation. Communities suffer from internal division or are set one against the other, and people are drawn into creating scapegoats to rationalize their own exclusion.[1]

The report goes on to say that the new World Trade Organization (WTO), the International Monetary Fund (IMF) and the World Bank have become "defenders of powerful economic and political interests", operated "in favour of the wealthy corporate sector". Despite the end of the cold war, there has been no meaningful reduction in arms expenditures. The UN Security Council increasingly represents these interests, which leads to a progressive weakening of the UN General Assembly.

If such developments continue, the result will be the removal of the majority of the world's population from economic participation, leading to outright hunger. Exclusion or the threat of exclusion could also cause racial and ethnic wars. This is why democratizing the UN system and strengthening its roles in peace-keeping, human rights, development and ecology — which coincide with the social objectives of the ecumenical movement and of many of the world's religions — are indispensable. For in spite of its evident weaknesses, the UN is likely to remain the only world political instrument which, if given support and some military means, can help to prevent further catastrophes and genocides.

In this effort the supportive role of religion in its local, regional and worldwide expression is indispensable. While religion does not and should not possess coercive political and military means, it must help to shape those mental and spiritual attitudes which make it possible for human persons and human communities to live in harmony. Christianity and other religions must learn from the disasters of the 20th century, to which (as we have seen in the previous chapters) they have so often contributed, either wilfully or by neglect, and become conscious and fearless protectors of all threatened communities, not only their own. It is not pious declarations which are needed but courageous confrontation with the reality of the world, the building up of solid socio-economic knowledge and the acquisition of a critical understanding of power structures (ethnic, local, nation-state, economic, military, global, etc.), guided by biblical-theological reflection. Above all, religion must have the courage to speak out and to act.

2. Ethnic conflict and the ambivalence of religion

But one may ask after reading the preceding nine chapters whether religion is capable of meeting such a challenge. All the personal courage of the signers of the Barmen declaration in 1934 does not take away the fact that the majority of Christians in Germany supported the National Socialist regime. Some of them said after the war that if they had "known" what was going on with regard to the Jews — to name only them — they might have gone into opposition. This may be so. But the problem was not limited to Germany. W.A. Visser 't Hooft, the first general secretary of the WCC, who was himself at the forefront of helping to save Jews, using the small Geneva headquarters of the World Council of Churches "in process of formation" as his centre for operations, later reflected ruefully on the blindness of Christians:

> As I look back on these attempts to help the Jews during the war years I feel far from proud. In some post-war publications my role has been presented as an example of active assistance to the Jews in their hour of crisis. But does this not amount to the truth that in the land of the blind the one-eyed man is king? For there was indeed an astonishing blindness in nearly all quarters with regard to the dimension and the meaning of the wholesale murder of European Jews. Here, if anywhere, the churches should have cried out, not only because fellow-men were persecuted to death, but also because an attempt was made to get rid once for all of the people through whom and from whom salvation had come to the world. But only a few Christians spoke out, and only a few went out of their way and stretched out a helping hand. I know that I should have done a great deal more, that I should have tried more persistently to break through the wall of apathy and indifference. In face of a crime and a tragedy of such magnitude the weight of the things one has not done is vastly greater than the weight of those which one has done.[2]

The apathy and indifference of churches in the face of racial, ethnic and other conflict and suffering continue to be a problem. A prime example was the reactions in many Christian communities to the WCC Programme to Combat Racism (PCR). No one, of course, ever opposed ecumenical *statements* condemning racism. But as soon as the WCC established PCR in 1969 and authorized an appeal for a Special Fund to give financial support to liberation movements in Southern Africa for humanitarian purposes (expressly excluding the purchase of arms), a storm of protest broke out throughout Western Europe, which soon degencrated into a diatribe. It was not only the WCC which came under severe attack, but also Latin American liberation theology, which arose at nearly the same moment. Even churches that had a reasonably good record in the struggle against Nazism joined the fray. The struggle was heated up further by powerful economic circles and the media.

Looking back on this controversy on the occasion of PCR's 25th anniversary, when apartheid had finally ended in South Africa, South African theologian Charles Villa-Vicencio identified five problem areas, which may also be applied to critical reflection on the relationship between ethnic conflicts and religion today:

First of all, the negative reactions from WCC member churches and others allowed the theological and ethical debate on liberation from racial and social injustice and oppression to be altered by powerful financial supporters of the WCC into something else. These forces imposed a debate of the issue on *their* terms.

Second, the racism which had precipitated the crisis in Southern Africa in the first place was consequently *not* discussed. Rather, the debate centred on the awarding of grants from the Special Fund to liberation movements, which was not the cause of the problem, but an attempt to meet it.

Third, at the same time, the accusation that the WCC was fostering violence meant that the oppressive violence of the police and the army against the poor and racially downtrodden in South Africa was neither examined nor condemned. Accordingly, the debate focussed almost exclusively on the counter-violence through which these populations tried to defend themselves.

Fourth, as result of these developments, the WCC allowed itself to be put on the defensive, with the consequence that the public ecumenical debate never really centred on liberation. The question of the need for an armed struggle which could not be avoided became separated from its social context.

Fifth, Villa-Vicencio concludes,

the debate about PCR exposed a disconcerting willingness by Christians to live with violence, reflective of the high tolerance of killing by the majority of the Christian churches. Implicit in aspects of the debate was a willingness simply to accept the political suffering of human beings as inevitable.[3]

The similar indifference and even hostility which many displayed regarding racism against European Jews in the 1930s and 1940s and racism against South Africa's blacks in the 1960s, 1970s and 1980s is disturbing. But there is no end to it. A careful examination of ethnic conflicts today, such as the ones illustrated by the seven contemporary case situations in this book, frequently shows the collusion of churches and other religions with the powers engaged in oppressive conflict. When these churches come under scrutiny for such collusion, they often resent it as "interference", just as do UN member states when challenged. If enough pressure is put on them, many subscribe to joint appeals calling for an end to the violence. But such statements are usually so well-balanced, with the issues soft-pedalled and rendered so harmless, that they carry little conviction and are often not even heard.

If Christianity wishes to shake off its ambivalence and become a truly prophetic instrument in God's hand, it must engage in a credible self-examination which acknowledges its disobedience and spells out its multiple forms of complicity. For example, if Christians object to the imposition of Islamic law and rightly protest death threats against and execution of Muslim dissenters, they must also bring to light and re-examine the long history of the persecution of Christian heretics and the burning of Jews and witches, which cost hundreds of thousands if not millions of lives. What finally ended these persecutions was secularism, not church initiatives. Until the time of the Enlightenment, the church turned over its victims to the state for execution. This tradition was initiated under the 4th-century Roman emperor Thedosius, who, at the request of church authorities, put to death not only unrepentant non-believers and Jews but also Christians who refused to accept official church dogma. Long after the church stopped turning *its* heretics over to the state, the state continued to punish and put to death those who questioned *its* ideology and *its* authority.

Like other religions, Christianity has undergone a great learning process, to which the Enlightenment, secularism, the "free church" and other protest movements, scientific advance, the communications revolution and the ecumenical movement have all contributed. But the effects of this development have been uneven. In some geographical areas the reflexes of the Constantinian era remain alive in the church. And in all churches and religions there are recesses in which age-old customs and ways of thought have been untouched by the claims of the gospel.

Part of the problem would thus seem to lie within religion itself. The Christian churches (to speak only of them) must be helped to face frankly their historical responsibility for the incendiary and often messianic fanaticism which they have implanted within society and whose cultural and political after-effects remain alive. The preceding chapters have attested to the impact of the East-West (Orthodox-Catholic) theological divide and power struggle, the Crusades of the Western church against Islam and Orthodoxy and the European (Catholic-Protestant) religious wars of the 16th and 17th centuries and their colonialist extension into the Americas and Southern Africa. The Enlightenment was a reaction to such religious fanaticism. Its adherents assumed that the extremist religious spirit could be overcome by reason and science. But fanaticism simply went underground, only to reappear later in the shape of secularized ideologies and nationalisms. In our own times, religious fanaticism has emerged anew as fundamentalism, combining religion with nationalism, ethnocentrism and racist ideologies. The spirit of Christ, shining through such movements as Eastern and Western monasticism, the Waldensians, the Quakers and the Anabaptists, or through such persons as St Benedict, St Francis, Bartolomé de Las Casas, Florence Nightingale and Albert Schweitzer (to name only a few), reminded Christians of the gospel's original call to peace and justice as part of the conversion of heart and mind.

Although the ambivalence of religion in ethnic conflicts remains a problem, there is doubtless greater awareness in the church today of the need to bring political struggles for justice into harmony with the search for religious unity. Within the ecumenical movement, this issue has, for example, been on the agenda of all of the assemblies of the World Council of Churches since Amsterdam 1948. The challenge is summarized well in the text on "What Unity Requires" adopted by the WCC's fifth assembly (Nairobi 1975), which describes the church as "a company under Christ's discipline", compelled, despite tensions over ethical and political decisions, to seek always "the way of obedience in each concrete situation":

> Open and honest controversy on political issues may lead to agreement or it may lead to polarization. When all things are brought into the light, some will find their refuge in a retreat into darkness. The church has to learn to distinguish in the light of God's word between sin which can be exposed and forgiven, and apostasy which rejects God's forgiveness and must therefore be rejected by the church. How can we learn to exercise this discipline and this discernment in situations where our churches are involved in racism, in social, political or religious oppression and in economic exploitation?[4]

3. Ecumenical action in local conflicts?

Each of the nine situations described in this book has international dimensions. Without outside interference, some of the conflicts might have happened on a greatly reduced scale or not at all. Such interference is usually covert, hidden from the public eye and denied. It involves elements such as the arms trade, intervention through the military and intelligence services, exploitative commercial treaties and practices and diplomatic pressures which may undermine the functioning of a weak state or threaten the existence of ethnic and tribal communities or under-privileged social sectors. This is one of the reasons that religious organizations tend to concentrate their attention on local and easily recognized problems: emergency relief and medical care, reconstruction and development. They are often at a loss to understand and act on the intricate international connections which have a direct bearing on the suffering they are trying to heal. To be sure, nongovernmental organizations for the defence of human rights like Amnesty International and bodies like the WCC's Commission of the Churches on International Affairs have made available a wealth of information and analysis in this field, but this generally reaches a limited concerned public, not the religious constituency at large.

Religious organizations in all countries, rich and poor, need to make fuller use of existing international networks to coordinate research, publicity and awareness-building in order to bring these hidden dimensions into the open and to help the search for realistic solutions. Political, ethical and theological questions must obviously be part of such reflection and action. It is evident that under authoritarian regimes such involvement may be dangerous, but the moral and technical support provided by international religious networks should not be underestimated.

In this spirit, a few lines of action in each of the nine case situations are suggested below. Similar methods can be proposed for other ethnic conflicts. Of course, in many of these situations, countless creative efforts are already underway, some of which we have referred to in earlier chapters. One might envisage, for example, a series of long-term informal ecumenical or inter-religious task forces to address situations of ethnic conflict. Over a period of time they would accompany and surround a community in conflict to defuse tensions and seek a measure of mutual understanding and if possible solutions. The structures, aims and methods of such task forces would vary according to the gravity and geographical extent of the problem. The quality of their work would depend on establishing a high degree of trust among the members of the task force and towards their local contacts.

1. *Armenia 1915*. While this massacre was planned and executed by the Turkish authorities, the Armenian people had previously been encouraged and supported by Britain, France and Russia, who, at the critical moment, abandoned them and delivered them to their fate. Germany, Turkey's ally during the first world war, kept silent, although its governing circles and most of its church leadership doubtless knew what was going on. Turkey's strategic importance in the global power game, due to its location, made it untouchable. In 1918 the US confirmed British and French policy, and this has remained basically unchanged throughout the years. An independent Armenia, apart from the small Soviet republic, was given no chance. Today the Kurds are also being sacrificed for nearly the same strategic reasons. Ninan Koshy's call (cited at the beginning of chapter 1) for Armenia's legitimate concerns to be recognized and for the churches to mobilize international support needs to be implemented, especially by the churches of the countries historically most directly involved: Britain, France, Russia, Germany and the USA. Concrete efforts need to be made to acknowledge responsibility for historic failure and to challenge Turkey's policy towards the Armenians and the Kurds — including the fulfilment of internationally certified commitments to protect Armenians in their ancient homeland (Treaty of Sèvres 1920, Treaty of Lausanne 1923) and the application of internationally agreed human rights principles in general.

2. *The Jewish holocaust*. While German churches have made a significant effort to face up to their nation's terrible guilt for massacres in occupied territories and the systematic destruction of European Jews, church reflection in most other countries ranges from partial acknowledgment to a complete absence of concern. By and large, the willful assistance of Christian communities in many Eastern European countries in the annihilation of the Jews by the occupying powers has not yet led to any official church acknowledgment of this guilt. Even today antisemitism is current in several countries. A concerted ecumenical effort to help these churches to face up to their responsibility is thus very important. At the same time, the churches in Western countries, including Britain, the US and those which remained neutral, must ask themselves why they did not warn their governments against the approaching danger even when information was available. Why did they not do more to prevent their governments from allowing the Evian refugee conference in 1938 to fail? In refusing entry to refugees, they effectively abandoned Europe's Jews to the gas chambers. Did the churches of the time not grasp the meaning of this betrayal, or did they not really care? This moral failure and failure of imagination needs to be rethought, not only for the sake of repentance, but in order to prepare for the future.

3. *Sudan*. The initial religious motivation of this destructive ethnic war is clear, even though Islam in Sudan today merely serves as a façade for a militarized government gone on a rampage. But the conflict cannot be understood without reference to Sudan's pre-colonial and colonial past. The Islamic community must not be absolved for having tolerated the slave trade for centuries, offending the human dignity of the black south. World religious organizations might well suggest that Sudanese Muslims acknowledge the historic guilt of slavery and ask for pardon, in the hope that this might in turn induce the southern rebels to ask for pardon for the excesses they have committed. British churches may also wish to engage in some historical house-cleaning. For the British colonial administration to have withdrawn without ensuring that adequate guarantees were provided to protect the integrity of the south — perhaps even in the form of granting separate statehood — was highly irresponsible. Why were the British churches at the time of the Sudanese independence negotiations not sufficiently alert when their government prepared the terms of this independence? And if they did realize what was happening, why did they fail to warn their government that the proposed terms were likely to lead to disaster, and to exert public political pressure? A fresh public debate on this question might help to bring the disastrous war in Sudan back onto the international agenda, as well as expose the hidden international arms trade and other forms of strategic cooperation which keep this bloody conflict, a key factor contributing to tension in East Africa, going.

4. *Rwanda*. The basic question is a theological one. How is it possible that this unspeakable mass murder took place in the "most Christian country of all of Africa"? How was it possible after nearly a century of Christian missions for religious and human barriers to break down so completely? This is a question addressed not only to Rwandan Christians but to the entire ecumenical community. Without an answer it is doubtful that reconstruction and reconciliation can truly take place. But in raising this question European Christians are certainly in no position to sit in judgment on their fellow Christians from Rwanda; after all, the similar failure of European Christianity during the 1930s and 1940s came after *fifteen hundred* years of Christianity. This has something to do with the unconverted "dark recesses" of religious existence mentioned above. A thorough ecumenical enquiry would have to involve the Roman Catholic White Fathers, the Anglican, Presbyterian and other churches and national and regional ecumenical bodies. It would have to explore issues of theology, church practice and the ethics of power. And its results would have to motivate self-examination, not only by churches in Rwanda, but also by those elsewhere in Africa and throughout the world.

5. *Palestine/Israel*. Without the European Jewish holocaust and the demise of British colonial power, Palestine today would probably be an independent state with an Arab majority and a Jewish minority. The chronic and multiple suffering caused by the present situation makes it urgent to recognize consciously the equality of the two peoples, on the basis of which a human and theological bridge can be built between Jewish suffering and Palestinian suffering, rather than to repeat *ad nauseam* religious and political dogmas regarding the land claims of both sides. To begin with, an effort should be made to see together as a single event the

immigration of hundreds of thousands of surviving Jews and the expulsion of hundreds of thousands of Arabs. It is also necessary to try to resolve the theological tension between the biblical pledges of land and the notion of the "chosen people" on the one hand and the obligation to be "a blessing to all nations" on the other. Christians have to clarify their own theological vacillation between guilt over the Jewish holocaust, guilt over complicity with Israel in the displacement of the Palestinians and fear that this conflict might touch off a wider conflagration in the already explosive Middle East. A final issue is the almost exclusive dependence of Israel on the United States, which is seen in the Middle East as permanent outside interference. Western Christians and the world Jewish community have not given sufficient thought to the long-term implications of this. Finally, the profound gap between Western and Middle Eastern Christians over the meaning of the biblical Israel and the modern state has to be sorted out.

Christianity, Judaism and Islam have obvious difficulties in establishing a serious meeting of minds over questions like these, and this impedes a frank and liberating theological dialogue. The divergences are obviously emotionally and politically highly charged; but if dialogue is impossible, continued warfare would seem to be the inescapable alternative. Since Christianity bears major responsibility for the origins of this issue, it would be important for churches from Eastern and Western Europe (the holocaust countries), the Middle East and North America to consult permanently not only with each other but also with Palestinians and Israelis.

6. *Lebanon*. France, Britain and the US have a long history of interference in Lebanon, and Israel and Syria have a strong military presence there. Each of these is related to a certain Lebanese clientele, which they support with both financial and military aid, often at the expense of the others. Beirut is also a key centre for all kinds of financial deals for the entire Middle East. This calls for a sustained effort by the churches in these countries to examine these relationships and to challenge their governments and economic powers to help strengthen the peace process. Only if these external connections with local ethnic groups are brought into the open can potentially dangerous developments be monitored. In the light of the power of vested interests that are embroiled in Lebanon, this suggestion may seem naive, but once again, what are the alternatives? Religious bodies, the ecumenical movement included, need to engage in a much more sustained effort than heretofore to work on the international dimensions of the Lebanon conflict, which is so closely related to the Palestine-Israel struggle.

7. *Sri Lanka*. The strategic position of this island in the Indian Ocean has always attracted the attention of foreign powers. Since independence British secret services have continued to train Sri Lankan secret services and armed forces, the US has maintained a naval base there, and India has kept its military and intelligence eyes on this island so close to its shores, sometimes backing the government and sometimes the Tamil rebels. This war would certainly not have lasted so long apart from this high level of outside interference. In addition to maintaining contacts based on former missionary connections and supporting church-related development, churches in Britain, the US and India need to pay closer attention to the political and military involvement of their governments

with Sri Lanka and to help the Sri Lankan churches to establish or strengthen contacts with the Buddhist and Hindu communities in Sri Lanka and India. The aim of such efforts must be the end of the civil war and the establishment of community.

8. *Bosnia-Herzegovina*. Without constant outside interference the Muslims, Serbs and Croats of Bosnia-Herzegovina could probably have evolved their own *modus vivendi*. The neighbours who have projected their own problems onto this troubled country thus have a primary responsibility and self-interest to do what they can to defuse the tensions. Efforts by the Conference of European Churches and the WCC to bring together religious leaders from opposing sides must be continued and strengthened. Each community needs to untangle religion from nationalism, and religious tolerance must penetrate to the level of local parishes. Much will be gained if the religious leaders unequivocally disavow any claim of their own ethnic community for hegemony, condemn every form of "ethnic cleansing" and call for the arrest and punishment of all war criminals. This could be supported by a corresponding political effort on the part of churches which supply the peace-keeping forces in Bosnia-Herzegovina. A special responsibility for fostering this dialogue falls on churches and Muslim communities in countries that have traditional ties with Bosnia-Herzegovina: Hungary, Austria, Italy, Greece, Turkey and Russia. Work is urgently needed on a common historical perspective, lay training and ecumenical theological education which stress the universality of God and new forms of ethics.

9. *Latin America*. The astonishing religious development of this continent seems to defy all logic. Even though Christianity was imposed by fire and by sword, resulting in the mass murder of tens of millions of Amerindians and the enslaving of countless young Africans, and even though neo-colonialism keeps exploiting Latin America's poor today, Christianity has taken deep roots. While the churches have traditionally preferred to address themselves to the rich and the mighty, they cannot prevent that "even the dogs eat the crumbs that fall from their masters' table" (Matt. 15:27). Because this historical development has been perceived only dimly if at all by the churches in Europe and North America, liberation theology is often misunderstood. The ecumenical movement must remove the layers of incomprehension that cover up the story of the conquest of the Indies and of African slavery if the churches are to understand the forms of Christian existence in contemporary Latin America. A series of convergent ecumenical encounters involving churches in Latin America, Africa, Europe and North America might consider such themes as the reality of conquest, Indian genocide and African slavery in the 16th and 17th centuries and their religious justification; evangelization within colonial economic and social structures; the poor — Indians, descendants of African slaves, indentured labour, rural and urban marginalized populations — and their religion in opposition to nefarious forms of modern development, the national security state and the globalized economy. Such encounters could help to prepare the ground for a common struggle for justice with and on behalf of those who have been oppressed since the dawn of colonialism. It is important that the churches bring the fate of the surviving Indian communities to world attention.

A comment by Charles Villa-Vicencio regarding the struggle against apartheid underscores the importance of the ecumenical involvement in such issues. In South Africa and elsewhere, the WCC has, before making any statement on injustice, carefully analyzed the ambiguities and processes that sustained racism, economic exploitation and human deprivation:

> The arms industry, the violation of the oil embargo and the collaboration of certain multinational companies with the apartheid regime were repeatedly brought under the spotlight of critical enquiry by the WCC. The Council's willingness to act on its insights gave the church a credibility among the poor that few can question or doubt. [5]

4. Religion and reconciliation

At the dawn of a new millennium the vast spiritual and intellectual resources which lie often dormant within Christianity and the other great world religions must be awakened and applied to the burning problem of ethnic conflict. A global ecumenical community needs to be created, marked by a spirit of discernment, mutual forgiveness and renewal, in gratitude to God for creation and for the fellow creatures which God has so generously placed at humanity's disposal.

The dramatic changes of the last few years have suggested that the assumption that religion is dying out — at least in the sense of being replaced by atheism or atheist ideologies — must be discarded. Nevertheless, one must be extremely cautious about the assumptions that the world is entering a "post-ideological" era, or that a substantial reversal of the secularized, non-church or "non-religious" life-style and refusal to adhere to institutional religion is likely, or that declining church structures (in the West at least) will soon be filled with new life. This may of course happen, but present signs point in the opposite direction. New religions and informal Christian communities are filling the vacuum. Many have democratic structures; some are led by charismatic figures who provide "meaning" and "direction". This is a complex phenomenon which has to be closely observed and carefully analyzed.

In this situation ecumenism must not remain on the defensive. But the new situation demands an honest examination of the *dual* role which religion plays in the world and in ethnic conflicts in particular. On the negative side, as we have seen repeatedly in the nine case situations, religion tends to side with government, no matter how authoritarian, tyrannical, reactionary and destructive its power. Religion thus contributes to injustice, fear, intolerance and violence even when it is silent and politically "neutral". On the positive side, religion also can and does work for peace, justice, reconciliation and solidarity; and many Christians have renewed their faith through ecumenical commitment, breaking out of the disillusion caused by ossified and claustrophobic religious communities.

Given this duality, it is indispensable that the churches assume their common responsibility and together act out their faith more decisively for the creation of new theological, structural and socio-political patterns. About this, the WCC's world conference on Church and Society (Geneva 1966) said:

> The church must accept a much more determined preaching and teaching role. The pulpit shares with the classroom the important task of giving instruction in the gospel

and its meaning for full brotherhood without discrimination... [It] must encourage the legitimate aspirations of suppressed minorities and majorities, and support all practicable measures aimed at changing any political and economic order which reflects the denial of political rights or economic opportunity, segregation, discrimination or other suppression.[6]

This does not mean that Christians should take no account of the secularization of originally religious conflicts, such as those in Northern Ireland, Lebanon or the former Yugoslavia, or that they should overestimate their own influence in the world. But because religion lies close to the roots of these and other conflicts, the churches and other religious faiths have a double duty in seeking peace.

The report on "What Unity Requires" of the WCC Nairobi assembly, cited earlier in this chapter, offers a pertinent theological framework for keeping the churches from limiting their attention too exclusively to the aspirations of their own class or community:

No church should become so identified with its own or another particular culture, present or past, as to frustrate its critical dialogue with that culture. When a church's loyalty to a given culture becomes uncritical, the oneness of the church universal suffers... Yet, the people of God will always find their first and primary identity through their baptism into the one body of Christ. How does this understanding of culture and unity shape our life in liturgy and mission, increase our understanding of diverse theological understandings of the one faith, free us in situations, such as Ireland, where cultural identification has become an imprisonment making it profoundly costly for the churches to exercise their ministry of reconciliation?[7]

At any rate, a new pattern of common action must be set up — away from the divisions within which the churches still exist, away from the mistrust and mutual hostility which keep determining their relationship, away from the burden of paralyzing memories of the past, away from intolerance and the refusal to accept religious freedom. In short, what is needed is a new ecumenical world order, an *oikoumene*, which means "the whole inhabited world". Without an *oikoumene* among religions, there will simply be no inhabited world.

A second, equally indispensable element is the establishment of peace among the world's religions. Even if the Armenian genocide or the Jewish holocaust did not have an immediate "religious" cause, traditional religious enmity had prepared the way for it. Even if fundamentalism, which may become a major contributor to future ethnic conflicts, grows out of unresolved social or psychological conditions, it is above all a religious phenomenon and it is seen as such by its adherents. The churches should therefore confront it first of all theologically and only then sociologically or psychologically.

In this connection some recent remarks of Hans Küng are worth pondering:

Those who carry on dialogue do not shoot. And by analogy that applies to religion and the church: those who engage in dialogue will not resort to disciplining in their own church or religion, and will abhor discrimination against anyone who thinks otherwise, even heresy-hunting. Those who engage in dialogue must have the inner power and strength to sustain dialogue and where necessary to respect the standpoint of others. For one thing is certain: that impatience with dissent which is constantly breaking out all over the world, in all religions, has no understanding of the virtue of a capacity for

dialogue. And yet: on this, literally on this, the whole of our spiritual and indeed physical survival will depend. For:
— There can be no peace among the nations without peace among the religions.
— There can be no peace among the religions without dialogue between the religions.
— There can be no dialogue between the religions without research into theological foundations. [8]

To be sure, Küng's remarks leave unanswered the significant question of how such theological insights can be effectively communicated to local faith communities within each religion. Moreover, before such suggestions can be implemented, some radical house-cleaning is needed *within* each religion. For instance, how are Jews and Christians to deal with the tension in biblical theology between "revealed truth" (which tends to exclusiveness) and the "universality" of God (which tends to inclusiveness)? Can one simply ignore those exclusive passages of scripture which are employed to defend claims to special privileges and rights? Similarly, Jews and Christians will surely have to take their unmistakeable distance from earlier traditions reflected in the Bible which advocated the extermination of "unbelievers" or of entire populations (for example Gen. 34; Num. 16:31-35; Josh. 6:21; 1 Sam. 15; 1 Kings 18:40) or the "purification" of Israel from all "foreign" family relations (Ezra 10) or severe punishment for erring members of the church (Acts 5:l-11).

While many Jews and Christians today are aware that such problematic passages reflect an earlier stage of religious thought and practice which can no longer be considered authoritative, these and similar texts have been used time and again over the centuries, until very recently, as divine sanction for destructive action against dissenters, adherents of other faiths and members of other ethnic groups or races. In contemporary fundamentalism, this spirit has found a refuge which is not to be underestimated. Historian Arnold Toynbee has summarized the problem as follows:

> The vein of exclusiveness and intolerance in Christianity is not, I should say, an especially Western deformation of Christianity; it is a congenital feature which is part of Christianity's and also part of Islam's heritage from Judaism. Just as the vision of God as being love is a heritage from Judaism, so is the other vision of God as being a jealous god, the god of my tribe as against the Gentiles outside my tribe or my church or whatever my community may be. Yet, however hard it may be to purge Christianity of its exclusive-mindedness, it seems imperative for Christians to achieve this spiritual feat. [9]

Toynbee takes Christianity to task for the self-centred arrogance which has caused the large Asian peoples such as the Indians, Chinese and Japanese to reject conversion after promising beginnings. In different forms, this same attitude has marked Christianity's relations with Judaism and Islam. It has finally turned off Europe's intellectual elite and labouring masses. Measured against the basic insights of faith gained through the ecumenical movement, this Christian arrogance must be seen as essentially un-Christian and anti-Christian. It belongs to the "unconverted" obscure side of Christianity. Christianity needs to come to terms with its own internal theological contradictions.

With the intermingling of the populations of the world, Toynbee sees the coming of some kind of "unification", which has to be spelled out more clearly:

> I think one form that this unification will take will be a unification of our different cultural heritages. Christians and Muslims are already familiar with the fact that the Jewish cultural heritage was, from the beginning, a part of the Christian and Islamic cultural heritage. I think one can foresee a time when the heritage of Islam and Buddhism will also have become part of the Christian society's background. The heritage of Christianity always has been, to some extent, a part of the Islamic society's background. One might also foresee its becoming part of the Buddhist society's background. And in our time already we have seen how the Christian heritage did become part of the background of a great Hindu saint, the Mahatma Gandhi.[10]

Summing up

Inevitably, deeply-rooted assumptions and behaviour patterns will be questioned and fundamental contradictions *within* and *between* religions examined in a self-critical way. This can lead to a creative, concrete, realistic and liberated process towards peace. It will help religious communities to detect danger signals at an early stage and to act upon them immediately and vigorously. They will become free to discover and eliminate those causes of conflict whose original roots lie in religion.

Such an ecumenical approach, in which theology is disciplined by scientific and interdisciplinary methods, can be neither church-sponsored nor produced in an ivory tower. The primary concern must be, in Küng's words, "with the fate of those individuals and communities of faith which are affected indeed, with the future of our divided and exploited world. Theologians should not be brake-blocks, but pioneers on the way to the future."[11]

NOTES

[1] Message of the consultation on "Church, Community, State in the Contemporary World", Seoul, Korea, 15-17 July 1996, Geneva, WCC Commission of the Churches on International Affairs, 1996.

[2] W. A. Visser 't Hooft, *Memoirs*, p.171.

[3] Charles Villa-Vicencio, "Church and Violence", in Pauline Webb, ed., *A Long Struggle: The Involvement of the World Council of Chuches in South Africa*, Geneva, WCC, 1994, pp.104-106.

[4] "What Unity Requires", in David M. Paton, ed., *Breaking Barriers: Official Report of the Fifth Assembly of the WCC*, Geneva, WCC, 1976, p.63.

[5] Villa-Vicencio, *loc. cit.*, p.106.

[6] *World Conference on Church and Society*, Geneva, WCC, 1966, p.150, paras 119f.

[7] *Loc. cit.*, p.64.

[8] Hans Küng, *Global Responsibility: In Search of a New World Ethic*, London, SCM Press, 1991, pp.104f.

[9] Arnold Toynbee, *Christianity among the Religions of the World*, New York, Scribners, 1957, p.97.

[10] *Ibid.*, p.102.

[11] Küng, *op. cit.*, p.132.

Ethnicity and Nationalism

A Challenge to the Churches

Introduction

In more than fifty places around the globe, violence has taken root between people who share the same terrain but differ in ethnicity, race, language or religion. Rapid population growth, diminishing resources, unemployment, migration to shantytowns and lack of education are steadily increasing pressures along many social fault-lines. Conditions seem ripe for more Bosnias, Rwandas or Sri Lankas, for more cities and villages to be destroyed, for more people to be left destitute, for more blood to flow. Along with other concerned groups, the church of Jesus Christ must reflect on this issue. And we must act.

From 15 to 19 November 1994, we have met — some 36 people from 21 countries — in Colombo, Sri Lanka, to discuss issues of ethnicity and nationalism and to discern the challenges these present to the witness and service of Christian churches and ecumenical bodies.

Jointly sponsored by the World Alliance of Reformed Churches, Lutheran World Federation and World Council of Churches, the consultation was hosted by the Ecumenical Institute for Study and Dialogue in Colombo and the National Christian Council of Sri Lanka. Our hosts made it possible for us to hear a presentation of the current situation in Sri Lanka itself; and we share the hopes and prayers of the people of Sri Lanka that recent developments may herald a peaceful resolution of the conflict that has torn their country apart and led to immense suffering in recent years.

Our discussions here have confirmed our awareness of the complexity and deep roots of many of today's conflicts, both those to which our attention is called daily by newspaper and television reports and those largely unnoticed by international media. The role of the Christian community in any situation of ethnic strife is always difficult and often ambiguous. In many of these conflicts, no solution is apparent; and we recognize that Christian faith offers no ready answers to them. Nevertheless, in what follows we have sought to distil from our discussions some insights and perspectives which we hope will be useful to the member churches of our organizations and to others concerned about these critical issues.

Our report is in three sections. We begin by drawing on accounts of particular situations presented at our meeting to suggest some general remarks about ethnic conflicts. This is followed by a presentation of biblical and theological perspectives; and we conclude with some practical suggestions for the churches. A separate section is appended, offering explanations of some of the terms used in our report and discussions.

I. Some types and elements of ethnicity

Participants shared case studies and more informal reports of ethnic tension or strife in Fiji, Hungary, Malaysia, Nagorno-Karabagh, Nigeria, Rwanda, Sri Lanka, Sudan, Taiwan and the former Yugoslavia. We regret that, due to circumstances beyond our control, it was not possible to hear a case study from Latin America.

• Text of the report drafted by participants in a consultation on this theme held in Colombo, Sri Lanka, November 1994, and co-sponsored by the Lutheran World Federation, World Alliance of Reformed Churches and World Council of Churches.

Any attempt to classify these situations highlights the wide diversity of individual cases. Christian churches within and outside of any situation must show humility and caution if they seek to respond to it with something more than a general appeal for nonviolent resolution of conflict, compassion for victims and justice for all. However, we note also that any such exercise in "understanding ethnic conflict" inevitably abstracts from the human experiences and often deep suffering of our brothers and sisters directly involved in these painful situations. If the discussion of ethnic tensions and conflicts is to be more than an academic exercise, our humility and caution in explaining events and identifying rights and wrongs must be matched by an abiding commitment to be artisans of peace.

No two situations of ethnic conflict are the same. The stories and case studies reported in our consultation revealed several specific areas in which the distinctive features of a particular tension or conflict may be found. Here are some of these elements:

• *Local factors.* Each situation grows in part out of the particularities of the context in which the various groups live, including their economic power and potential, sociological makeup, demographic realities, geographical factors. In cases involving indigenous peoples, it is important to recognize that their relationship to the land is an intimate component of their spirituality.

• *History.* Each situation evolves out of specific historical circumstances, with which those from outside are often unfamiliar. As part of the ongoing stream of history, no situation is static. More importantly, there are often deep differences of opinion about the historical record (in most cases, history is "written by the winners") and how it is to be interpreted.

• *External influences.* No situation is insulated from outside forces, who act out of various interests. Frequently it is the past actions of outside forces which have created the present tension, as in the case of colonialism; but similar intervention from outside comes with expansionist policies of neighbouring nations and with the economic domination of "neo-colonialism". Often the action of outside forces is overt and evident, but they may also intervene covertly, creating further suspicion and mistrust.

• *Images of the other.* In every situation of ethnic tension or conflict, the behaviour of each side is most likely to be determined by negative images of the other, without any serious attempt to verify these images. As tensions between groups intensify, people increasingly act according to their distorted images of the self and the other, and ethnicity is increasingly invoked as a factor in the group rivalry. Conflict is exacerbated when the general perception is of the other as inferior, or threatening, or demonic.

• *Occasion for conflict and opportunity for resolution.* Ethnic mistrust or tension often escalates into conflict because of a specific event or episode. Any attempt to resolve the conflict must deal with what touched off the conflict. Merely resolving that episode will not solve the underlying conflict, however, since the conflict will have opened old wounds and is likely to have created new fears, hatreds and enemy-images.

• *Who speaks for the group?* From each side in a case of ethnic tension or conflict many voices may be heard, offering divergent explanations of the issues at stake and different proposals for how they are to be dealt with. Frequently it will be difficult to verify which if any of these voices is in fact speaking for those who are most vulnerable. While seeking to listen carefully and objectively to all voices, those outside the situation must remember that co-option and "divide and rule" are strategies often used by opponents to weaken and discredit groups.

• *Myths and visions.* Many ethnic conflicts are intensified and complicated by the deep convictions held by ethnic groups about their place in history and in their region. These visions may not respond to "objective" judgments made by those outside the group.

On the basis of the cases presented to us, we would identify two main categories of ethnic conflict: ideological conflicts and conflicts concerning minority-majority relationships. Both are embedded in the struggle of ethnic groups over economic resources and political power. The following list of types of such conflict is not exhaustive, and in any given case several categories may overlap:

Ideological conflicts
  • Some cases are often described as "inter-religious" or "intra-religious", because each of the parties is identified with a different religious or "sectarian" affiliation, even if it is clear to all that the teachings and religious practices of both sides have little if anything to do with the dispute.
  • Some cases involve groups with identifiably different "ethnic" consciousness, often supported by a perception of distinctiveness in language, race, customs and values or cultural identity.

Majority-minority relationships
  • Some cases involve ethnic groups of relatively equal size or power each struggling for dominance in a national state.
  • Some cases arise because of the historical movement of people, as refugees or as migrants, into the territory of another nation-state.
  • Some cases arise because an ethnic group, nation or part of a nation finds itself within the borders of a nation-state which it did not choose, whether because of boundaries drawn by colonial authorities or as a result of earlier treaties.
  • Some cases arise within nation-states in which a large majority is of one ethnic group and one or more minority groups struggle for recognition of rights which they are not able to achieve through parliamentary or other democratic means because of their minority status.
  • Some cases arise when a minority ethnic group achieves and maintains dominance over the majority by economic, political and military power.
  • Some cases involve indigenous peoples who have been increasingly marginalized, reduced to a minority and threatened with extinction by the colonial powers and their descendants or by other ethnic groups brought in to serve the economic interests of the colonial powers.

II. Biblical and theological perspectives
  God the Creator has made humankind in God's image; all human beings share equal dignity and are owed equal respect (Gen. 1:26-28). This image of God is expressed in the relationship of female and male (Gen. 1:27). The image of God is marred when the relationship between two or more people or peoples is broken (Genesis 4:1-16).
  In God's providence and for our good we have come to speak different languages, inhabit different cultural spaces (Gen. 11:1-10). God is the author both of our common humanity and of our diversity.
  Estranged from the God of peace, human beings have made wholesome ethnic differences a source of deadly conflict. In greed for wealth and power, land and its fruits, one ethnic group oppresses another, excluding it from the things that rightfully belong to it, suppressing cultural distinctiveness, plundering material goods, sometimes even threatening and obliterating its very existence.
  By sending Jesus Christ into this world, God the Redeemer calls the whole of humanity to respond to the proclamation of the good news of the reign of God, of the coming new creation of God. The promise of the new creation is that people from every tribe and nation with all their cultural goods will be gathered around the throne of the Triune God in a new

heaven and a new earth (Rev. 21-22). But before this promise is received, a note of judgment is struck (Rev. 21:27): that all cultures will be refined and renewed.

As the gospel has been preached to many nations, the church has taken root in many cultures, transforming them as well as being profoundly shaped by them. Yet the church does not have its own specific culture; rather, to be church is a way of living the life of the new creation within a given culture. The church must have its feet firmly planted in any culture in which it lives, and its arms stretched out towards God and God's future, the new creation.

Pentecost, the day the church was born, is not a reversal of the experience of the Tower of Babel (Gen. 11:1-10). Before Babel all of humanity spoke *one* language; in Jerusalem at Pentecost the new community speaks *many* languages (Acts 2). When the Spirit comes, all understand each other; yet each speaks his or her own language. Pentecost is not a reversion to the unity of cultural uniformity; it is an advance towards the harmony of cultural diversity.

We wish to affirm not only the unity of humanity but also the cultural diversity that ethnic groups bring to our societies. One of the tasks of the church in a given culture is to contribute to the flowering of that culture, as well as to make sure that the salutary sense of ethnic belonging does not turn into ethnic aggressions towards the "stranger who is within the gates" or towards neighbouring ethnic groups. It is therefore the responsibility of the church to work towards genuine community, in which each ethnic group remains faithful to its dynamic and changing identity and yet is enriched by and enriches others. In this way, the churches must seek to contribute not only to the development of each culture but also to harmony among all.

The church is called to participate in the mission of God to establish God's new creation, to bring everything together under Christ as head (Eph. 1:10), by inviting people to repent and believe the gospel of Jesus Christ, as well as by struggling together for justice, peace and the integrity of creation. The churches therefore need to challenge structures and practices of economic, political, sexual, racial, ethnic and other kinds of oppression, recognizing the intersecting nature of these oppressions and their specific impact on equality within communities.

Yet as we face the ethnic conflicts that are surfacing around the globe today, our first act as churches and Christians must be to repent for the fact that too often we have been accomplices in ethnic wars rather than agents of peace. Finding it difficult to distance themselves from their own culture, churches too often echo its reigning opinions and mimic its practices, sometimes to the point of repeating nationalistic slogans and propaganda.

In seeking to find harmony with others in the Spirit of love while remaining true to themselves, churches must strive for justice and truth. A peace between ethnic groups without truth is a false peace; harmony without justice is an unjust harmony. Yet the search for truth and justice must be a common search in which all parties in conflict participate. If each ethnic group simply insists on its own account of truth and justice, conflict will continue. As each group seeks peace and communion with the other, each must not only be faithful to its own account of justice and truth but be willing to have these accounts corrected by the convictions of other groups.

In seeking the resolution of ethnic conflicts, churches should pay special attention to those who are particularly vulnerable to the denial of political or economic power. While continuing to affirm a preferential option for the poor, they should carefully analyze conflicts which arise, sustaining the capacity to be critical of groups and movements fighting for liberation but violating human rights and perpetrating injustice.

"The churches are called to move towards visible unity in order to proclaim the gospel of hope and reconciliation for all people and show a credible model of that life God offers to all" (*The Unity of the Church as Koinonia: Gift and Calling*, statement by the seventh assembly of the World Council of Churches, Canberra, 1991). For the sake of ethnic harmony the churches are invited to respond to this gift and calling. Above the commitment to their respective cultures and nations the churches must place not only their commitment to their common Lord Jesus Christ and to God's new creation, but also their commitment to one another as Christian communions.

"You were slaughtered and by your blood you ransomed for God saints from every tribe and language and people and nation" (Rev. 5:9). "There is no longer Jew or Greek, there is no longer slave or free, there is no longer male and female; for all of you are one in Christ Jesus" (Gal. 3:28).

All the churches of Jesus Christ, scattered in diverse cultures, have been redeemed for God by the blood of the Lamb to form one multi-cultural community of faith. The "blood" that binds them as brothers and sisters is more precious than the "blood", the language, the customs, the political allegiances or economic interests that may separate them.

III. Challenges to the churches

In a world in which ethnic strife and nationalism threaten the human rights of so many ethnic communities and their members, these biblical and theological perspectives point to a clear challenge to the church as a whole and in its local expressions.

The church is challenged constantly and critically to search the scriptures as it seeks to understand ethnicity and nationalism, opening itself to new insights and honestly acknowledging where it has abused scripture to justify its own understanding of ethnicity and nationalism. In searching the scriptures and seeking to live as the body of Christ, the church is called to repent and to walk the path of Christian discipleship, which is always under the shadow of the cross and may often lead to the cross.

The church is challenged to reassess critically its own history and evaluate its own involvement in ethnic conflicts and in nationalistic desires for power. This is not a simple matter. It may involve a painful process of naming and unmasking diabolical and dehumanizing powers. Breaking down walls of division and being reconciled with another group is especially difficult when there has been long and bitter enmity between groups. Yet as the church listens to the Spirit of Christ, it will be challenged to abandon old ways and to move in new directions under the leading of that Spirit, growing closer together with the various members of its family. The term "kingdom [reign, realm] of God", as understood by the various Christian traditions, should be explored anew as a key to understanding nationalism, ethnicity and the church.

The church is challenged to examine and explore its relations with people of other faiths, moving beyond passive tolerance to constant, critical and creative dialogue with them. This is important whenever religion is mobilized in an ethnic conflict, especially when nation-states seek to meet their need for legitimation by drawing on and exploiting the beliefs and traditions of religious communities. All world faiths include visions of and resources for the just and harmonious living together of all human beings and for the care and preservation of creation. These resources for life must be marshalled in interfaith encounter, particularly when claims by some adherents of these religions are leading to oppression, injustice and violence. Interfaith dialogue in situations of conflict may not be possible and will certainly be less fruitful if relationships of trust have not already been built before conflict breaks out.

The church is challenged to respond to the increase in missionary activity and the phenomenal growth of new religious movements in many countries. Often these groups promote a kind of faith which is alien to the cultural identity of the communities to which they come, offer simplistic responses to complex and critical issues and serve as vehicles for the economic and political interests of other powers.

The church is challenged to live as a prophetic sign of the new creation and servant of the reconciliation of God at the local level. The local congregation should be a community characterized in its life, mission and worship by inclusiveness and advocacy for the rights of others, thereby underlining the reconciling work of Christ, who has broken down barriers of ethnicity and race, creating a new people in the Spirit in whom there is "neither Jew nor Greek" (Gal. 3:28). This gospel message provides a clear and risky challenge, particularly to churches built on ethnic lines and living in a wider community where those divisions are embroiled in struggles for power.

Church leaders are often caught between their own understanding and knowledge of the gospel of reconciliation and their ethnic ties and obligations. They must be encouraged and supported to stand for the gospel which is above ethnic ties and to work for peace in their communities. In order to develop wise leadership in these matters, there is a clear need for theological seminaries and church educational activities and programmes to include peace education programmes in their curricula.

If they are to carry out a role as peacemaker and mediator in conflict situations, churches must equip themselves to face questions of ethnicity and nationalism by being politically and economically informed, historically and culturally aware and sensitive. In the service of justice and peace, churches must continue to hear the call to have "the mind of Christ" (Phil. 2:5). Their identification with vulnerable communities should lead to an acknowledgment and renunciation of all forms of power as domination.

Churches need to stand by the weak and disadvantaged and to provide healing for the victims of power. In practical terms, this may mean taking steps such as these:
— familiarizing themselves with the ethnic composition of their own community and being especially aware of the minority ethnic groups in their society;
— as resources are available, providing opportunity, space and facilities for such minority groups to gather together;
— supporting by prayer and other means sisters and brothers in those churches which are vulnerable to and are experiencing the consequences of ethnic strife and nationalism;
— supporting and encouraging their own members who are involved, often at great personal risk, in struggles for the rights of vulnerable groups;
— sharing from their own resources, whether local resources or those of the wider church, when food and other basic necessities of life are needed;
— supporting non-church groups and organizations working for the well-being of ethnic groups that are disadvantaged;
— listening to the concerns of groups in conflict and if need be representing peoples before government and standing with and for them in their desire for peace and justice.

At heart the Christian church is to be a welcoming and open community to all those who are powerless and helpless. The church is called to be the people of God, the body of Christ. It is challenged to break down the walls of hostility among groups and to unmask the dehumanizing powers often inherent in nationalistic programmes. It lives in the hope of joining in that "great multitude that no one could count, from every nation, from all tribes and peoples and languages" (Rev. 7:9) in the worship of the one who was slain to bring them peace and to unite them as the people of God.

Appendix: Explanation of some terms

How are ethnicity, nationalism and religion linked? Modern Europe claimed that the nation-state represents the normal or even "natural" form of political self-organization; and nation-states have been exported to many parts of the world as a legacy of colonial history.

To give legitimacy to nation-states, elites have often tapped the resources of the people's history, religion and local traditions. Such ideas as "we are the chosen people", "this land is our land" and "our noble tradition" are galvanized into ideologies. It is in this perspective that the problems we have discussed arise.

Identity. Many factors shape human identity, including religion, culture, gender, class. Identity is about a sense of belonging. From birth, every person requires socialization in a culture for development. Identity is therefore derived in part from membership in a socio-cultural system.

Ethnicity is collective group consciousness defined by reference to a configuration of elements such as language, homeland, descent, religion, values. The collective group identity or ethnicity of a group is often asserted relationally, in comparison to or contrast with other neighbouring groups. Although specific characteristics of an ethnic identity, such as religion or homeland, may shift over time, the need for that identity seems to be permanent, fulfilling the need for belonging. Ethnic identity may provide economic advantages and protection; it also confers symbolic satisfactions of emotional bonding and personal meaning. In cases of group conflicts, ethnicity may be mobilized and become a factor aggravating such conflicts.

Religion is a key factor that shapes the identity and character of many communities. Every religion includes, among other elements, the following: a body of oral and written doctrines, a set of rituals, a communal structure and a code of behaviour and values.

State is the name of the sovereign territorial entities which constitute the main units in the international system. Typically a state is composed of a population, land and an independent government. Prior to the emergence of the state, kingdoms, tribes and the like were the main units of social organization. Today, state boundaries are being challenged by new forms of organization such as the European Union, ASEAN, etc.

Nation refers to a group that possesses its own cultural practices and institutions. A state may contain many nations. This is what is meant by the idea of a "multi-ethnic state". There are only a few states which are constituted entirely by one cultural group or nation.

A *nation-state* in the modern sense is an overarching structure in which political power is concentrated in the hands of one or more ethnic communities within its territory. The nation-state has been challenged by new concepts, structures and practices such as movements for civil rights and self-determination, cooperative trade and supra-governmental structures and the impact of global capitalism.

Nationalism is collective group consciousness built around the boundaries of an actual or perceived nationhood. In many countries, internal cultural fragmentation means that collective nationalist sentiments representing all the people cannot arise; instead, ethno-nationalisms of the separate sub-state communities exist. The appeal to nationalism and ethno-nationalism may serve as an ideology for a group's claims.

Colombo, 19 November 1994

Index of People

Abboud, Ibrahim 34, 35
Abd-el-Malik (caliph) 60
Abdul Hamid (sultan) 4, 5, 6, 9
Abdullah (successor of the Mahdi) 31, 32
Abdullah (emir) 62
Abraham 13, 25, 56, 57, 58
Ahmed Riza 8
Alexander the Great 1, 74
Alexander I (king) 108
Alexander II (czar) 4
Alexander III (czar) 16
Alexander IV (pope) 122
Ali (Muhammed's son-in-law) 78
Allenby, Edmund 62
Allende, Isabel 128
Ana Maria (comandante) 121
Arafat, Yassir 68
Aram I xiv
Ariarajah, Wesley 96, 97
Araujo, Elias 130
Arzu, Alvaro 130
Ashoka (emperor) 89

Baker, Sir Samuel 30
Balasuriya, Tissa 98
Balboa, Vasco Nuñez de 116
Balfour (Lord) 63
Bandaranaike, S.W.R.D. 93
Bandel, Ehud 70
Barahinyura, Jean 47
Barot, Madeleine 19
Barth, Karl 18
Bartholomew (apostle) 2
Bashir, Omar Hassan Ahmad al- 28
Ben-Gurion, David 64, 66
Benedict, Saint 140
Ben Zakkai (rabbi) 58
Beshir Shebab II 79
Boegner, Marc 19
Bonhoeffer, Dietrich 18

Boris II 23
Born, Friedrich 23
Bshara al-Khouri 81
Buddha 89

Candace (queen) 29
Cardoso, Fernando Henrique 130
Carr, Dhyanchand 97
Casas, Bartolomé de Las 118, 123, 140
Castillo Cardenas, Gonzalo 121
Cavert, Samuel McCrae 18
Chamoun, Camille 82
Charles V (emperor) 118
Chipenda, José 54
Chmielnicki, Bogdan 15
Chofsky, Nathan 69
Christian X (king) 23
Classe, Léon-Paul 43, 44
Clémenceau, Georges 81
Clement XIV (pope) 118
Columbus, Christopher 15, 116, 121, 122
Condorcanqui, José Gabriel
    (Tupac Amaru II) 120
Constantine 57, 59
Corm, Georges 73, 85
Cortés, Hernan 116
Coughlin, Charles 19

Darazi 78
David (king) 57
Dayan, Moshe 69
Decius (emperor) 2
Dessalines, Jean-Jacques 125
Dharmapala, Anagarika 92
Diocletian 75
Dreyfus, Alfred 16, 63
Durayappah, Alfred 87
Dusan, Lazar 104
Dussel, Enrique, 117, 119, 131, 133

Merusanes (bishop) 2
Messiah 25, 58, 59, 64
Mihailovic, Dragomir 108
Milosevic, Slobodan 104, 110, 112, 113
Mitri, Tarek 84
Mitterand, François 51, 52
Mladic, Ratko 100, 110, 111, 113
Mojzes, Paul 114
Moses 57, 135
Muhammed (the prophet) 6, 59, 78, 85
Muhammed II (sultan) 3
Muhammed V (sultan) 6
Muhammed Ali (khedive) 29, 30, 61, 79
Muhammed Rey (son-in-law
    of Muhammed Ali) 30
Müller, Ludwig 18
Musinga (mwami) 42, 44
Mussolini, Benito 108
Mustafa Kemal Pasha (Atatürk) 7, 9
Mutura III (mwami) 45
Mwinyi, Ali Hassan 50

Naguib (general) 33
Napoleon Bonaparte 61, 101, 122
Nasir, Hanna 69
Nasser, Gamal Abdel 35, 82
Ndadaye, Melchior 49
Nestorius 75
Netanyahu, Benjamin 68
Niemöller, Martin 18
Nightingale, Florence 140
Noah 1, 42
Nsengiyumva, Thadée 51
Nsengiyumva, Vincent 47
Nshamihigo, Augustin 52, 54
Ntaryamira, Cyprien 51
Numeiri, Ga'afar al- 35, 36, 37

Oldham, J.H. xiii
Omar (caliph) 59
Osman (sultan) 3

Parakramabahu (king) 89
Paul (apostle) 2, 13, 59, 75
Paul VI 132
Pavelic, Ante 106
Peiris, Chandra 96
Perraudin, André 45, 46, 47
Peter (apostle) 59
Petherick, John 30

Philip (apostle) 29
Pilate 14
Pinochet (general) 132
Pinsker, Leo 63
Pius XI 20
Pius XII 20
Pizarro, Francisco 116
Prabhakaran, Velupillai 87, 94, 95
Prien, Hans-Jürgen 121, 132
Princip, Gavril 105

Rama (Hindu hero) 88
Ratzinger, Joseph 98
Raznatovic, "Arkan" Zeljko 109
Reagan, Ronald 84
Ricci, Matteo 117, 122
Riad as-Sol 81
Rotta, Angelo 23
Rubenstein, Richard L. 25
Rudahigwa, Charles 44
Rummel, R.J. ix, 135
Rwabugiri (mwami) 42

Said (successor of Muhammed Ali) 30
Said Halim Pasha 8
Saint-Exupéry 135
Saul of Tarsus 13
Schäfer, Heinrich 132
Schweitzer, Albert 140
Selim I (sultan) 3
Sennacherib (king) 74
Seselj, Voislav 109
Sheba, Queen of 58
Sheikh-ul-Islam 8
Silva, Colin R. de 92
Simon Bar Kokhba 57
Sinbad the seafarer 87
Smolenskin, Perez 63
Solano López, Francisco 121
Solomon (king) 57, 58, 74
Stalin, Joseph 10, 24
Suleiman the Magnificent 3, 61

Taffeng (general) 35
Talaat Bey 7
Tamerlane 2
Temple, William 18
Thaddaeus (apostle) 2
Theodosius (emperor) 14, 140
Tiridates III (king) 2